Journeys Through Ethnography

Realistic Accounts of Fieldwork

edited by

Annette Lareau
Temple University

and

Jeffrey Shultz
Beaver College

A Member of the Perseus Books Group

Copyright © 1996 by Westview Press., A Member of the Perseus Books Group

Published in 1996 in the United States of America by Westview Press, 5500 Central Avenue, Boulder, Colorado 80301-2877, and in the United Kingdom by Westview Press, 12 Hid's Copse Road, Cumnor Hill, Oxford OX2 9JJ

Library of Congress Cataloging-in-Publication Data
Journeys through ethnography : realistic accounts of fieldwork /
    edited by Annette Lareau and Jeffrey Shultz.
      p. cm.
    Includes bibliographical references and index.
    ISBN 0-8133-2637-0 (hc) —ISBN 0-8133-2638-9 (pb)
    1. Ethnology—Field work.   2. Ethnology—Methodology.   I. Lareau,
Annette.   II. Shultz, Jeffrey J.
GN346.J68   1996
305.8´00723—dc20   96-15890
                                                                        CIP

The paper used in this publication meets the requirements of the American National Standard for Permanence of Paper for Printed Library Materials Z39.48-1984.

PERSEUS
POD
ON DEMAND   10   9   8   7   6   5

To our teachers:
Michael Burawoy, Courtney Cazden,
Troy Duster, Frederick Erickson,
Arlie Russell Hochschild,
Milbrey McLaughlin, Victoria Steinitz,
and Beatrice Whiting

Contents

Acknowledgments

This book shows the social side of research. Although bringing together a collection of essays is a more modest undertaking than doing fieldwork, throughout the process we have benefited from the thoughts, support, and good humor of friends and colleagues. We are particularly grateful to Hugh Mehan for his encouragement in the early stages of the project. Dean Birkenkamp, our editor at Westview Press, has been a model editor: He has been helpful, focused, critical, and patient. Laurie Milford, our project editor at Westview, also provided much-needed support and assistance in the preparation of the manuscript. The contributors graciously agreed to participate in the project and, in several instances, provided helpful comments. A number of people have commented on various drafts, including Patricia Berhau, Robert Kidder, and David Watt. We are grateful to them as well as to Frederick Erickson, Evelyn Jacob, and Christina Ager for conversation and good ideas. For bibliographic research and general assistance we appreciate the help of Ginny Blaisdell, Karen Forgeng, Mimi Keller, and Jonathan Shaw. We, of course, remain responsible for any errors. The Office of Graduate Studies at Beaver College graciously provided financial support for the project. Finally, we are indebted to Samuel Freeman and Janet Theophano for their companionship and support throughout this journey.

Annette Lareau
Jeffrey Shultz

Credits

Introduction

ANNETTE LAREAU AND JEFFREY SHULTZ

"The longest journey begins with one step."

At one point or another in our lives, we are all beginners. We begin college, a first job, a first love affair, and a first research project. We bring a great deal to these new situations, including our temperament, previous education, and family situations. Yet, as adults, we also learn. In romantic relationships, couples report having to learn how to interact successfully with their partners. College students report being better at reading, studying, paper writing, and test taking as seniors than as freshmen. They have learned how to be students while they were students. Now close to graduating, some view they have finally mastered the role.

Ideally, of course, we would have the necessary information in hand before we needed it. We would already know, without being told, what makes a loved one angry or frustrated. All students would be spared the frustration of working hard on a paper and having it not be well received. Especially, researchers would never make mistakes.

Indeed, some individuals go through life believing that they should know how to do something ahead of time. In this view, mistakes are aberrations. After making a mistake, individuals can torture themselves with repeated accusations and self-blame. They see their foibles as an indication of their own lack of capability as a person. Some plunge into despair and conclude they will never sustain a romantic relationship, succeed in college, or complete a valuable research project.

Nevertheless, the reality is that learning is a process and that mistakes, including costly ones, are integral to that process. Although reading, teaching, and guidance are helpful, there are key aspects—for example, of romantic relationships, college course work, and research methodology—

that are mastered through experience. Usually, although not always, humans get better at something through practice. This learning process can be exhilarating, difficult, boring, uplifting, lonely, exciting, frustrating, and scary.

This book is about learning to do research variously called "ethnography," "naturalistic studies," "qualitative research," and "case studies."[1] This methodological approach is used by anthropologists, sociologists, and folklorists as well as students of cultural studies, educational studies, and religious studies. We are dissatisfied with the state of the current methodological books in this genre. With few exceptions, we find the books on qualitative research to be overly general in their expositions; many are filled with platitudes. Standard methodological texts extol a set of virtues: Researchers using participant-observation should build rapport, gain the trust of the people in the study, provide detailed and accurate field notes, interpret the results in a theoretically informed manner, and write it up in a vivid and engaging style. We agree with these standards.

Yet, participant-observation necessarily brings the researcher into varied and unpredictable situations. In an effort to be with people and to understand their lives, researchers sometimes react in ways that they are pleased about; other times they say or do things that they regret. There is always a gap between instruction and implementation, but this pattern of success and regret has been traditionally private. Though often acknowledging briefly that there were some aspects of the project that did not proceed as anticipated, researchers—including those who use field research techniques—often skimmed across and minimized the inevitable difficulties in the field.[2]

In part, these omissions in the presentation of self are driven by fear. Researchers correctly fear that revelations of weaknesses in the collection and analysis of data will be seized upon by readers and reviewers as weaknesses in the project. Because researchers want their results to be well received, the norm has been to reveal a minimum of difficulty. In addition, accepted social science practice is to introduce problems in the study and then attempt to explain to the reader how these problems were overcome and do not threaten the integrity of the results.

This collection provides a different vantage point. All of the authors write of being beginners in one fashion or another; most were beginning a senior thesis or doctoral dissertation. They show us how individuals learned to be researchers in the process of carrying out their projects. The chapters are "confessional" (Van Maanen 1988) in the sense they reveal foibles. More to the point, they show how research actually gets done. We believe that revelations of the unevenness of the process are helpful. They provide comfort to beginners who know that even distinguished scholars, including William F. Whyte, sometimes made foolish mistakes as they learned how to do research. They provide clarity of how methodological goals such as building rapport are translated into action. They provide insight into the kinds of factors other researchers considered when they stumbled into difficulty and the strategies—for example, of reflection and data analysis—that researchers used to extract themselves from their temporary woes. More to the point, they highlight the uncertainty and confusion that inevitably accompany field research. It is, as we explain in more detail further on, appropriate to be confused at various points of the project.

What Do We Mean by Ethnographic Methods?

Reasonable people disagree about the definition of ethnography. Traditionally, in anthropology, ethnographic studies had a host of characteristics including the use of participant-observation to study a community for an extended period of time, a holistic approach, the portrayal of the community from the perspective of the participants, a focus on culture (particularly the lived culture of the setting), and a focus on context (Agar 1980; Fetterman 1989; Spindler 1982). In other fields—including sociology, religious studies, and education—ethnography has been defined more loosely. Almost all definitions, however, include the use of participant-observation as well as in-depth interviews with key informants. There is an effort to understand the view of the participants; researchers seek to be in the setting long enough to acquire some notion of acceptance and understanding.

In this collection, we have taken a broader rather than narrower definition of ethnography. We include works from both perspectives. The only works we would exclude from our definition are those using ethnographic methods (participant observation and in-depth interviewing) but for such a short amount of time (e.g., one week per site) that a rich understanding of the setting could not possibly be obtained.

Moreover, ethnographic methods can be distinguished from other approaches such as survey or experimental research. There is, clearly, a difference in scale. Whereas a survey researcher might give a standardized questionnaire to one thousand students, a researcher using participant-observation might "hang out" with a few individuals. There are also differences in how the research is carried out and the data are analyzed. Survey researchers seek to control almost all aspects of their study. They "select" in a sample who they study, and they ensure that the "respondents" are asked the exact same question. They also standardize the answer categories in an effort to improve comparability among respondents ("Do you strongly agree, somewhat agree, neither agree nor disagree, somewhat disagree, or strongly disagree with the following statement").

In particular, survey researchers seek to assess the frequency of behavior in a population. They report, for example, the proportion of individuals who voted in the last election, used drugs in high school, graduated from college, and are employed.

Researchers who use participant-observation have a different set of goals. Rather than being interested in how frequent a behavior is, they wonder about the meaning of a behavior. They seek, generally, to understand the character of the day-to-day life of the people in the study. Ethnographers often ask, "What is going on here?" The research is labor intensive; most studies cover a few individuals, one or two classrooms, or one tribe. Sometimes decisions are made, but once in the setting researchers end up collecting more data on some aspects of life than others. This "sample" often is the result of serendipity. Participant-observers do not center their work on fixed-answer questions. They generally try to get to know respondents and to spend time with them over and over again. Thus they are interested in the character of social life. Rather than a survey showing X percentage of high school students smoked marijuana once in the last month, they explore what it is like to be a drug peddler and how it shapes the contours of one's life (Adler 1993). Instead of reporting by race, gender, and family background the number of students who stayed in college, they describe the day-to-day character of what it is like to be a student (Komarovsky 1985; Moffat 1989). Unlike survey research, where a large number of persons review and adjust the research "instrument," in participant-observation the person is the "instrument." How a researcher acts in the field shapes the contours of the results.

A Short Map of the Contents

Different aspects of the process of doing field research are examined in each of the chapters that follow (see Table I.1). In order to begin the research process, the researcher must choose a question to explore. The question chosen must address the concerns of the researcher and must be answerable within the setting in which the research is to be carried out. Lareau, MacLeod, and Whyte in each of their chapters discuss the ways in which they went about choosing the question they used to frame their research.

Having chosen a question, the researcher must set about the delicate process of negotiating entry into the setting in which the research will be carried out. This complicated task often sets the tone for the remainder of the research project. As such, it is one that must be carried out with diplo-

TABLE I.1   Guide to Themes by Chapter

	Chap. 1 Whyte	Chap. 2 Gottlieb & Graham	Chap. 3 MacLeod	Chap. 4 Theophano & Curtis	Chap. 5 Krieger	Chap. 6 Lareau
Choosing a question	√		√			√
Entry	√	√	√	√		√
Ethical issues	√	√	√	√	√	√
Data collection	√	√	√	√	√	√
Relations with those studied	√	√	√	√	√	√
Doing research as a student	√	√	√	√		√
Collaboration with other researchers				√		
Data analysis	√				√	√
Writing up findings	√				√	√

macy and tact. The chapters written by Whyte, Gottlieb and Graham, MacLeod, Theophano and Curtis, and Lareau each examine the process of negotiating entry.

Because field research involves working with people in the settings in which they normally interact, researchers must attend closely to the relationships they establish with those being studied and, in particular, with ethical concerns that might arise as a result of this interaction. These are such important issues that they are discussed in all six of the chapters that follow. Additionally, the process of data collection itself can be problematic. When and where to observe, who should be interviewed, how much time should be spent in the field, and how (physically) the data should be collected are among the questions that field researchers grapple with on a regular basis. All of the authors address issues of data collection in their discussion of the research process.

Once the data are collected, researchers must deal with how they are to be analyzed and written up. Making decisions about how to categorize data, how to reduce it and summarize it, how to combine data from various sources (observation, interviews, videotapes, for example), and how to write about those being studied in a manner that does justice to what was experienced in the field are among the issues that present challenges for even the most seasoned of researchers. Whyte, Krieger, and Lareau address issues of data analysis and problems they faced in writing the reports of their research.

In addition to the topics generally dealt with in field research projects, the chapters in this book examine a variety of other issues. Several of the authors (Whyte, MacLeod, Gottlieb, Theophano and Curtis, and Lareau) were students while they were doing their research. They all discuss the particular problems that students face in the field in balancing their responsibilities to their advisors, to their own work and families, and to the people they were studying. Although doing field research is often a solitary activity, Theophano and Curtis also examine, in some detail, the benefits accrued and the problems encountered in doing research collaboratively. And, finally, the issue of subjectivity plays a central role in the chapter written by Krieger.

Conclusion

In recent decades, there has been a major transformation in the research process among social scientists in the university. Efforts to emulate the natural sciences and to make social science research "scientific" have come under serious attack. Although the basis of the critiques vary, most center on the failure to capture the subjective experience of individuals and, especially, the meaning of events in individuals' lives. As a result, there has been a renaissance of interest in interpretative methods in a wide range of fields including sociology, education, social work, nursing, and psychology as well as anthropology and folklore.

Nevertheless the literature on interpretative methods, as with much of academic research, does not generally acknowledge failure as part of the research process. Nor do many studies provide concrete details of the process. This silence around the research process inevitably distorts and ultimately isolates researchers in training. Many students have a clear idea of the final goal (e.g., rapport) but an inadequate understanding of the steps one takes in reaching this goal. The following chapters provide realistic accounts of the research process. In the honest reflections of the process, our hope is that new students and seasoned scholars will find the collection a source of knowledge and support as they use ethnographic methods to deepen our understanding of the social world.

Notes

1. See the epilogue of this collection for a more detailed, albeit selective, guide to this literature.

2. As Van Maanen points out (1988) there is a genre of confessional essays where researchers lay bare their journeys and their foibles. Nevertheless, most ethnographic studies are not accompanied by such essays. Although there are notable exceptions, including the chapters in this volume, many of the confessional essays are quite limited in size and scope.

1

Introduction to Chapter 1

[The researcher] has a role to play, and he has his own personality needs that must be met in some degree if he is to function successfully. . . . A real explanation, then, of how the research was done necessarily involves a rather personal account of how the researcher lived during the period of the study.

(Whyte, 1981: 279)

William F. Whyte was a pioneer. In 1936, as a recent graduate of Swarthmore College and the recipient of a fellowship from Harvard, he set out to do a study of a "slum community." He was looking for ways of improving the living conditions of the inhabitants of such communities and was particularly concerned with issues of housing. As he began his study, he looked for helpful guides or other sources of inspiration and information. Such accounts were not available; in fact, novice researchers did not have many resources of any sort at their disposal. In order to help remedy this situation, Whyte wrote an appendix to his now classic study, *Street Corner Society*, in which he described in great detail his experiences in the community of Cornerville.

In this appendix, written twelve years after the publication of the first edition, Whyte provides us with a detailed account of all facets of his research project. Beginning with how and why he chose to do this sort of a study in the first place, Whyte traces his thoughts and actions as he developed both his research questions and methods. He gives us insights into all aspects of doing field research: We learn about his attempts to find a suitable community and, once he found it, his often inept and inappropriate efforts at meeting and being accepted by members of the community. He tells of his first meeting with Doc, who was to become his most important informant, and of how he secured his room with a family in this overcrowded community. He describes the struggles—personal, emotional and intellectual—that he faced as he did his work. And he does all of this with humor, grace, and humility; in so doing, he humanizes the research process.

In addition to describing how he went about doing his research, Whyte writes about his return to Cornerville after the research had been published in *Street Corner Society*. He was somewhat surprised to learn that few people in the community appeared to have read his book. Additionally, he did not know what to make of Doc's response: His prime informant appeared to have been both pleased at being one of the key players in the book and embarrassed by the attention that was focused on him. One of the more poignant aspects of the appendix is Whyte's realization that Doc had such ambivalent feelings both about him and the research. In discussing this issue, he raises concerns about some of the unforeseen and unimagined consequences that can result from the publication of field research.

Whyte's research was then considered to be an unusual sort, and finding a publisher for the manuscript was not easy. With the encouragement of faculty in the Sociology Department at the University of Chicago (where Whyte had gone to complete his Ph.D.), he approached the University of Chicago Press. The Press agreed to publish but, as they expected the book would not sell many copies, insisted that Whyte subsidize the publication by contributing $1,300, an enormous sum of money in the early 1940s, to help defray the production costs. Little did anyone know that *Street Corner Society* would become one of the best selling books in the field of sociology, with sales of over 200,000 copies.

The work Whyte describes in *Street Corner Society* has achieved the status of a classic in the field of small group studies in sociology. It served as the foundation for the work of Merton, Homans, and Parsons. Prior to this research, poor communities were portrayed as disorganized and pathological. Whyte's description of street-corner gangs and their relationships with the political and economic structures of the community paints a very different picture: He found a very complex set of relationships among these various components, leading to a highly developed social structure.

His research focused on the gangs of young men in their twenties who hung around the street corners in a tightly knit Italian-American community. He paid particularly close attention to the Nortons, whose leader, Doc, was one of the first members of the community he met and the person who was able to introduce him to others and allowed him to gain access to many other individuals, groups, and institutions in Cornerville. He examines in close detail the interactions among group members—the patterns of reciprocity and exchange among them. He also explores the relationships of these groups to the political structure of the community and to the racketeers who transacted business there. On the basis of these observations, he provides a comprehensive and detailed portrait of the intricacies of the social structure of this neighborhood.

On the Evolution of *Street Corner Society*

WILLIAM FOOTE WHYTE

In the years since completing *Street Corner Society* I have several times sought to teach students the research methods needed for field studies of communities or organizations. Like other instructors in this field, I have been severely handicapped by the paucity of reading matter that I can assign to students.

There are now many good published studies of communities or organizations, but generally the published report gives little attention to the actual process whereby the research was carried out. There have also been some useful statements on methods of research, but, with a few exceptions, they place the discussion entirely on a logical-intellectual basis. They fail to note that the researcher, like his informants, is a social animal. He has a role to play, and he has his own personality needs that must be met in some degree if he is to function successfully. Where the researcher operates out of a university, just going into the field for a few hours at a time, he can keep his personal social life separate from field activity. His problem of role is not quite so complicated. If, on the other hand, the researcher is living for an extended period in the community he is studying, his personal life is inextricably mixed with his research. A real explanation, then, of how the research was done necessarily involves a rather personal account of how the researcher lived during the period of study.

This account of living in the community may help also to explain the process of analysis of the data. The ideas that we have in research are only in part a logical product growing out of a careful weighing of evidence. We do not generally think problems through in a straight line. Often we have the experience of being immersed in a mass of confusing data. We study the data carefully, bringing all our powers of logical analysis to bear upon them. We come up with an idea or two. But still the data do not fall in any coherent pattern. Then we go on living with the data—and with the people—until perhaps some chance occurrence casts a totally different light upon the data, and we begin to see a pattern that we have not seen before. This pattern is not purely an artistic creation. Once we think we see it, we must reexamine our notes and perhaps set out to gather new data in order to determine whether the pattern adequately represents the life we are observing or is simply a product of our imagination. Logic, then, plays an important part. But I am convinced that the actual evolution of research ideas does not take place in accord with the formal statements we read on research methods. The ideas grow up in part out of our immersion in the data and out of the whole process of living. Since so much of this process of analysis proceeds on the unconscious level, I am sure that we can never present a full account of it. However, an account of the way the research was done may help to explain how the pattern of *Street Corner Society* gradually emerged.

I am not suggesting that my approach to *Street Corner Society* should be followed by other researchers. To some extent my approach must be unique to myself, to the particular situation, and to the state of knowledge existing when I began research. On the other hand, there must be some common elements of the field research process. Only as we accumulate a series of accounts of how research was actually done will we be able to go beyond the logical-intellectual picture and learn to describe the actual research process. What follows, then, is simply one contribution toward that end.

1. Personal Background

I come from a very consistent upper-middle-class background. One grandfather was a doctor; the other, a superintendent of schools. My father was a college professor. My upbringing, therefore, was very far removed from the life I have described in Cornerville.

At Swarthmore College I had two strong interests: economics (mixed with social reform) and writing. In college I wrote a number of short stories and one-act plays. During the summer after college I made an attempt at a novel. This writing was valuable to me largely in what it taught me about myself. Several of the stories appeared in the college literary magazine, and one was accepted for publication (but never published) in *Story* magazine. Three of the one-act plays were produced at Swarthmore in the annual one-act playwriting contest. Not a bad start for someone who had hopes, as I did then, for a writing career. But yet I felt uneasy and dissatisfied. The plays and stories were all fictionalized accounts of events and situations I had experienced or observed myself. When I attempted to go beyond my experience and tackle a novel on a political theme, the result was a complete bust. Even as I wrote the concluding chapters, I realized that the manuscript was worthless. I finished it, I suppose, just so that I could say to myself that I had written a novel.

Now I had read the often-given advice to young writers that they should write out of their own experience, so I had no reason to be ashamed of this limitation. On the other hand, it was when I reflected upon my experience that I became uneasy and dissatisfied. My home life had been very happy and intellectually stimulating—but without adventure. I had never had to struggle over anything. I knew lots of nice people, but almost all of them came from good, solid middle-class backgrounds like my own. In college, of course, I was associating with middle-class students and middle-class professors. I knew nothing about the slums (or the gold coast for that matter). I knew nothing about life in the factories, fields, or mines—except what I had gotten out of books. So I came to feel that I was a pretty dull fellow. At times this sense of dulness became so oppressive that I simply could not think of any stories to write. I began to feel that, if I were really going to write anything worth while, I would somehow have to get beyond the narrow social borders of my existence up to that time.

My interest in economics and social reform also led in the direction of *Street Corner Society.* One of my most vivid college memories is of a day spent with a group of students in visiting the slums of Philadelphia. I remember it not only for the images of dilapidated buildings and crowded people but also for the sense of embarrassment I felt as a tourist in the district. I had the common young man's urge to do good to these people, and yet I knew then that the situation was so far beyond anything I could realistically attempt at the time that I felt like an insincere dabbler even to be there. I began to think sometimes about going back to such a district and really learning to know the people and the conditions of their lives.

My social reform urges came out in other forms on the campus. In my sophomore year I was one of a group of fifteen men who resigned from their fraternities amid a good deal of fanfare. This was an exciting time on the campus, and some of the solid fraternity men were fearful lest the structure would crumble under their feet. They should not have worried. Fraternities went right along without us. In my senior year I became involved in another effort at campus reform. This time we were aiming at nothing less than a reorganization of the whole social life of the campus. The movement got off to a promising start but then quickly petered out.

These abortive reform efforts had one great value to me. I saw that reform was not so easy. I recognized that I had made a number of mistakes. I also came to the realization that some of the people who had fought against me the hardest were really pretty nice fellows. I did not conclude from this that they were right and I was wrong, but I came to recognize how little I really knew about the forces that move people to action. Out of my own reflections about the failures of my campus reform efforts grew a keener interest in understanding other people.

There was also a book that I had read, which weighed most heavily with me at this time. It was the *Autobiography of Lincoln Steffens.* I got my hands on it during the year I spent in Germany between high school and college. In my efforts to master German, this was the only thing written in English that I read for some time, so perhaps it weighed more heavily with me than it otherwise would. In any case, I was fascinated by it and read it through several times. Steffens had begun as a reformer, and he never abandoned this urge to change things. Yet he had such an unending curiosity about the world around him that he became more and more interested in discovering how society actually functioned. He demonstrated that a man of a background similar to my own could step out of his own usual walks of life and gain an intimate knowledge of individuals and groups whose activities and beliefs were far different from his own. So you could actually get these "corrupt politicians" to talk to you. This I needed to know. It helped me sometimes when I had the feeling that the people I was interviewing would much rather have me get out of there altogether.

2. Finding Cornerville

When I was graduated from Swarthmore in 1936, I received a fellowship from the Society of Fellows at Harvard. This provided me with a unique sort of opportunity—three years of support for any line of research I wished to pursue. The only restriction was that I was not allowed to accumulate credits toward a Ph.D. degree. I am grateful now for this restriction. If I had been allowed to work for the Ph.D., I suppose I should have felt that I must take advantage of the time and the opportunity. With this avenue cut off, I was forced to do what I wanted to do, regardless of academic credits.

I began with a vague idea that I wanted to study a slum district. Eastern City provided several possible choices. In the early weeks of my Harvard fellowship I spent some of my time walking up and down the streets of the various slum districts of Eastern City and talking with people in social agencies about these districts.

I made my choice on very unscientific grounds: Cornerville best fitted my picture of what a slum district should look like. Somehow I had developed a picture of run-down three- to five-story buildings crowded in together. The dilapidated wooden-frame buildings of some other parts of the city did not look quite genuine to me. To be sure, Cornerville did have one characteristic that recommended it on a little more objective basis. It had more people per acre living in it than any other section of the city. If a slum meant overcrowding, this was certainly it.

3. Planning the Study

As soon as I had found my slum district, I set about planning my study. It was not enough for me at the time to plan for myself alone. I had begun reading in the sociological literature and thinking along the lines of the Lynds' *Middletown*. Gradually I came to think of myself as a sociologist or a social anthropologist instead of an economist. I found that, while slums had been given much attention in the sociological literature, there existed no real community study of such a district. So I set out to organize a community study for Cornerville. This was clearly a big job. My early outline of the study pointed to special researches in the history of the district, in economics (living standards, housing, marketing, distribution, and employment), politics (the structure of the political organization and its relation to the rackets and the police), patterns of education and recreation, the church, public health, and—of all things—social attitudes. Obviously, this was more than a one-man job, so I designed it for about ten men.

With this project statement in hand I approached L. J. Henderson, an eminent biochemist who was secretary of the Society of Fellows.

We spent an hour together, and I came away with my plans very much in a state of flux. As I wrote to a friend at this time: "Henderson poured cold water on the mammoth beginning, told me that I should not cast such grandiose plans when I had done hardly any work in the field myself. It would be much sounder to get in the field and try to build up a staff slowly as I went along. If I should get a ten-man project going by fall, the responsibility for the direction and co-ordination of it would inevitably fall upon me, since I would have started it. How could I direct ten people in a field that was unfamiliar to me? Henderson said that, if I did manage to get a ten-man project going, it would be the ruination of me, he thought. Now, the way he put all this it sounded quite sensible and reasonable."

This last sentence must have been written after I had had time to recover from the interview, because I remember it as being a crushing experience. I suppose good advice is just as hard to take as poor advice, and yet in a very short time I realized that Henderson was right, and I abandoned the grandiose plan I had made. Since people who offer painful but good advice so seldom get any thanks for it, I shall always be glad that I went to see Henderson again shortly before his death and told him that I had come to feel that he had been absolutely right.

While I abandoned the ten-man project, I was reluctant to come down to earth altogether. It seemed to me that, in view of the magnitude of the task I was undertaking, I must have at least one collaborator, and I began to cast about for means of getting a college friend of mine to join me in the field. There followed through the winter of 1936–37 several revisions of my outline of the community study and numerous interviews with Harvard professors who might help me to get the necessary backing.

As I read over these various research outlines, it seems to me that the most impressive thing about them is their remoteness from the actual study I carried on. As I went along, the outlines became gradually more sociological, so that I wound up this phase planning to devote major emphasis to a sort of sociometric study of the friendship patterns of people. I would start with one family and ask them who their friends were and who the people were that they were more or less hostile to. Then I would go to these friends and get the list of their friends and learn in the process something of their activities together. In this way, I was to chart the social structure of at least some of the community. Even this, of course, I did not do, for I came to find that you could examine social structure directly through observing people in action.

When, a year later in the fall of 1937, John Howard, also a Harvard junior fellow, changed his field from physical chemistry to sociology, I invited him to join me in the Cornerville study. We worked together for two years, with Howard particularly concentrating on one of the churches and its Holy Name Society. The discussions between us helped immensely in clarifying my ideas. But only a few months after I had begun Cornerville field work, I had completely abandoned the thought of building up a Cornerville staff. I suppose that I found Cornerville life so interesting and rewarding that I no longer felt a need to think in large-scale terms.

Although I was completely at sea in planning the study, at least I had valuable help in developing the field research methods which were eventually to lead to a study plan as well as to the data here reported.

It is hard to realize now how rapid has been the development of sociological and anthropological studies of communities and organizations since 1936, when I began my work in Cornerville. At that time nothing had yet been published on W. Lloyd Warner's "Yankee City" study. I had read the Lynds' *Middletown* and Carolyn Ware's *Greenwich Village* with interest and profit, and yet I began to realize, more and more as I went along, that I was not making a community study along those lines. Much of the other sociological literature then available tended to look upon communities in terms of social problems so that the community as an organized social system simply did not exist.

I spent my first summer following the launching of the study in reading some of the writings of Durkheim and Pareto's *The Mind and Society* (for a seminar with L. J. Henderson, which I was to take in the fall of 1937). I had a feeling that these writings were helpful but still only in a general way. Then I began reading in the social anthropological literature, beginning with Malinowski, and this seemed closer to what I wanted to do even though the researchers were studying primitive tribes and I was in the middle of a great city district.

If there was then little to guide me in the literature, I needed that much more urgently to have the help of people more skilled and experienced than I in the work I was undertaking. Here I was extraordinarily fortunate in meeting Conrad M. Arensberg at the very outset of my Harvard appointment. He also was a junior fellow, so that we naturally saw much of each other. After having worked for some months with W. Lloyd Warner in the Yankee City study, he had gone with Solon Kimball to make a study of a small community in Ireland. When I met him, he had just returned from this field trip and was beginning to write up his data. With Eliot Chapple, he was also in the process of working out a new approach to the analysis of social organization. The two men had been casting about together for ways of establishing such social research on a more scientific basis. Going over the Yankee City data and the Irish study, also, they had set up five different theoretical schemes. One after the other each of the first four schemes fell to the ground under their own searching criticism or under the prods of Henderson or Elton Mayo or others whom they consulted. At last they began to develop a theory of interaction. They felt that, whatever else might be subjective in social research, one could establish objectively the pattern of interaction among people: how often A contacts B, how long they spend together, who originates action when A, B, and C are together, and so on. Careful observation of such interpersonal events might then provide reliable data upon the social organization of a community. At least this was the assumption. Since the theory grew out of research already done, it was natural that these previous studies did not contain as much of the quantitative data as the theory would have required. So it seemed that I might be one of the first to take the theory out into the field.

Arensberg and I had endless discussions of the theory, and in some of these Eliot Chapple participated. At first it seemed very confusing to me—I am not sure I have it all clear yet—but I had a growing feeling that here was something solid that I could build upon.

Arensberg also worked with me on field research methods, emphasizing the importance of observing people in action and getting down a detailed report of actual behavior completely divorced from moral judgments. In my second semester at Harvard, I took a course given by Arensberg and Chapple concerning social anthropological community studies. While this was helpful, I owed much more to the long personal conversations I had with Arensberg throughout the Cornerville research, particularly in its early stages.

In the fall of 1937 I took a small seminar with Elton Mayo. This involved particularly readings from the works of Pierre Janet, and it included also some practice in interviewing psychoneurotics in an Eastern City hospital. This experience was too brief to carry me beyond the amateur stage, but it was helpful in developing my interviewing methods.

L. J. Henderson provided a less specific but nevertheless pervasive influence in the development of my methods and theories. As chairman of the Society of Fellows, he presided over our Monday-night dinners like a patriarch in his own household. Even though the group included A. Lawrence Lowell, Alfred North Whitehead, John Livingston Lowes, Samuel Eliot Morrison, and Arthur Darby Nock, it was Henderson who was easily the most imposing figure for the junior fellows. He seemed particularly to enjoy baiting the young social scientists. He took me on at my first Monday-night dinner and undertook to show me that all my ideas about society were based upon softheaded sentimentality. While I often resented Henderson's sharp criticisms, I was all the more determined to make my field research stand up against anything he could say.

4. First Efforts

When I began my work, I had had no training in sociology or anthropology. I thought of myself as an economist and naturally looked first toward the matters that we had taken up in economics courses, such as economics of slum housing. At the time I was sitting in on a course in slums and housing in the Sociology Department at Harvard. As a term project I took on a study of one block in Cornerville. To legitimize this effort, I got in touch with a private agency that concerned itself in housing matters and offered to turn over to them the results of my survey. With that backing, I began knocking on doors, looking into flats, and talking to the tenants about the living conditions. This brought me into contact with Cornerville people, but it would be hard now to devise a more inappropriate way of beginning a study such as I was eventually to make. I felt ill at ease at this intrusion, and I am sure so did the people. I wound up the block study as rapidly as I could and wrote it off as a total loss as far as gaining a real entry into the district.

Shortly thereafter I made another false start—if so tentative an effort may even be called a start. At the time I was completely baffled at the problem of finding my way into the district. Cornerville was right before me and yet so far away. I could walk freely up and down its streets, and I had even made my way into some of the flats, and yet I was still a stranger in a world completely unknown to me.

At this time I met a young economics instructor at Harvard who impressed me with his self-assurance and his knowledge of Eastern City. He had once been attached to a settlement house, and he talked glibly about his associations with the tough young men and women of the district. He also described how he would occasionally drop in on some drinking place in the area and strike up an acquaintance with a girl, buy her a drink, and then encourage her to tell him her life-story. He claimed that the women so encountered were appreciative of this opportunity and that it involved no further obligation.

This approach seemed at least as plausible as anything I had been able to think of. I resolved to try it out. I picked on the Regal Hotel, which was on the edge of Cornerville. With some trepidation I climbed the stairs to the bar and entertainment area and looked around. There I encountered a situation for which my adviser had not prepared me. There were women present all right, but none of them was alone. Some were there in couples, and there were two or three pairs of women together. I pondered this situation briefly. I had little confidence in my skill at picking up one female, and it seemed inadvisable to tackle two at the same time. Still, I was determined not to admit defeat without a struggle. I looked around me again and now noticed a threesome: one man and two women. It occurred to me that here was a maldistribution of females which I might be able to rectify. I approached the group and opened with something like this: "Pardon me. Would you mind if I joined you?" There was a moment of silence while the man stared at me. He then offered to throw me downstairs. I assured him that this would not be necessary and demonstrated as much by walking right out of there without any assistance.

I subsequently learned that hardly anyone from Cornerville ever went into the Regal Hotel. If my efforts there had been crowned with success, they would no doubt have led somewhere but certainly not to Cornerville.

For my next effort I sought out the local settlement houses. They were open to the public. You could walk right into them, and—though I would not have phrased it this way at the time—they were manned by middle-class people like myself. I realized even then that to study Cornerville I would have to go well beyond the settlement house, but perhaps the social workers could help me to get started.

As I look back on it now, the settlement house also seems a very unpromising place from which to begin such a study. If I had it to do over again, I would probably make my first approach through a local politician or perhaps through the Catholic church, although I am not myself Catholic. John Howard, who worked with me later, made his entry very successfully through the church, and he, too, was not a Catholic—although his wife was.

However that may be, the settlement house proved the right place for me at this time, for it was here that I met Doc. I had talked to a number of the social workers about my plans and hopes to get acquainted with the people and study the district. They listened with varying degrees of interest. If they had suggestions to make, I have forgotten them now except for one. Somehow, in spite of the vagueness of my own explanations, the head of girls' work in the Norton Street House understood what I needed. She began describing Doc to me. He was, she said, a very intelligent and talented person who had at one time been fairly active in the house but had dropped out, so that he hardly ever came in any more. Perhaps he could understand what I wanted, and he must have the contacts that I needed. She said she frequently encountered him as she walked to and from the house and sometimes stopped to chat with him. If I wished, she would make an appointment for me to see him in the house one evening. This at last seemed right. I jumped at the chance. As I came into the district that evening, it was with a feeling that here I had my big chance to get started. Somehow Doc must accept me and be willing to work with me.

In a sense, my study began on the evening of February 4, 1937, when the social worker called me in to meet Doc. She showed us into her office and then left so that we could talk. Doc waited quietly for me to begin, as he sank down into a chair. I found him a man of medium height and spare build. His hair was a light brown, quite a contrast to the more typical black Italian hair. It was thinning around the temples. His cheeks were sunken. His eyes were a light blue and seemed to have a penetrating gaze.

I began by asking him if the social worker had told him about what I was trying to do.

"No, she just told me that you wanted to meet me and that I should like to meet you."

Then I went into a long explanation which, unfortunately, I omitted from my notes. As I remember it, I said that I had been interested in congested city districts in my college study but had felt very remote from them. I hoped to study the problems in such a district. I felt I could do very little as an outsider. Only if I could get to know the people and learn their problems first hand would I be able to gain the understanding I needed.

Doc heard me out without any change of expression, so that I had no way of predicting his reaction. When I was finished, he asked: "Do you want to see the high life or the low life?"

"I want to see all that I can. I want to get as complete a picture of the community as possible."

"Well, any nights you want to see anything, I'll take you around. I can take you to the joints—gambling joints—I can take you around to the street corners. Just remember that you're my friend. That's all they need to know. I know these places, and, if I tell them that you're my friend, no-body will bother you. You just tell me what you want to see, and we'll arrange it."

The proposal was so perfect that I was at a loss for a moment as to how to respond to it. We talked a while longer, as I sought to get some pointers as to how I should behave in his company. He warned me that I might have to take the risk of getting arrested in a raid on a gambling joint but added that this was not serious. I only had to give a false name and then would get bailed out by the man that ran the place, paying only a five-dollar fine. I agreed to take this chance. I asked him whether I should gamble with the others in the gambling joints. He said it was unnecessary and, for a greenhorn like myself, very inadvisable.

At last I was able to express my appreciation. "You know, the first steps of getting to know a community are the hardest. I could see things going with you that I wouldn't see for years otherwise."

"That's right. You tell me what you want to see, and we'll arrange it. When you want some information, I'll ask for it, and you listen. When you want to find out their philosophy of life, I'll start an argument and get it for you. If there's something else you want to get, I'll stage an act for you. Not a scrap, you know, but just tell me what you want, and I'll get it for you."

"That's swell. I couldn't ask for anything better. Now I'm going to try to fit in all right, but, if at any time you see I'm getting off on the wrong foot, I want you to tell me about it."

"Now we're being too dramatic. You won't have any trouble. You come in as my friend. When you come in like that, at first everybody will treat you with respect. You can take a lot of liberties, and nobody will kick. After a while when they get to know you they will treat you like anybody else—you know, they say familiarity breeds contempt. But you'll never have any trouble. There's just one thing to watch out for. Don't spring [treat] people. Don't be too free with your money."

"You mean they'll think I'm a sucker?"

"Yes, and you don't want to buy your way in."

We talked a little about how and when we might get together. Then he asked me a question. "You want to write something about this?"

"Yes, eventually."

"Do you want to change things?"

"Well—yes. I don't see how anybody could come down here where it is so crowded, people haven't got any money or any work to do, and not want to have some things changed. But I think a fellow should do the thing he is best fitted for. I don't want to be a reformer, and I'm not cut out to be a politician. I just want to understand these things as best I can and write them up, and if that has any influence. . . ."

"I think you can change things that way. Mostly that is the way things are changed, by writing about them."

That was our beginning. At the time I found it hard to believe that I could move in as easily as Doc had said with his sponsorship. But that indeed was the way it turned out.

While I was taking my first steps with Doc, I was also finding a place to live in Cornerville. My fellowship provided a very comfortable bedroom, living-room, and bath at Harvard. I had been attempting to commute from these quarters to my Cornerville study. Technically that was possible, but socially I became more and more convinced that it was impossible. I realized that I would always be a stranger to the community if I did not live there. Then, also, I found myself having difficulty putting in the time that I knew was required to establish close relations in Cornerville. Life in Cornerville did not proceed on the basis of formal appointments. To meet people, to get to know them, to fit into their activities, required spending time with them—a lot of time day after day. Commuting to Cornerville, you might come in on a particular afternoon and evening only to discover that the people you intended to see did not happen to be around at the time. Or, even if you did see them, you might find the time passing entirely uneventfully. You might just be standing around with people whose only occupation was talking or walking about to try to keep themselves from being bored.

On several afternoons and evenings at Harvard, I found myself considering a trip to Cornerville and then rationalizing my way out of it. How did I know I would find the people whom I meant to see? Even if I did so, how could I be sure that I would learn anything today? Instead of going off on a wild-goose chase to Cornerville, I could profitably spend my time reading books and articles to fill in my woeful ignorance of sociology and social anthropology. Then, too, I had to admit that I felt more comfortable among these familiar surroundings than I did wandering around Cornerville and spending time with people in whose presence I felt distinctly uncomfortable at first.

When I found myself rationalizing in this way, I realized that I would have to make the break. Only if I lived in Cornerville would I ever be able to understand it and be accepted by it. Finding a place, however, was not easy. In such an overcrowded district a spare room was practically nonexistent. I might have been able to take a room in the Norton Street Settlement House, but I realized that I must do better than this if possible.

I got my best lead from the editor of a weekly English-language newspaper published for the Italian-American colony. I had talked to him before about my study and had found him sympathetic. Now I came to ask him for help in finding a room. He directed me to the Martinis, a family which operated a small restaurant. I went there for lunch and later consulted the son of the family. He was sympathetic but said that they had no place for any additional person. Still, I liked the place and enjoyed the food. I came back several times just to eat. On one occasion I met the editor, and he invited me to his table. At first he asked me some searching questions about my study: what I was after, what my connection with Harvard was, what they had expected to get out of this, and so on. After I had answered him in a manner that I unfortunately failed to record in my notes, he told me that he was satisfied and, in fact, had already spoken in my behalf to people who were suspicious that I might be coming in to "criticize our people."

We discussed my rooming problem again. I mentioned the possibility of living at the Norton Street House. He nodded but added: "It would be much better if you could be in a family. You would pick up the language much quicker, and you would get to know the people. But you want a nice family, an educated family. You don't want to get in with any low types. You want a real good family."

At this he turned to the son of the family with whom I had spoken and asked: "Can't you make some place for Mr. Whyte in the house here?"

Al Martini paused a moment and then said: "Maybe we can fix it up. I'll talk to Mama again."

So he did talk to Mama again, and they did find a place. In fact, he turned over to me his own room and moved in to share a double bed with the son of the cook. I protested mildly at this imposition, but everything had been decided—except for the money. They did not know what to charge me, and I did not know what to offer. Finally, after some fencing, I offered fifteen dollars a month, and they settled for twelve.

The room was simple but adequate to my purposes. It was not heated, but, when I began to type my notes there, I got myself a small oil-burner. There was no bathtub in the house, but I had to go out to Harvard now and then anyway, so I used the facilities of the great university (the room of my friend, Henry Guerlac) for an occasional tub or shower.

Physically, the place was livable, and it provided me with more than just a physical base. I had been with the Martinis for only a week when I discovered that I was much more than a roomer to them. I had been taking many of my meals in the restaurant and sometimes stopping in to chat with the family before I went to bed at night. Then one afternoon I was out at Harvard and found myself coming down with a bad cold. Since I still had my Harvard room, it seemed the sensible thing to do to stay overnight there. I did not think to tell the Martinis of my plan.

The next day when I was back in the restaurant for lunch, Al Martini greeted me warmly and then said that they had all been worried when I did not come home the night before. Mama had stayed up until two o'-clock waiting for me. As I was just a young stranger in the city, she could visualize all sorts of things happening to me. Al told me that Mama had come to look upon me as one of the family. I was free to come and go as I pleased, but she wouldn't worry so much if she knew of my plans.

I was very touched by this plea and resolved thereafter to be as good a son as I could to the Martinis.

At first I communicated with Mama and Papa primarily in smiles and gestures. Papa knew no English at all, and Mama's knowledge was limited to one sentence which she would use when some of the young boys on the street were making noise below her window when she was trying to get her afternoon nap. She would then poke her head out of the window and shout: "Goddam-sonumabitcha! Geroutahere!"

Some weeks earlier, in anticipation of moving into the district, I had begun working on the Italian language myself with the aid of a Linguaphone. One morning now Papa Martini came by when I was talking to the phonograph record. He listened for a few moments in the hall trying to make sense out of this peculiar conversation. Then he burst in upon me with fascinated exclamations. We sat down together while I demonstrated the machine and the method to him. After that he delighted in working with me, and I called him my language professor. In a short time we reached a stage where I could carry on simple conversations, and, thanks to the Linguaphone and Papa Martini, the Italian that came out apparently sounded authentic. He liked to try to pass me off to his friends as *paesano mio*—a man from his own home town in Italy. When I was careful to keep my remarks within the limits of my vocabulary, I could sometimes pass as an immigrant from the village of Viareggio in the province of Tuscany.

Since my research developed so that I was concentrating almost exclusively upon the younger, English-speaking generation, my knowledge of Italian proved unnecessary for research purposes. Nevertheless, I feel certain that it was important in establishing my social position in Cornerville—even with that younger generation. There were schoolteachers and social workers who had worked in Cornerville for as much as twenty years and yet had made no effort to learn Italian. My effort to learn the language probably did more to establish the sincerity of my interest in the people than anything I could have told them of myself and my work. How could a researcher be planning to "criticize our people" if he went to the lengths of learning the language? With language comes understanding, and surely it is easier to criticize people if you do not understand them.

My days with the Martinis would pass in this manner. I would get up in the morning around nine o'clock and go out to breakfast. Al Martini told me I could have breakfast in the restaurant, but, for all my desire to fit in, I never could take their breakfast of coffee with milk and a crust of bread.

After breakfast, I returned to my room and spent the rest of the morning, or most of it, typing up my notes regarding the previous day's events.

I had lunch in the restaurant and then set out for the street corner. Usually I was back for dinner in the restaurant and then out again for the evening.

Usually I came home again between eleven and twelve o'clock, at a time when the restaurant was empty except perhaps for a few family friends. Then I might join Papa in the kitchen to talk as I helped him dry the dishes, or pull up a chair into a family conversation around one of the tables next to the kitchen. There I had a glass of wine to sip, and I could sit back and mostly listen but occasionally try out my growing Italian on them.

The pattern was different on Sunday, when the restaurant was closed at two o'clock, and Al's two brothers and his sister and the wives, husband, and children would come in for a big Sunday dinner. They insisted that I eat with them at this time and as a member of the family, not paying for my meal. It was always more than I could eat, but it was delicious, and I washed it down with two tumblers of Zinfandel wine. Whatever strain there had been in my work in the preceding week would pass away now as I ate and drank and then went to my room for an afternoon nap of an hour or two that brought me back completely refreshed and ready to set forth again for the corners of Cornerville.

Though I made several useful contacts in the restaurant or through the family, it was not for this that the Martinis were important to me. There is a strain to doing such field work. The strain is greatest when you are a stranger and are constantly wondering whether people are going to accept you. But, much as you enjoy your work, as long as you are observing and interviewing, you have a role to play, and you are not completely relaxed. It was a wonderful feeling at the end of a day's work to be able to come home to relax and enjoy myself with the family. Probably it would have been impossible for me to carry on such a concentrated study of Cornerville if I had not had such a home from which to go out and to which I might return.

5. Beginning with Doc

I can still remember my first outing with Doc. We met one evening at the Norton Street House and set out from there to a gambling place a couple of blocks away. I followed Doc anxiously down the long, dark hallway at the back of a tenement building. I was not worried about the possibility of a police raid. I was thinking about how I would fit in and be accepted. The door opened into a small kitchen almost bare of furnishings and with the paint peeling off the walls. As soon as we went in the door, I took off my hat and began looking around for a place to hang it. There was no place. I looked around, and here I learned my first lesson in participant observation in Cornerville: Don't take off your hat in the house—at least not when you are among men. It may be permissible, but certainly not required, to take your hat off when women are around.

Doc introduced me as "my friend Bill" to Chichi, who ran the place, and to Chichi's friends and customers. I stayed there with Doc part of the time in the kitchen, where several men would sit around and talk, and part of the time in the other room watching the crap game.

There was talk about gambling, horse races, sex, and other matters. Mostly I just listened and tried to act friendly and interested. We had wine and coffee with anisette in it, with the fellows chipping in to pay for the refreshments. (Doc would not let me pay my share on this first occasion.) As Doc had predicted, no one asked me about myself, but he told me later that, when I went to the toilet, there was an excited burst of conversation in Italian and that he had to assure them that I was not a G-man. He said he told them flatly that I was a friend of his, and they agreed to let it go at that.

We went several more times together to Chichi's gambling joint, and then the time came when I dared to go in alone. When I was greeted in a natural and friendly manner, I felt that I was now beginning to find a place for myself in Cornerville.

When Doc did not go off to the gambling joint, he spent his time hanging around Norton Street, and I began hanging with him. At first, Norton Street meant only a place to wait until I could go somewhere else. Gradually, as I got to know the men better, I found myself becoming one of the Norton Street gang.

Then the Italian Community Club was formed in the Norton Street Settlement, and Doc was invited to be a member. Doc maneuvered to get me into the club, and I was glad to join, as I could see that it represented something distinctly different from the corner gangs I was meeting.

As I began to meet the men of Cornerville, I also met a few of the girls. One girl I took to a church dance. The next morning the fellows on the street corner were asking me: "How's your steady girl?" This brought me up short. I learned that going to the girl's house was something that you just did not do unless you hoped to marry her. Fortunately, the girl and her family knew that I did not know the local customs, so they did not assume that I was thus committed. However, this was a useful warning. After this time, even though I found some Cornerville girls exceedingly attractive, I never went out with them except on a group basis, and I did not make any more home visits either.

As I went along, I found that life in Cornerville was not nearly so interesting and pleasant for the girls as it was for the men. A young man had complete freedom to wander and hang around. The girls could not hang on street corners. They had to divide their time between their own homes, the homes of girl friends and relatives, and a job, if they had one. Many of them had a dream that went like this: some young man, from outside of Cornerville, with a little money, a good job, and a good education would come and woo them and take them out of the district. I could hardly afford to fill this role.

6. Training in Participant Observation

The spring of 1937 provided me with an intensive course in participant observation. I was learning how to conduct myself, and I learned from various groups but particularly from the Nortons.

As I began hanging about Cornerville, I found that I needed an explanation for myself and for my study. As long as I was with Doc and vouched for by him, no one asked me who I was or what I was doing. When I circulated in other groups or even among the Nortons without him, it was obvious that they were curious about me.

I began with a rather elaborate explanation. I was studying the social history of Cornerville—but I had a new angle. Instead of working from the past up to the present, I was seeking to get a thorough knowledge of present conditions and then work from present to past. I was quite pleased with this explanation at the time, but nobody else seemed to care for it. I gave the explanation on only two occasions, and each time, when I had finished, there was an awkward silence. No one, myself included, knew what to say.

While this explanation had at least the virtue of covering everything that I might eventually want to do in the district, it was apparently too involved to mean anything to Cornerville people.

I soon found that people were developing their own explanation about me: I was writing a book about Cornerville. This might seem entirely too vague an explanation, and yet it sufficed. I found that my acceptance in the district depended on the personal relationships I developed far more than upon any explanations I might give. Whether it was a good thing to write a book about Cornerville depended entirely on people's opinions of me personally. If I was all right, then my project was all right; if I was no good, then no amount of explanation could convince them that the book was a good idea.

Of course people did not satisfy their curiosity about me simply by questions that they addressed to me directly. They turned to Doc, for example, and asked him about me. Doc then answered the questions and provided any reassurance that was needed.

I learned early in my Cornerville period the crucial importance of having the support of the key individuals in any groups or organizations I was studying. Instead of trying to explain myself to everyone, I found I was providing far more information about myself and my study to leaders such as Doc than I volunteered to the average corner boy. I always tried to give the impression that I was willing and eager to tell just as much about my study as anyone wished to know, but it was only with group leaders that I made a particular effort to provide really full information.

My relationship with Doc changed rapidly in this early Cornerville period. At first he was simply a key informant—and also my sponsor. As we spent more time together, I ceased to treat him as a passive informant. I discussed with him quite frankly what I was trying to do, what problems were puzzling me, and so on. Much of our time was spent in this discussion of ideas and observations, so that Doc became, in a very real sense, a collaborator in the research.

This full awareness of the nature of my study stimulated Doc to look for and point out to me the sorts of observations that I was interested in. Often when I picked him up at the flat where he lived with his sister and brother-in-law, he said to me: "Bill, you should have been around last night. You would have been interested in this." And then he would go on to tell me what had happened. Such accounts were always interesting and relevant to my study.

Doc found this experience of working with me interesting and enjoyable, and yet the relationship had its drawbacks. He once commented: "You've slowed me up plenty since you've been down here. Now, when I do something, I have to think what Bill Whyte would want to know about it and how I can explain it. Before, I used to do things by instinct."

However, Doc did not seem to consider this a serious handicap. Actually, without any training he was such a perceptive observer that it only needed a little stimulus to help him to make explicit much of the dynamics of the social organization of Cornerville. Some of the interpretations I have made are his more than mine, although it is now impossible to disentangle them.

While I worked more closely with Doc than with any other individual, I always sought out the leader in whatever group I was studying. I wanted not only sponsorship from him but also more active collaboration with the study. Since these leaders had the sort of position in the community that enabled them to observe much better than the followers what was going on and since they were in general more skilful observers than the followers, I found that I had much to learn from a more active collaboration with them.

In my interviewing methods I had been instructed not to argue with people or pass moral judgments upon them. This fell in with my own inclinations. I was glad to accept the people and to be accepted by them. However, this attitude did not come out so much in interviewing, for I did little formal interviewing. I sought to show this interested acceptance of the people and the community in my everyday participation.

I learned to take part in the street corner discussions on baseball and sex. This required no special training, since the topics seemed to be matters of almost universal interest. I was not able to participate so actively in discussions of horse-racing. I did begin to follow the races in a rather general and amateur way. I am sure it would have paid me to devote more study to the *Morning Telegraph* and other racing sheets, but my knowledge of baseball at least insured that I would not be left out of the street corner conversations.

While I avoided expressing opinions on sensitive topics, I found that arguing on some matters was simply part of the social pattern and that one could hardly participate without joining in the argument. I often found myself involved in heated but good-natured arguments about the relative merits of certain major-league ball players and managers. Whenever a girl or a group of girls would walk down the street, the fellows on the corner would make mental notes and later would discuss their evaluations of the females. These evaluations would run largely in terms of shape, and here I was glad to argue that Mary had a better "build" than Anna, or vice versa. Of course, if any of the men on the corner happened to be personally attached to Mary or Anna, no searching comments would be made, and I, too, would avoid this topic.

Sometimes I wondered whether just hanging on the street corner was an active enough process to be dignified by the term "research." Perhaps I should be asking these men questions. However, one has to learn when to question and when not to question as well as what questions to ask.

I learned this lesson one night in the early months when I was with Doc in Chichi's gambling joint. A man from another part of the city was regaling us with a tale of the organization of gambling activity. I had been told that he had once been a very big gambling operator, and he talked knowingly about many interesting matters. He did most of the talking, but the others asked questions and threw in comments, so at length I began to feel that I must say something in order to be part of the group. I said: "I suppose the cops were all paid off?"

The gambler's jaw dropped. He glared at me. Then he denied vehemently that any policemen had been paid off and immediately switched the conversation to another subject. For the rest of that evening I felt very uncomfortable.

The next day Doc explained the lesson of the previous evening. "Go easy on that 'who,' 'what,' 'why,' 'when,' 'where' stuff, Bill. You ask those questions, and people will clam up on you. If people accept you, you can just hang around, and you'll learn the answers in the long run without even having to ask the questions."

I found that this was true. As I sat and listened, I learned the answers to questions that I would not even have had the sense to ask if I had been getting my information solely on an interviewing basis. I did not abandon questioning altogether, of course. I simply learned to judge the sensitiveness of the question and my relationship to the people so that I only asked a question in a sensitive area when I was sure that my relationship to the people involved was very solid.

When I had established my position on the street corner, the data simply came to me without very active efforts on my part. It was only now and then, when I was concerned with a particular problem and felt I needed more information from a certain individual, that I would seek an opportunity to get the man alone and carry on a more formal interview.

At first I concentrated upon fitting into Cornerville, but a little later I had to face the question of how far I was to immerse myself in the life of the district. I bumped into that problem one evening as I was walking down the street with the Nortons. Trying to enter into the spirit of the small talk, I cut loose with a string of obscenities and profanity. The walk came to a momentary halt as they all stopped to look at me in surprise. Doc shook his head and said: "Bill, you're not supposed to talk like that. That doesn't sound like you."

I tried to explain that I was only using terms that were common on the street corner. Doc insisted, however, that I was different and that they wanted me to be that way.

This lesson went far beyond the use of obscenity and profanity. I learned that people did not expect me to be just like them; in fact, they were interested and pleased to find me different, just so long as I took a friendly interest in them. Therefore, I abandoned my efforts at complete immersion. My behavior was nevertheless affected by street corner life. When John Howard first came down from Harvard to join me in the Cornerville study, he noticed at once that I talked in Cornerville in a manner far different from that which I used at Harvard. This was not a matter of the use of profanity or obscenity, nor did I affect the use of ungrammatical expressions. I talked in the way that seemed natural to me, but what was natural in Cornerville was different from what was natural at Harvard. In Cornerville, I found myself putting much more animation into my speech, dropping terminal g's, and using gestures much more actively. (There was also, of course, the difference in the vocabulary that I used. When I was most deeply involved in Cornerville, I found myself rather tongue-tied in my visits to Harvard. I simply could not keep up with the discussions of international relations, of the nature of science, and so on, in which I had once been more or less at home.)

As I became accepted by the Nortons and by several other groups, I tried to make myself pleasant enough so that people would be glad to have me around. And, at the same time, I tried to avoid influencing the group, because I wanted to study the situation as unaffected by my presence as possible. Thus, throughout my Cornerville stay, I avoided accepting office or leadership positions in any of the groups with a single exception. At one time I was nominated as secretary of the Italian Community Club. My first impulse was to decline the nomination, but then I reflected that the secretary's job is normally considered simply a matter of dirty work—writing the minutes and handling the correspondence. I accepted and found that I could write a very full account of the progress of the meeting as it went on under the pretext of keeping notes for the minutes.

While I sought to avoid influencing individuals or groups, I tried to be helpful in the way a friend is expected to help in Cornerville. When one of the boys had to go downtown on an errand and wanted company, I went along with him. When somebody was trying to get a job and had to write a letter about himself, I helped him to compose it, and so on. This sort of behavior presented no problem, but, when it came to the matter of handling money, it was not at all clear just how I should behave. Of course, I sought to spend money on my friends just as they did on me. But what about lending money? It is expected in such a district that a man will help out his friends whenever he can, and often the help needed is financial. I lent money on several occasions, but I always felt uneasy about it. Naturally, a man appreciates it at the time you lend him the money, but how does he feel later when the time has come to pay, and he is not able to do so? Perhaps he is embarrassed and tries to avoid your company. On such occasions I tried to reassure the individual and tell him that I knew he did not have it just then and that I was not worried about it. Or I even told him to forget about the debt altogether. But that did not wipe it off the books; the uneasiness remained. I learned that it is possible to do a favor for a friend and cause a strain in the relationship in the process.

I know no easy solution to this problem. I am sure there will be times when the researcher would be extremely ill advised to refuse to make a personal loan. On the other hand, I am convinced that, whatever his financial resources, he should not look for opportunities to lend money and should avoid doing so whenever he gracefully can.

If the researcher is trying to fit into more than one group, his field work becomes more complicated. There may be times when the groups come into conflict with each other, and he will be expected to take a stand. There was a time in the spring of 1937 when the boys arranged a bowling match between the Nortons and the Italian Community Club. Doc bowled for the Nortons, of course. Fortunately, my bowling at this time had not advanced to a point where I was in demand for either team, and I was able to sit on the sidelines. From there I tried to applaud impartially the good shots of both teams, although I am afraid it was evident that I was getting more enthusiasm into my cheers for the Nortons.

When I was with members of the Italian Community Club, I did not feel at all called upon to defend the corner boys against disparaging remarks. However, there was one awkward occasion when I was with the corner boys and one of the college boys stopped to talk with me. In the course of the discussion he said: "Bill, these fellows wouldn't understand what I mean, but I am sure that you understand my point." There I thought I had to say something. I told him that he greatly underestimated the boys and that college men were not the only smart ones.

While the remark fitted in with my natural inclinations, I am sure it was justified from a strictly practical standpoint. My answer did not shake the feelings of superiority of the college boy, nor did it disrupt our personal relationship. On the other hand, as soon as he left, it became evident how deeply the corner boys felt about his statement. They spent some time giving explosive expressions to their opinion of him, and then they told me that I was different and that they appreciated it and that I knew much more than this fellow and yet I did not show it.

My first spring in Cornerville served to establish for me a firm position in the life of the district. I had only been there several weeks when Doc said to me: "You're just as much of a fixture around this street corner as that lamppost." Perhaps the greatest event signalizing my acceptance on Norton Street was the baseball game that Mike Giovanni organized against the group of Norton Street boys in their late teens. It was the old men who had won glorious victories in the past against the rising youngsters. Mike assigned me to a regular position on the team, not a key position perhaps (I was stationed in right field), but at least I was there. When it was my turn to bat in the last half of the ninth inning, the score was tied, there were two outs, and the bases were loaded. As I reached down to pick up my bat, I heard some of the fellows suggesting to Mike that he ought to put in a pinch-hitter. Mike answered them in a loud voice that must have been meant for me: "No, I've got confidence in Bill Whyte. He'll come through in the clutch." So, with Mike's confidence to buck me up, I went up there, missed two swings, and then banged a hard grounder through the hole between second and short. At least that is where they told me it went. I was so busy getting down to first base that I did not know afterward whether I had reached there on an error or a base hit.

That night, when we went down for coffee, Danny presented me with a ring for being a regular fellow and a pretty good ball player. I was particularly impressed by the ring, for it had been made by hand. Danny had started with a clear amber die discarded from his crap game and over long hours had used his lighted cigarette to burn a hole through it and to round the corners so that it came out a heart shape on top. I assured the fellows that I would always treasure the ring.

Perhaps I should add that my game-winning base hit made the score 18–17, so it is evident that I was not the only one who had been hitting the ball. Still, it was a wonderful feeling to come through when they were counting on me, and it made me feel still more that I belonged on Norton Street.

As I gathered my early research data, I had to decide how I was to organize the written notes. In the very early stage of exploration, I simply put all the notes, in chronological order, in a single folder. As I was to go on to study a number of different groups and problems, it was obvious that this was no solution at all.

I had to subdivide the notes. There seemed to be two main possibilities. I could organize the notes topically, with folders for politics, rackets, the church, the family, and so on. Or I could organize the notes in terms of the groups on which they were based, which would mean having folders on the Nortons, the Italian Community Club, and so on. Without really thinking the problem through, I began filing material on the group basis, reasoning that I could later redivide it on a topical basis when I had a better knowledge of what the relevant topics should be.

As the material in the folders piled up, I came to realize that the organization of notes by social groups fitted in with the way in which my study was developing. For example, we have a college-boy member of the Italian Community Club saying: "These racketeers give our district a bad name. They should really be cleaned out of here." And we have a member of the Nortons saying: "These racketeers are really all right. When you need help, they'll give it to you. The legitimate businessman—he won't even give you the time of day." Should these quotes be filed under "Racketeers, attitudes toward"? If so, they would only show that there are conflicting attitudes toward racketeers in Cornerville. Only a questionnaire (which is hardly feasible for such a topic) would show the distribution of attitudes in the district. Furthermore, how important would it be to know how many people felt one way or another on this topic? It seemed to me of much greater scientific interest to be able to relate the attitude to the *group* in which the individual participated. This shows why two individuals could be expected to have quite different attitudes on a given topic.

As time went on, even the notes in one folder grew beyond the point where my memory would allow me to locate any given item rapidly. Then I devised a rudimentary indexing system: a page in three columns containing, for each interview or observation report, the date, the person or people interviewed or observed, and a brief summary of the interview or observation record. Such an index would cover from three to eight pages.

When it came time to review the notes or to write from them, a five- to ten-minute perusal of the index was enough to give me a reasonably full picture of what I had and of where any given item could be located.

7. Venture into Politics

July and August, 1937, I spent away from Cornerville with my parents. Perhaps I was just too accustomed to the family summer vacation to remain in Cornerville, but at least I rationalized that I needed some time to get away and do some reading and get some perspective upon my study. The perspective was not easy to come by at that time. I still did not see the connecting link between a broad study of the life of the community and intensive studies of groups.

I came back feeling that I must somehow broaden my study. That might have meant dropping my contacts with the Nortons and the Italian Community Club in order to participate more heavily in other areas. Perhaps that would have been the logical decision in terms of the way I saw my Cornerville study at the time. Fortunately, I did not act that way. The club took only one evening a week, so there was no great pressure to drop that. The Nortons took much more time, and yet it meant something important to me to have a corner and a group where I was at home in Cornerville. At the time I did not clearly see that there was much more to a study of a group than an examination of its activities and personal relationships at a particular point in time. Only as I began to see changes in these groups did I realize how extremely important it is to observe a group over an extended period of time.

While I wandered along with the Nortons and the Italian Community Club more or less by a process of inertia, I decided I should expand the study by getting a broader and deeper view of the political life of the community. Street corner activities and politics in Cornerville were inextricably intertwined. There were several political organizations seeking to build up rival candidates. I felt that I could best gain an inside view of politics if I aligned myself actively with one political organization, yet I was afraid this might so label me that I would have difficulty with my study afterward in relation to people who were against this particular politician.

The problem solved itself for me. In the fall of 1937 there was a mayoralty contest. An Irish politician who had formerly been mayor and governor of the state was running again. Among the good Yankees, Murphy's name was the personification of corruption. However, in Cornerville, he had a reputation for being a friend of the poor man and of the Italian people. Most of the Cornerville politicians were for him, and he was expected to carry the district by a tremendous majority. I therefore decided that it would be a good thing for my study if I could get my start in politics working for this man. (Among my Harvard associates, this new political allegiance led to some raised eyebrows, but I rationalized that a complete novice could hardly be of any influence in securing the election of the notorious politician.)

In order to enlist in the campaign, I had to have some sort of local connection. I found this with George Ravello, state senator representing our ward and two others. At the restaurant where I lived, I met Paul Ferrante, who was Ravello's secretary and also a friend of the Martini family. Ferrante's services to Ravello were entirely on a volunteer basis. Paul was unemployed at the time and was working for the politician in hopes that he would some day get a political job out of it.

After a little preliminary discussion, I enlisted as the unpaid secretary of the state senator for the duration of the mayoralty campaign. When that election was over, I re-enlisted, for there was a special election for a vacant seat in Congress, and George Ravello was running for that office. Fortunately for my study, all the other Cornerville politicians were at least officially for Ravello, since he was running against several Irishmen. I therefore felt that I could be active in his campaign without creating barriers for myself anywhere else in the district.

As a campaign worker for the state senator, I was a complete anomaly. Most workers in such campaigns can at least claim to be able to deliver substantial numbers of votes; I could not pledge anything but my own. It was hard for the organization to get used to this. On one occasion, George Ravello gave me a ride up to the State House, in the course of which he wanted to know when I was going to deliver him the indorsement of the Italian Community Club. This was quite a touchy topic within the club at the time. On the one hand, all the members were interested in seeing an Italian-American advance to higher office, and yet they were embarrassed by being identified with George Ravello. The language he used in public was hardly refined, and he had gained publicity that had embarrassed the young men on several occasions. There was, for example, the time when a woman was testifying against a bill introduced into the senate by Ravello. Ravello got angry in the midst of the hearing and threatened to throw the good woman off the wharf and into the harbor if she ever set foot in his district. On another occasion, the newspapers carried a picture of Ravello with a black eye, which he had received in a fight with a member of the State Parole Board.

I explained to Ravello that it was against the policy of the club to indorse candidates for any public office. While this happened to be true, it was hardly a satisfactory explanation to the Senator. Still, he did not press the matter further, perhaps recognizing that the support of the Italian Community Club did not count for very much anyway.

Not being able to deliver votes, I sought to make myself useful by running errands and doing various odd jobs, such as nailing up Ravello posters in various parts of the district.

I am sure no one thought I was any real help to the Senator's campaign, but neither did I appear to be doing any harm, so I was allowed to hang around in the quarters which served as a combination political office and funeral parlor.

I found this one of the more unpleasant places to hang around, because I never was able to gain complete scientific detachment regarding funeral parlors. One of my most vivid and unpleasant memories of Cornerville stems from this period. One of the Senator's constituents had died. The stairs to his flat being too narrow to accommodate the casket, the deceased was laid out for friends and family in the back room of the funeral parlor. Unfortunately, he was laid out in two pieces, since he had had his leg amputated shortly before his death. The rest of his body had been embalmed, but I was told that there was no way of embalming a detached leg. The gangrenous leg gave off a most sickening odor. While family and friends came in to pay their last respects, we political workers sat in the front part of the office trying to keep our attention on politics. Now and then Paul Ferrante went about the room spraying perfume. The combination of perfume with the gangrenous stench was hardly an improvement. I stayed at my post through the day but finished up a trifle nauseated.

Since the politicians did not know what to do with my services and yet were willing to have me hang around, I found that I could develop my own job description. Before one of the meetings of the political workers, I suggested to Carrie Ravello—the candidate's wife and the real brains of the family—that I serve as secretary for such meetings. I then took notes while the meeting proceeded and typed her out a summary for later use. (The invention of carbon paper enabled me to retain my own copy of all the records.)

Actually, it was of no importance for the organization to have such a record. Although they were officially considered meetings to discuss political strategy and tactics, they were only pep rallies for the second string of political powers supporting Ravello. I never did get in on the top-level political discussions where the real decisions were made. However, my note-taking at these political meetings did give me a fully documented record of one area of activity. From here I went on to the large-scale political rally, where I sought to record on the spot the speeches and other activities of the leading Ravello supporters.

When election day came, I voted as the polls opened and then reported for duty at the candidate's headquarters. There I found I had been assigned to work with Ravello's secretary in another ward. I spent the first part of election day outside of Cornerville following Ferrante around and being of no real use to myself or to the organization. I did not worry about my contribution, because I was getting a growing impression that a lot of what passed under the name of political activity was simply a waste of time. On election-day morning we stopped in to chat with a number of friends of Paul Ferrante and had a drink or a cup of coffee here and there. Then we drove around to offer voters transportation to the polls, which in such a crowded district would be just around the corner. We made about thirty stops and took one voter to the polls, and she said she had been going to walk down in five minutes anyway. The others were either not home or told us they were going to walk down later.

At two o'clock I asked if it would be all right for me to leave and return to my ward. This was readily granted, so I was able to spend the rest of the day in Cornerville.

When I got home, I began hearing alarming reports from the home ward of the Irish politician who was Ravello's chief rival. He was said to have a fleet of taxicabs cruising about his ward so that each of his repeaters would be able to vote in every precinct of the ward. It became clear that, if we did not steal the election ourselves, this low character would steal it from us.

Around five o'clock one of the senator's chief lieutenants rushed up to a group of us who were hanging on the corner across the street from my home polling place. He told us that Joseph Maloney's section of our ward was wide open for repeaters, that the cars were ready to transport them, and that all he needed were a few men to get to work. At the moment the organization was handicapped by a shortage of manpower to accomplish this important task. The senator's lieutenant did not ask for volunteers; he simply directed us to get into the cars to go to the polling places where the work could be done. I hesitated a moment, but I did not refuse.

Before the polls had closed that night, I had voted three more times for George Ravello—really not much of a feat, since another novice who had started off at the same time as I managed to produce nine votes in the same period of time. Two of my votes were cast in Joseph Maloney's end of the ward; the third was registered in my home polling place.

I was standing on the corner when one of the politician's henchmen came up to me with the voting list to ask me to go in. I explained that this was my home polling place and that I had already voted under my own name. When they learned that this had been when the polls opened, they told me that I had nothing to worry about and that a new shift was now on duty. They had the name of Frank Petrillo picked out for me. They told me that Petrillo was a Sicilian fisherman who was out to sea on election day, so we were exercising his democratic rights for him. I looked at the voting list to discover that Petrillo was forty-five years old and stood five feet nine. Since I was twenty-three and six feet three, this seemed implau-

sible to me, and I raised a question. I was assured that this made no difference at all, since the people inside the polling place were Joe Maloney's
people. I was not completely reassured by this, but, nevertheless, I got in
line to wait my new turn in the rush of the hour before the polls closed.

I gave my name, and the woman at the gate checked me in, I picked up
my ballot, went back to the booth, and marked it for George Ravello. As I
was about to put the ballot into the box, this woman looked me over and
asked me how old I was. Suddenly the ridiculousness of my masquerade
struck home to me. I knew I was supposed to say forty-five, but I could
not voice such an absurd lie. Instead, I compromised on twenty-nine. She
asked how tall I was, and again I compromised, giving the figure as six
feet. They had me all right, but still the questioning went on. The woman
asked me how I spelled my name. In the excitement I spelled it wrong.
The other woman checker now came over and asked me about my sisters.
I thought I had recalled seeing the names of some female Petrillos on the
list, and, in any case, if I invented names that did not appear, they could
be names of women who were not registered. I said, "Yes, I have two sisters." She asked their names. I said, "Celia and Florence."

She leered at me and asked, "What about this Marie Petrillo?"

I took a deep breath and said, "She's my cousin."

They said they would have to challenge my vote. They called for the
warden in charge of the polling place.

I had a minute to wait before he stepped forward, and that was plenty
of time to mull over my future. I could see before my eyes large headlines
on the front pages of Eastern City's tabloids—HARVARD FELLOW AR-
RESTED FOR REPEATING. Why wouldn't they play it up? Indeed, this was
an ideal man-bites-dog newspaper story. In that moment I resolved that
at least I would not mention my connection with Harvard or my Cornerville study when I was arrested.

The warden now stepped up, said he would have to challenge my vote,
and asked me to write my name on the back of the ballot. I went over to
the booth. But, by this time, I was so nervous that I forgot what my first
name was supposed to be and put down "Paul." The warden took my
ballot and looked at the back of it. He had me swear that this was my
name and that I had not voted before. I did so. I went through the gate.
He told me to stop. As I looked over the crowd coming in, I thought of
trying to run for it, but I did not break away. I came back. He looked at the
book of registered voters. He turned back to the booth, and for a moment
his back was to me. Then I saw him scratch out the name I had written on
the back of the ballot. He put the ballot into the box, and it registered with
a ring of the bell. He told me I could go out, and I did, trying to walk in a
calm and leisurely manner.

When I was out on the street, I told the politician's lieutenant that my
vote had been challenged. "Well, what do you care? We didn't lose any-

thing by it." Then I told him that the vote had finally gone through. "Well, so much the better. Listen, what could they have done to you? If the cops had taken you in, they wouldn't hold you. We would fix you up."

I did not eat well that night. Curiously enough, I did not feel nearly so guilty over what I had done until I had thought that I was going to be arrested. Up to that point, I had just gone numbly along. After supper, I went out to look up Tony Cardio of the Italian Community Club. As I had walked into his home precinct to repeat, I encountered him coming out of the polling place. As we passed, he grinned at me and said: "They're working you pretty hard today, aren't they?" I immediately jumped to the conclusion that he must know that I was going in to repeat. Now I felt that I must see him as soon as possible to explain in the best way that I could what I had been doing and why. Fortunately for me, Tony was not home that night. As my anxiety subsided, I recognized that, simply because I knew my own guilt, it did not necessarily follow that everybody else and Tony knew what I had done. I confirmed this indirectly when I had a conversation with Tony later about the election. He raised no question concerning my voting activities.

That was my performance on election day. What did I gain from it? I had seen through firsthand personal experience how repeating was accomplished. But this was really of very little value, for I had been observing these activities at quite close range before, and I could have had all the data without taking any risk. Actually, I learned nothing of research value from the experience, and I took a chance of jeopardizing my whole study. While I escaped arrest, these things are not always fixed as firmly as the politician's henchman think they are. A year later, when I was out of town at election time, somebody was actually arrested for voting in *my* name.

Even apart from the risk of arrest, I faced other possible losses. While repeating was fairly common in our ward, there were only relatively few people who engaged in it, and they were generally looked down upon as the fellows who did the dirty work. Had the word got around about me, my own standing in the district would have suffered considerable damage. So far as I know, my repeating never did become known beyond some of the key people in Ravello's organization. Most of my repeating had been done outside of Cornerville, and my Norton Street friends did not vote in the same precinct where I put in my second Cornerville vote. I had not been observed by anyone whose opinion could damage me. Furthermore, I was just plain lucky that I did not reveal myself to Tony Cardio; in fact, I was lucky at every point.

The experience posed problems that transcended expediency. I had been brought up as a respectable, law-abiding, middle-class citizen. When I discovered that I was a repeater, I found my conscience giving me serious trouble. This was not like the picture of myself that I had been trying to build up. I could not laugh it off simply as a necessary part of the field work. I knew that it was not necessary; at the point where I began to repeat, I could have refused. There were others who did refuse to do it. I had simply got myself involved in the swing of the campaign and let myself be carried along. I had to learn that, in order to be accepted by the people in a district, you do not have to do everything just as they do it. In fact, in a district where there are different groupings with different standards of behavior, it may be a matter of very serious consequence to conform to the standards of one particular group.

I also had to learn that the field worker cannot afford to think only of learning to live with others in the field. He has to continue living with himself. If the participant observer finds himself engaging in behavior that he has learned to think of as immoral, then he is likely to begin to wonder what sort of a person he is after all. Unless the field worker can carry with him a reasonably consistent picture of himself, he is likely to run into difficulties.

8. Back on Norton Street

When the campaign was over, I went back to Norton Street, I did not sever my ties with the Ravello organization altogether. For this there were two reasons: I wanted to maintain my connections for possible further research in politics; but then also I did not want them to think of me as just another of those "phonies" who made a fuss over the politician when he seemed to have a chance to win and abandoned him when he lost. Still, I had no strong personal tie to hold me to the organization. Carrie Ravello I liked and respected; the Senator puzzled and interested me, but I never felt that I got to know him. His one-time secretary just dropped out of sight for a while after the election—still owing me ten dollars. The others did not really matter to me personally. And, as I review my notes today, even their names have little meaning.

As I became more active once again on Norton Street, the local world began to look different. The world I was observing was in a process of change. I saw some of the members of the Italian Community Club establishing contacts with the upper world of Yankee control as I followed them to All-American Night at the Women's Republican Club. I saw the stresses and strains within the Nortons growing out of contacts with the Aphrodite Club and the Italian Community Club. I watched Doc, completely without scientific detachment, as he prepared for his doomed effort to run for public office.

Then in April, 1938, one Saturday night I stumbled upon one of my most exciting research experiences in Cornerville. It was the night when the Nortons were to bowl for the prize money; the biggest bowling night of the whole season. I recall standing on the corner with the boys while they discussed the coming contest. I listened to Doc, Mike, and Danny making their predictions as to the order in which the men would finish. At first, this made no particular impression upon me, as my own unexpressed predictions were exactly along the same lines. Then, as the men joked and argued, I suddenly began to question and take a new look at the whole situation. I was convinced that Doc, Mike, and Danny were basically correct in their predictions, and yet why should the scores approximate the structure of the gang? Were these top men simply better natural athletes than the rest? That made no sense, for here was Frank Bonnelli, who was a good enough athlete to win the promise of a tryout with a major-league baseball team. Why should not Frank outdo us all at the bowling alley? Then I remembered the baseball game we had had a year earlier against the younger crowd on Norton Street. I could see the man who was by common consent the best baseball player of us all striking out with long, graceful swings and letting the grounders bounce through his legs. And then I remembered that neither I nor anyone else seemed to have been surprised at Frank's performance in this game. Even Frank himself was not surprised, as he explained: "I can't seem to play ball when I'm playing with fellows I know like that bunch."

I went down to the alleys that night fascinated and just a bit awed by what I was about to witness. Here was the social structure in action right on the bowling alleys. It held the individual members in their places—and I along with them. I did not stop to reason then that, as a close friend of Doc, Danny, and Mike, I held a position close to the top of the gang and therefore should be expected to excel on this great occasion. I simply felt myself buoyed up by the situation. I felt my friends were for me, had confidence in me, wanted me to bowl well. As my turn came and I stepped up to bowl, I felt supremely confident that I was going to hit the pins that I was aiming at. I have never felt quite that way before—or since. Here at the bowling alley I was experiencing subjectively the impact of the group structure upon the individual. It was a strange feeling, as if something larger than myself was controlling the ball as I went through my swing and released it toward the pins.

When it was all over, I looked at the scores of all the other men. I was still somewhat bemused by my own experience, and now I was excited to discover that the men had actually finished in the predicted order with only two exceptions that could readily be explained in terms of the group structure.

As I later thought over the bowling-alley contest, two things stood out in my mind. In the first place, I was convinced that now I had something important: the relationship between individual performance and group structure, even though at this time I still did not see how such observation would fit in with the over-all pattern of the Cornerville study. I believed then (and still believe now) that this sort of relationship may be observed in other group activities everywhere. As an avid baseball fan, I had often been puzzled by the records of some athletes who seemed to be able to hit and throw and field with superb technical qualifications and yet were unable to make the major-league teams. I had also been puzzled by cases where men who had played well at one time suddenly failed badly, whereas other men seemed to make tremendous improvements that could not be explained simply on the basis of increasing experience. I suspect that a systematic study of the social structure of a baseball team, for example, will explain some of these otherwise mysterious phenomena. The other point that impressed me involved field research methods. Here I had the scores of the men on that final night at the bowling alleys. This one set of figures was certainly important, for it represented the performance of the men in the event that they all looked upon as the climax of the year. However, this same group had been bowling every Saturday night for many months, and some of the members had bowled on other nights in between. It would have been a ridiculously simple task for me to have kept a record for every string bowled by every man on every Saturday night of that season and on such other evenings as I bowled with the men. This would have produced a set of statistics that would have been the envy of some of my highly quantitative friends. I kept no record of these scores, because at this time I saw no point to it. I had been looking upon Saturday night at the bowling alleys as simply recreation for myself and my friends. I found myself enjoying the bowling so much that now and then I felt a bit guilty about neglecting my research. I was bowling with the men in order to establish a social position that would enable me to interview them and observe important things. But what were these important things? Only after I passed up this statistical gold mine did I suddenly realize that the behavior of the men in the regular bowling-alley sessions was the perfect example of what I should be observing. Instead of bowling in order to be able to observe something else, I should have been bowling in order to observe bowling. I learned then that the day-to-day routine activities of these men constituted the basic data of my study.

9. Replanning the Research

The late spring and summer of 1938 brought some important changes into my research.

On May 28, I was married to Kathleen King, and three weeks later we returned to Cornerville together. Kathleen had visited me at the restaurant and had met some of my friends. Even as a married man, I did not want to move out of the district, and Kathleen, fortunately, was eager to move in. This presented problems, because, while we were not asking for everything, we did hope to find an apartment with a toilet and bathtub inside it. We looked at various gloomy possibilities until at last we found a building that was being remodeled on Shelby Street. Some of my Norton Street friends warned us against the neighborhood, saying that the place was full of Sicilians who were a very cutthroat crowd. Still, the apartment had the bathtub and toilet and was clean and relatively airy. It had no central heating, but we could be reasonably comfortable with the kitchen stove.

Now that we were two, we could enter into new types of social activities, and Kathleen could learn to know some of the women as I had become acquainted with the men. However, these new directions of social activity were something for the future. My problem now was to find where I was and where I was going. This was a period of stocktaking.

In describing my Cornerville study, I have often said I was eighteen months in the field before I knew where my research was going. In a sense, this is literally true. I began with the general idea of making a community study. I felt that I had to establish myself as a participant observer in order to make such a study. In the early months in Cornerville I went through the process that sociologist Robert Johnson has described in his own field work. I began as a nonparticipating observer. As I became accepted into the community, I found myself becoming almost a nonobserving participant. I got the feel of life in Cornerville, but that meant that I got to take for granted the same things that my Cornerville friends took for granted. I was immersed in it, but I could as yet make little sense out of it. I had a feeling that I was doing something important, but I had yet to explain to myself what it was.

Fortunately, at this point I faced a very practical problem. My three-year fellowship would run out in the summer of 1939. The fellowship could be renewed for a period up to three years. Applications for renewal were due in the early spring of 1939.

I was enjoying Cornerville, and I felt that I was getting somewhere, yet at the same time I felt that I needed at least three more years. I realized that so far I had little to show for the time I had spent. When I submitted my application for renewal, I must also submit some evidence that I had acquitted myself well in the first three-year period. I would have to write something. I had several months in which to do the writing, but the task at first appalled me. I sat down to ask myself what it was in Cornerville upon which I had reasonably good data. Was there anything ready to be written up? I pondered this and talked it over with Kathleen and with John Howard, who was working with me in the district.

Still thinking in terms of a community study, I recognized that I knew very little about family life in Cornerville, and my data were very thin upon the church, although John Howard was beginning to work on this area. I had been living with the restaurant family in a room that overlooked the corner where T. S., the most prominent Cornerville racketeer, sometimes was seen with his followers. I had looked down upon the group many times from my window, and yet I had never met the men. Racketeering was of obvious importance in the district, yet all I knew about it was the gossip I picked up from men who were only a little closer to it than I. I had much more information regarding political life and organization, but even here I felt that there were so many gaps that I could not yet put the pieces together.

If these larger areas were yet to be filled in, what on earth did I have to present? As I thumbed through the various folders, it was obvious that the Norton and Community Club folders were fatter than the rest. If I knew anything about Cornerville, I must know it about the Nortons and the Italian Community Club. Perhaps, if I wrote up these two stories, I would begin to see some pattern in what I was doing in Cornerville.

As I wrote the case studies of the Nortons and of the Italian Community, a pattern for my research gradually emerged in my mind.

I realized at last that I was not writing a community study in the usual sense of that term. The reader who examines *Middletown* will note that it is written about people in general in that community. Individuals or groups do not figure in the story except as they illustrate the points that the authors are making (the sequel, *Middletown in Transition,* presents one exception to this description with a chapter on the leading family of the community). The reader will further note that *Middletown* is organized in terms of such topics as getting a living, making a home, training the young, and using leisure.

The Lynds accomplished admirably the task they set out to accomplish. I simply came to realize that my task was different. I was dealing with particular individuals and with particular groups.

I realized also that there was another difference that I had stumbled upon. I had assumed that a sociological study should present a description and analysis of a community at one particular point in time, supported of course by some historical background. I now came to realize that *time* itself was one of the key elements in my study. I was observing, describing, and analyzing groups as they evolved and changed through time. It seemed to me that I could explain much more effectively the behavior of men when I observed them over time than would have been the case if I had got them at one point in time. In other words, I was taking a moving picture instead of a still photograph.

But, if this was a study of particular individuals and there were more than twenty thousand people in the district, how could I say anything significant about Cornerville on this individual and group basis? I came to realize that I could only do so if I saw individuals and groups in terms of their positions in the social structure. I also must assume that, whatever the individual and group differences were, there were basic similarities to be found. Thus I would not have to study every corner gang in order to make meaningful statements about corner gangs in Cornerville. A study of one corner gang was not enough, to be sure, but, if an examination of several more showed up the uniformities that I expected to find, then this part of the task became manageable.

On the Italian Community Club, I felt that I needed no additional data. There were few enough college men in Cornerville at the time, so that this one group represented a large sample of people in this category. It also seemed to me that they represented significant points in the social structure and in the social mobility process. There would certainly be others like them coming along after they had left the district, even as the Sunset Dramatic Club had gone before them. Furthermore, examination of their activities showed up important links with Republican politics and with the settlement house.

I now began to see the connection between my political study and the case study of the corner gang. The politician did not seek to influence separate individuals in Cornerville; consciously or unconsciously he sought out group leaders. So it was men like Doc who were the connecting links between their groups and the larger political organization. I could now begin writing my study by examining particular groups in detail, and then I could go on to relate them to the larger structures of the community. With this pattern in mind, I came to realize that I had much more data on politics than I had thought.

There were still important gaps in my study. My knowledge of the role of the church in the community was fragmentary, and this I hoped to fill in. I had done no systematic work upon the family. On the one hand, it seemed inconceivable that one could write a study of Cornerville without discussing the family; yet, at the same time, I was at a loss as to how to proceed in tying family studies into the organization of the book as it was emerging in my mind. I must confess also that for quite unscientific reasons I have always found politics, rackets, and gangs more interesting than the basic unit of human society.

The gap that worried me most was in the area of the rackets and the police. I had a general knowledge of how the rackets functioned, but nothing to compare with the detailed interpersonal data I had upon the corner gang. As my book was evolving, it seemed to me that this was the gap that simply must be filled, although at the time I had no idea how I would get the inside picture that was necessary.

I finished the writing of my first two case studies and submitted them in support of my application for a renewal of the fellowship. Some weeks later I received my answer. The fellowship had been renewed for one year instead of the three for which I had been hoping. At first, I was bitterly disappointed. As I was just beginning to get my bearings, I did not see how it would be possible to finish an adequate study in the eighteen months that then remained.

I am now inclined to believe that this one year cut-off was a very good thing for me and my research. In a sense, the study of a community or an organization has no logical end point. The more you learn, the more you see that there is to learn. If I had had three years instead of one, my study would have taken longer to complete. Perhaps it might have been a better study. On the other hand, when I knew I had just eighteen months to go, I had to settle down and think through my plans more thoroughly and push ahead with the research and writing much more purposefully.

10. Again the Corner Gang

The most important steps I took in broadening my study of street corner gangs grew out of Doc's recreation center project, although at first I had some other interests in mind. It began with one of my periodic efforts to get Doc a job. When I heard that the Cornerville House had finally been successful in getting its grant to open three store-front recreation centers, I sought to persuade Mr. Smith, the director, to man them with local men who, like Doc, were leaders in their groups. I found that he had planned to man them with social workers trained in group work. When I realized that it was hopeless to get him to select three local men, I tried to urge at least Doc upon him. I could see that Mr. Smith was tempted by the idea and afraid of it at the same time. When I brought Doc in to meet him, I found that I lost ground instead of gaining it, for, as Doc told me later, he had got a dizzy spell there in the settlement-house office, and he had been in no condition to make a favorable personal impression. If Doc and I had figured out correctly the underlying causes for his dizzy spells, then a steady job and the money that would enable him to resume his customary pattern of social activity would cure these neurotic symptoms. On the other hand, I could hardly explain this to Mr. Smith. I was afraid that it appeared that I was simply trying to do a favor for a friend. As my last effort in this direction, I turned over to Mr. Smith a copy of my case study of the Nortons—and asked him please to keep it confidential, since I was not ready to publish.

This made the difference. Mr. Smith agreed to hire Doc.

As the preliminary activities of setting up the recreation centers got under way, I began to worry about my confident predictions of Doc's success. In the preliminary meetings to discuss plans for the centers, Doc was passive and apparently apathetic. Nevertheless, almost from the moment that Doc's center opened, it became apparent that it was to be a success.

On one of my early visits to Doc's center, he introduced me to Sam Franco, who was to play a far more important part in my study than brief mentions of him in the book indicate. Doc met Sam the night his center opened. Sam's gang was hanging around outside of the center looking the place over. Sam came in as the emissary of his group—a move which immediately identified him as the leader to Doc. The two men discussed the center briefly, and then Sam went out and brought his gang in. By the second night of the center, Sam had become Doc's lieutenant in its administration. Doc knew a few people in this part of the district, but Sam knew everybody.

Doc knew that I was trying to extend my corner gang study, and he suggested that Sam might be the man to help me. Doc had already learned that Sam had been keeping a scrapbook with newspaper accounts of Cornerville activities and some personal material on his own group.

I invited Sam and his scrapbook up to our apartment. There I learned that Sam had got started on his scrapbook after an experience on a National Youth Administration Project, where he had been working for a man who was writing a study of the problems of youth in this region. The scrapbook was completely miscellaneous and undirected, but it did have one part that particularly interested me. Sam had a section for his own gang with one page for each member. At the top of the page was a line drawing (from memory) of the individual, and then he wrote in such points as age, address, education, job, and ambition. (Usually he had written "none" opposite the heading, "ambition.")

My task was now to persuade Sam that, while it was fine to look upon these men as individuals, it was even better to look upon them in terms of their relations with each other. I had only begun my explanation when Sam got the point and accepted it with enthusiasm. Of course, this was the sort of thing he knew; he had so taken it for granted that it had not occurred to him how important it might be. From this point on until the end of my study Sam Franco was my research assistant. I even managed to get Harvard to pay a hundred dollars for his services.

We began with an analysis of Sam's own gang, the Millers. We also looked at other gangs that came into Doc's recreation center. Here we had the great advantage of having two sharp observers checking each other on the same groups. I was reassured to find that they were in complete

agreement on the top-leadership structure of every gang—with one exception. This one exception did trouble me until the explanation presented itself.

I had spent part of one afternoon listening to Doc and Sam argue over
the leadership of one gang. Doc claimed that Carl was the man; Sam argued that it was Tommy. Each man presented incidents that he had observed in support of his point of view. The following morning Sam
rushed up to my house with this bulletin: "You know what happened last
night? Carl and Tommy nearly had it out. They got into a big argument,
and now the gang is split into two parts with some of them going with
Carl and the rest going with Tommy." So their conflicting views turned
out to be an accurate representation of what was taking place in the gang.

As I worked on these other gang studies, I assumed that I had finished
my research on the Nortons. Still, I kept in close touch with Doc, and, just
for recreation, I continued to bowl with the remnants of the Nortons on
some Saturday nights.

With my attention directed elsewhere, I failed to see what was happening among the Nortons right before my eyes. I knew Long John was not
bowling as he had in previous years, and I also knew that he was not as
close to Doc, Danny, and Mike as he had been. I had noticed that, when
Long John was on Norton Street, the followers badgered him more aggressively than they ever had before. I must have assumed some connection among these phenomena, and yet I did not make much of the situation until Doc came to me and told me of Long John's psychological
difficulties.

It was as if this information set off a flash bulb in my head. Suddenly all
the pieces of the puzzle fell together. The previous season, I had stumbled
upon the relationship between position in the group and performance at
the bowling alleys. I now saw the three-way connection between group
position, performance, and mental health. And not only for Long John.
Doc's dizzy spells seemed to have precisely the same explanation.

We could put it more generally in this way. The individual becomes accustomed to a certain pattern of interaction. If this pattern is subject to a
drastic change, then the individual can be expected to experience mental
health difficulties. That is a very crude statement. Much further research
would be needed before we could determine the degree of change necessary, the possibilities of compensating with interactions in other social
areas, and so on. But here at least was one way of tying together human
relations and psychological adjustment.

Furthermore, here was an opportunity to experiment in therapy. If my
diagnosis was correct, then the line of treatment was clear: re-establish
something like Long John's pre-existing pattern of interaction, and the neurotic symptoms should disappear. This was the first real opportunity to test
my conclusions on group structure. I embraced it with real enthusiasm.

Convinced as I was of the outcome that should follow, I must confess that I was somewhat awestruck when, under Doc's skilfully executed therapy program, Long John not only lost his neurotic symptoms but also closed out the season by winning the prize money in the final bowling contest. Of course, this victory was not necessary to establish the soundness of the diagnosis. It would have been enough for Long John to have re-established himself *among* the top bowlers. His five-dollar prize was just a nice bonus for interaction theory.

11. Studying Racketeering

My meeting with Tony Cataldo, the prominent Cornerville racketeer, came about almost by chance. I dropped in one afternoon at the restaurant where I had first lived in Cornerville. Ed Martini, Al's older brother, was there at the time. He was grumbling about a pair of banquet tickets he had had to buy from a local policeman. He said that his wife did not want to go to banquets; perhaps I might like to accompany him.

I asked what the occasion was. He told me that the banquet was in honor of the son of the local police lieutenant. The young man had just passed his bar examinations and was starting out on his legal career. I thought a moment. It was perfectly obvious what sorts of people would be present at the banquet: mainly policemen, politicians, and racketeers. I decided that this might be an opportunity for me.

At the banquet hall, Ed and I took up our position in the lounge outside the men's room. Here we encountered Tony Cataldo and one of his employees, Rico Deleo. It turned out that Ed Martini knew Tony slightly and that Rico lived right across the street from me. Rico asked what I was doing, and I said something about writing a book on Cornerville. Tony said he had seen me around taking photographs of the *feste* that had been staged on Shelby Street the previous summer. This proved to be a fortunate association in his mind, since I could talk quite freely about what I had been trying to learn of the *feste*—which were actually just a minor interest in the research.

The four of us went up to a banquet table together, where we had to wait more than an hour for our food. We munched on olives and celery and sympathized with one another over the poor service. After the dinner we stepped downstairs and bowled three strings together. By this time, Tony was quite friendly and invited me to stop in at his store any time.

I paid several visits to the back room of the store from which Tony operated some of his business. A week after we had met, Tony invited Kathleen and me to dinner at his home. His wife, an attractive young girl, told us later that he had spoken of us as a Harvard professor and a commercial artist. She was very upset that he gave her only one day's notice for the dinner when she felt she needed at least a week to prepare for such important personages. The food was nevertheless quite elaborate, and each course seemed like a whole meal. After dinner, Tony drove us out to meet some of his relatives in one of the suburbs. Then we all went bowling together.

We had dinner twice at their home, and they came to ours twice. On each occasion, apart from the small talk, the research pattern was similar. We talked some about the *feste*, about the club life of the *paesani* from the old country, and about such things which Tony associated with my study. Then, I gradually eased him into a discussion of his business. The discussion seemed to move naturally in this direction. It was just like a friend asking a legitimate businessman about the progress he was making and the problems he was meeting. Tony seemed glad to unburden himself.

I now felt optimistic about my future in racketeering. We seemed to be getting along very well with the Cataldos, and I was ready to follow Tony into the new field. However, after the first exchanges of sociability, Tony seemed to lose interest in us.

I was puzzled by this sudden cooling-off. I am not sure I have the full explanation, but I think there were at least two parts of it.

In the first place, Tony ran into a business crisis at about this time. Some men broke into his horse room one afternoon, held it up, and took all the money from the customers and from Tony. In order to maintain good relations with his customers, Tony had to reimburse them for the robbery, so that afternoon was doubly costly. It was also most frustrating, because, as the men were making their getaway, Tony could look out of the window and see them running right beneath him. He had a clear shot at them, yet he could not shoot, because he knew that a shooting would close down gambling in Cornerville like nothing else. As long as these things were done quietly, the "heat" was not so likely to be on.

This might have accounted for an interruption in our social life together but hardly for a complete cessation. It seems to me that the other factor was a problem in social status and mobility. At first, Tony had built me up to his wife—and probably to friends and relatives also—as a Harvard professor. Both the Cataldos were highly status-conscious. They did not allow their young son to play with the local riffraff. They explained that they only lived in the district because it was necessary for business reasons and that they still hoped to move out. When we were their guests, they introduced us to their friends and relatives who lived in more fashionable parts of the city.

On the other hand, when the Cataldos came to our house for dinner they just met with us and nobody else. Furthermore, Tony was now seeing me associating with the men on Shelby Street who were distinctly small fry to him. At first, he had thought that his contact with me was something important; now, perhaps, he considered it insignificant.

To some extent, I was aware of this risk and thought of the possibility of having Harvard friends in to dinner with the Cataldos. I had been keeping the two worlds apart. One Harvard friend, a symbolic logician, had once asked me to introduce him to a crap game. He explained that he had figured out mathematically how to win in a crap game. I explained that my crap-shooting friends had reached the same mathematical conclusion by their rule-of-thumb method, and I begged off from this adventure. On another occasion, we had the wife of one of my Harvard associates visiting us when one of the local men dropped in. Sizing up his new audience, he began regaling her with accounts of famous murders that had taken place in Cornerville in recent years. She listened with eyes wide open. At the end of one particularly hair-raising story she asked, "Who killed him?"

Our Cornerville friend shook his head and said: "Lady! Lady! Around here you don't ask them things."

That incident did us no damage, for the man knew us well enough to take it all as a joke. Still, I was hesitant about mixing Harvard and Cornerville. I did not worry about what Cornerville would do to Harvard, but I did worry lest some Harvard friend would unintentionally make a blunder that would make things awkward for me or would act in such a way as to make the local people ill at ease. For that reason, I kept the two worlds separate, but that meant that Tony could not improve his social standing through associating with us.

When it became evident that I was at a dead end with Tony, I cast about for other avenues leading to a study of racketeering. Two possibilities seemed open. Tony had an older brother who worked for him. I reasoned that, since the two men were brothers and worked so closely together, Henry would know almost as much about racket developments as Tony. I already had seen something of Henry, and I set about building the relationship further. This went along smoothly with visits back and forth from house to house as well as conversations in the back room of the store. (This indicates that Tony did not drop us out of suspicion, for in that case he could have seen to it that we did not take up with his brother.)

This led to a good deal of discussion of Tony's racket organization, which was exceedingly valuable to me. Still, I had an uneasy feeling that I was not getting what I needed. I was not yet ready to give up the possibility of getting close to Tony and of observing him in action. I understood that he was a member of the Cornerville Social and Athletic Club, which was located right across the street from our apartment. I joined the club then in order to renew my pursuit of Tony Cataldo.

At first I was disappointed in the fruits of my decision. While officially a member, Tony was rarely in the clubroom. In a few weeks it became evident that I was not going to cement relations with him in this area. What next? I considered dropping out of the club. Perhaps I would have done so if there had been other research openings then demanding my attention. Since I had planned to concentrate upon the role of the racketeer and had no other plans at the time, I rationalized that I should stay with the club. I did not record the reasons for my decision at the time. Perhaps I had a hunch that interesting things would break here. Or perhaps I was just lucky.

At least, I recognized that the club presented some new angles in research. It was far larger than any corner gang I had studied. Here was an opportunity to carry further the observational methods I had used on the Nortons.

When I wrote my first draft of this present statement, I described how I developed these new methods to a point where I had systematic knowledge of the structure of the club *before* the election crisis. In other words, when Tony entered and sought to manipulate the club, I already had a full picture of the structure he was attempting to manipulate. I must now admit, following a review of my notes, that this is a retrospective falsification. What I first wrote was what I *should* have done. Actually, I began my systematic observations of the club several weeks before the election. When the crisis arrived, I had only an impressionistic picture of group structure. The notes I had then justified no systematic conclusions.

There were two factors that propelled me into more systematic efforts at charting the organizational structure. In the first place, when I began spending time in the club, I also began looking around for *the* leader. Naturally, I did not find *him*. If Tony was not around much, then somebody must take over in his absence. The club had a president, but he was just an indecisive nice guy who obviously did not amount to much. Of course, I did not find *the* leader because the club consisted of two factions with two leaders and—just to make matters more confusing for me—Carlo Tedesco, the leader of one faction, was not even a member of the club when I began my observations. Since I was completely confused in my crude efforts to map the structure, it followed that I must get at the data more systematically.

Then the political crisis underlined the necessity of pushing ahead with such observations. I had to learn more about the structure that Tony was seeking to manipulate.

Here I had a more complicated task than any I had faced before. The club had fifty members. Fortunately, only about thirty of them were frequent attenders, so that I could concentrate on that smaller number, but even that number presented a formidable problem.

I felt I would have to develop more formal and systematic procedures than I had used when I had been hanging on a street corner with a much smaller group of men. I began with positional mapmaking. Assuming that the men who associated together most closely socially would also be those who lined up together on the same side when decisions were to be made, I set about making a record of the groupings I observed each evening in the club. To some extent, I could do this from the front window of our apartment. I simply adjusted the venetian blind so that I was hidden from view and so that I could look down and into the store-front club. Unfortunately, however, our flat was two flights up, and the angle of vision was such that I could not see past the middle of the clubroom. To get the full picture, I had to go across the street and be with the men.

When evening activities were going full blast, I looked around the room to see which people were talking together, playing cards together, or otherwise interacting. I counted the number of men in the room, so as to know how many I would have to account for. Since I was familiar with the main physical objects of the clubroom, it was not difficult to get a mental picture of the men in relation to tables, chairs, couches, radio, and so on. When individuals moved about or when there was some interaction between these groupings, I sought to retain that in mind. In the course of an evening, there might be a general reshuffling of positions. I was not able to remember every movement, but I tried to observe with which members the movements began. And when another spatial arrangement developed, I went through the same mental process as I had with the first.

I managed to make a few notes on trips to the men's room, but most of the mapping was done from memory after I had gone home. At first, I went home once or twice for mapmaking during the evening, but, with practice, I got so that I could retain at least two positional arrangements in memory and could do all of my notes at the end of the evening.

I found this an extremely rewarding method, which well compensated me for the boring routines of endless mapping. As I piled up these maps, it became evident just what the major social groupings were and what people fluctuated between the two factions of the club. As issues arose within the club, I could predict who would stand where.

In the course of my observations I recorded 106 groupings. Upon inspecting the data, I divided the club tentatively into the two factions I thought I was observing. Then, when I re-examined the data, I found that only 40, or 37.7 per cent, of the groupings observed contained members of both factions. I found further that only 10 out of these 40 groupings contained two or more members of each faction. The other 30 were cases where a single individual of the other faction joined in the card game or conversation. I then divided the groupings into two columns, placing in one column those which were predominantly of one faction and in the other column those which were predominantly of the other faction. Then

I underlined in red those names which did not "belong" in the column where I found them. Out of a total of 462 names, 75, or approximately 16 per cent, were underlined in red. Of course, we would not expect a pure separation of two cliques in any club, but the figures, crude as they were, seemed to demonstrate that the two factions were real entities which would be important in understanding any decisions made by the club.

This observation of groupings did not, in itself, point out the influential people in the club. For that purpose, I tried to pay particular attention to events in which an individual originated activity for one or more others—where a proposal, suggestion, or request was followed by a positive response. Over a period of six months, in my notes I tabulated every observed incident where A had originated activity for B. The result of this for pair events (events involving only two people) was entirely negative. While I might have the impression that, in the relationship between A and B, B was definitely the subordinate individual, the tabulation might show that B originated for A approximately as much as A for B. However, when I tabulated the set events (those involving three or more people), the hierarchical structure of the organization clearly emerged.

As this phase of the research proceeded, I saw more clearly how to relate together the large racket organization and the street corner gang or club. In fact, the study of the role of Tony Cataldo in this setting provided the necessary link, and the observational methods here described provided the data for the analysis of this linkage.

While I was working up these research methods, I committed a serious blunder. It happened during the political crisis. Tony had been trying to persuade the club to invite his candidate in to address us, although nearly all the members were disposed to support Fiumara. At this crucial point, I participated actively, saying that, while we were all for Fiumara, I thought it was a good idea to hear what other politicians had to say. The vote was taken shortly after I spoke, and it went for Tony against Carlo. That led to the rally for Mike Kelly in our clubroom and to the most serious dissension within the club.

Here I violated a cardinal rule of participant observation. I sought actively to influence events. In a close and confused contest such as this, it is quite likely that my indorsement of Tony's position was a decisive factor. Why did I so intervene?

At the time, I was still hoping to re-establish close relations with Tony Cataldo, and I wanted to make some move that would build in that direction. So I sought to do the impossible: to take a stand which would not antagonize Carlo and his boys but would be appreciated by Tony. It was a foolish and misguided attempt. I did antagonize Carlo, and he forgave me only on the assumption that I was ignorant of the situation in which I was acting. Ignorance being preferable to treachery, I accepted this excuse.

Ironically enough, my effort to win favor with Tony was a complete failure. Before the political crisis, he had hardly known Carlo and had not recognized his leadership position in the club. When Carlo opposed him so vigorously and effectively, Tony immediately recognized Carlo's position and made every effort to establish closer relations with him. As I had taken a position on his side in the crisis, Tony needed to make no efforts to establish closer relations with me.

I did not have to speak in this situation at all. If I had spoken against Tony, it seems likely that this would have done more to re-establish our close relations than what I actually did.

As I thought over this event later, I came to the conclusion that my action had not only been unwise from a practical research standpoint; it had also been a violation of professional ethics. It is not fair to the people who accept the participant observer for him to seek to manipulate them to their possible disadvantage simply in order to seek to strengthen his social position in one area of participation. Furthermore, while the researcher may consciously and explicitly engage in influencing action with the full knowledge of the people with whom he is participating, it is certainly a highly questionable procedure for the researcher to establish his social position on the assumption that he is not seeking to lead anyone anywhere and then suddenly throw his weight to one side in a conflict situation.

12. Marching on City Hall

I suppose no one goes to live in a slum district for three and a half years unless he is concerned about the problems facing the people there. In that case it is difficult to remain solely a passive observer. One time I gave in to the urge to do something. I tried to tell myself that I was simply testing out some of the things I had learned about the structure of corner gangs, but I knew really that this was not the main purpose.

In all my time in Cornerville I had heard again and again about how the district was forgotten by the politicians, how no improvements were ever made, how the politicians just tried to get themselves and their friends ahead. I heard a good deal about the sporadic garbage collections, but perhaps the bitterest complaint concerned the public bathhouse, where in the summer of 1939 as well as in several earlier summers there was no hot water available. In a district where only 12 per cent of the flats had bathtubs, this was a matter of serious moment.

People complained to each other about these matters, but apparently it did no good to try to work through the local politicians, who were primarily concerned about doing favors for friends and potential friends. If you could not go through the local politicians, why not go direct to the mayor—and on a mass basis? If, as I assumed, the corner gang leaders were able to mobilize their gangs for action in various directions, then it should be possible through working with a small number of individuals to organize a large demonstration.

I talked this over with Sam Franco, who was enthusiastic and ready to act at once. He promised me the support of his section of Cornerville. For the Norton Street area I called on Doc. For the area around George Ravello's headquarters, I picked one of the local leaders. With my new acquaintances on Shelby Street, I was able to cover that end of the district.

Then began the complicated task of organizing the various groups, bringing them together, and getting them ready to march at the same time. And who was going to lead this demonstration? Since I was the connecting link among most of these corner gang leaders and since I had begun the organizing activity, I was the logical man to take over. But I was not then prepared to depart so far from my observer's role. I agreed with the others that I would serve on the organizing committee, but we would have to have a different chairman. I proposed Doc, and all the others agreed to this. But, as I talked with Doc, I found that, while he was happy to go along with us, he was not prepared to accept the leadership responsibility. I then proposed Mike Giovanni, and he too was acceptable to the small group with whom I was working in preparing the demonstration. Mike said that he would conduct a public meeting in Cornerville in getting people together for the march, but he thought that the chairman from that point on should be elected by the representatives of the different corners who were there assembled. We agreed on this.

But then we had a misunderstanding as to the composition of this public meeting. Sam Franco brought just several representatives from his end of the district, while a large part of the Shelby section marched en masse down to the meeting. Thus, when there were nominations for chairman, a man from Shelby Street who had previously taken no part in the planning was nominated and elected. Sam Franco's friends were considerably annoyed by this, for they felt they could have elected one of their candidates if they had simply brought their boys along. Sam and several of the other men also suspected our chairman's motives. They were convinced that he would try to turn the demonstration to his personal advantage, and I had to concede that there was a good possibility of this. From this point on, part of the efforts of our committee were to hem in the chairman so that he would have no opportunity to go off on his own tangent.

In this election meeting we had been misled by our own conception of democratic processes. It makes sense to elect a chairman only from a regularly constituted group or constituency. In this case the election had turned out quite fortuitously because of the overrepresentation of Shelby Street.

We next had difficulty with the date on which we were to march. It had been set about a week from the election meeting, but now the men on Shelby Street were telling me that their people were all steamed up and wanted to march much sooner. I consulted Sam Franco and one or two other members of the committee but was not able to get all the committee together. In spite of this, I told them that maybe we should move the march up a couple of days. We then scheduled a meeting of the full committee to take place the night before the march. When the committee began assembling, it became evident that some of them were annoyed that they had been bypassed, and I realized that I had made a serious blunder. Fortunately, at this point one of the local politicians came in and tried to argue against the march. This was a great morale booster. Instead of arguing with each other as to how we had been handling the plan, we got all our aggressions off against the politician.

The next morning we assembled in the playground in front of the bathhouse. We had had mimeographed handbills distributed through the neighborhood the day before; the newspapers had been notified. We had our committee ready to lead the march, and we had the playground pretty well filled. Some of the older generation were there lining the sides of the playground. I assumed they would be marching with us, but, significantly enough, they did not. We should have realized that, if we wanted to get the older generation, we had to work through their leadership too. As the march got under way, young boys from all over the district thronged in among us carrying their home-made banners. And so we set off for city hall right through the center of the business district. We had the satisfaction of stopping traffic all along the route, but it was not for long, since the parade moved very fast. We had made the mistake of having all our committee up in front, and it seemed that everybody behind us was trying to get to the front, so that we leaders were almost stampeded. And some of the women pushing baby carriages were unable to keep up.

We had no opposition from the police, who were only concerned with an orderly demonstration as we assembled in the courtyard below the city hall. Then the ten committee members went up to see the mayor, while the rest of the marchers sang "God Bless America" and other songs to the accompaniment of an improvised band. We had known that the mayor was out of town, but our demonstration could not wait, so we talked to the acting mayor. He got our names and a list of our grievances, treating us seriously and respectfully. As our committee members began to speak, I heard Sam saying behind me in a low voice: "Get out of here, you cheap racketeer." I turned to see the local politician, Angelo Fiumara, elbowing his way in. Fiumara stood his ground and spoke up at the first opportunity: "I would like to add my voice to the protest as a private citizen. . . ." Sam interrupted, calling out: "He's got nuttin' to do with us. He's just trying to chisel in." Mike Giovanni reiterated Sam's remarks, and the acting mayor ruled that he would not hear Fiumara at that time. While the speaking was going on, I distributed a prepared statement to the reporters. At the end of our session the acting mayor promised that all our protests would be seriously considered and that any possible action would be taken.

We then marched to the bathhouse playground, where we told our followers what had taken place in the mayor's office. Here again, Angelo Fiumara tried to address the crowd, and we elbowed him out. The next day's newspapers carried big stories with pictures of our demonstration. We were given credit for having three hundred to fifteen hundred marchers with us in the various papers. The fellows happily accepted the figure of fifteen hundred, but I suspect three hundred was closer to the truth. The day after the demonstration, engineers were examining the boilers in the bathhouse, and in less than a week we had hot water. The street-cleaning and the garbage collections also seemed to be pepped up, for at least a short time. For all the mistakes we had made, it was evident that the demonstration had brought results. But now the problem was: What next? We had got an organization together, and we had staged a demonstration. Somehow, we must keep Cornerville working together.

In this effort we were completely unsuccessful. Several committee meetings petered out without any agreements on concerted action. I think there were several difficulties here. In the first place, the committee members were not accustomed to meeting together or working together personally. There was nothing to bring them together except the formal business of the meeting. Their ties were on their various street corners. In the second place, we had started off with such a sensational performance that anything else would be anticlimax. It seemed hard to get up enthusiasm for any activity that would be dwarfed beside our protest march.

I came to realize that any over-all street corner organization would have to be built around some sort of continuing activity. The softball league developed the following spring and met this need to some extent. In fact, I worked with the same men in setting up the league, so in a sense the march on city hall did have continuing consequences, though they fell far short of our fond hopes.

13. Farewell to Cornerville

Through the spring and summer of 1940, most of my time was spent in writing the first draft of *Street Corner Society*. I already had the case studies of the Nortons and the Italian Community Club. I followed these with three manuscripts which I then called "Politics and the Social Structure," "The Racketeer in the Cornerville S. and A. Club," and "The Social Structure of Racketeering."

As I wrote, I showed the various parts to Doc and went over them with him in detail. His criticisms were invaluable in my revision. At times, when I was dealing with him and his gang, he would smile and say: "This will embarrass me, but this is the way it was, so go ahead with it."

When I left Cornerville in midsummer of 1940, the Cornerville S. and A. Club had a farewell beer party for me. We sang "God Bless America" three times and the "Beer Barrel Polka" six times. I have moved around many times in my life, and yet I have never felt so much as though I were leaving home. The only thing that was missing was a farewell from the Nortons, and that was impossible, for the Nortons were no more by this time.

14. Cornerville Revisited

As I write this, more than forty years after leaving the district, there seems no longer any reason to maintain its fictional name, nor to maintain the pseudonyms of some of the principal characters. I was studying the North End of Boston, one of the most historic sections of this country, where tourists can still visit Paul Revere's home on North Street and the Old North Church on Salem Street. On the southern edge of the North End is Faneuil Hall, where leaders of the American Revolution sometimes met. A peninsula in the harbor, the North End is the scene of the Boston Tea Party.

The North End also figures importantly in political history in the nineteenth and early twentieth centuries. It was located in the Third Ward and was then dominated by the Hendricks Club in the West End, the area studied by Herbert Gans in *Urban Villagers*. There Lincoln Steffens's favorite ward boss, Martin Lomasney, held sway through the early decades of this century. When I began my study in 1937, Lomasney had passed on, and under the leadership of John I. Fitzgerald, the Irish-dominated club was losing its hold on district politics.

By 1980, the North End was in the process of transformation. It was still predominantly an Italian-American district, but gentrification had set in. Some decades earlier, the elevated tracks had been torn down, thus opening up the view of the waterfront. This stimulated the growth of fine restaurants and condominiums along the wharves. At the other end of the district, the extraordinarily attractive redevelopment of the Quincy Market gave added appeal to the North End, already within easy walking distance of the commercial, banking, and political center of Boston.

Physically, most of the district appeared unchanged. North Bennett Street (Norton Street) looked in 1980 just as when I left it in 1940. The Capri Restaurant of the Orlandi family had long since disappeared, but the building in which I first lived, at 7 Paramenter Street, on the corner of Hanover Street, appeared unchanged. The building where Kathleen and I began our married life, half a block from the waterfront, at 477 Hanover Street, still stands, but across the street the Hanover Association (Cornerville S. and A. Club) has disappeared, and the building that once housed it has been rebuilt into a condominium.

What impact did the book have on the North End? I have no evidence of any major influence or even that it was widely read in the district. For more than ten years after publication, the book jacket to the first edition (designed by Kathleen Whyte) was on the bulletin board of the branch library under the heading Recent Books of Interest, but among the corner boys, Ralph Orlandella (Sam Franco) could not find anyone who had read it beyond those to whom I had sent copies.

The local social workers did, of course, read the book, but it had no dramatic effect upon their institutions. I heard indirectly that, with one exception, the workers in the North Bennett Street Industrial School (Norton Street House) were upset because they had befriended me and then I had turned against them and embarrassed them before other social workers and their elite supporters. I took some comfort from the one exception, the head of girls' work, who had introduced me to Ernest Pecci (Doc). I heard that she judged my study an accurate picture of the institution and the district. By the 1950s, the Industrial School at last had acquired, for work with young boys, a full-time staff member, one who had been born and raised in the North End but who had a college degree and some social-work education beyond that.

Reactions at the North End Union (Cornerville House) appeared to be ambivalent. Frank Havey (Mr. Kendall) told me in 1953 that he did not question the accuracy of the book, but he was uncertain as to what extent the settlement house could attract corner boys without losing its established clientele. He then told about getting a grant to hire a local World War II hero who had organized a basketball league of forty-two teams and made the Union the liveliest place in its history—apparently without disruption of the regular settlement-house programs. Unfortunately, when the grant ran out, the local man was let go. By the early 1950s, the Union did have two Italian-American staff members, but both men were from outside of the district.

Havey confessed that he found himself in a bind between his recognition of the value of indigenous leadership and the standards being promoted by those evaluating social-work programs. Schools of social work have been striving to enhance the professional prestige of their graduates.

How can social work be regarded as a profession if its institutions hire young men who got their basic training on the street corner?

Havey knew of no one who had been threatened with a cut off of funds if he hired anyone who did not have an M.S.W. degree. Still, he was often asked how many people on his staff had this degree, and he had been hearing references to other institutions which were not "measuring up." Upon inquiry, he would learn that these substandard institutions were those which persisted in hiring people without the advanced degree.

As I was preparing this third edition, I talked again with Frank Havey. By the time of his retirement in 1974, after forty years at the North End Union, he was regarded with admiration and affection throughout social-work circles in the Boston area. Recognition went beyond an impressive ceremonial dinner in his honor: a professor at Boston University began an oral history project about his four decades in the North End and conducted extensive interviews with him. Havey hopes one day to turn these reminiscences into a book—which I shall read with great interest.

Havey reported that the problems of relating settlement house to street corner had not changed during the 1970s. He himself had made several efforts to include North End men with street-corner backgrounds in his staff. He recalled particularly two men who were doing good jobs for the Union, but after some months, they both quit. His explanation: they were caught in a bind between the standards of the settlement house and the standards of the street corner. He added that there was no problem in hiring people for jobs that were not thought to require social-work education. But, of course, a man hired to run a basketball program or a woman hired to conduct sewing classes would be in a dead-end job with no prospects for career advancement.

In spite of the good reputation the Union enjoyed in social-work circles, for many years Havey was unable to persuade any of Boston's major social agencies to place students or staff members part time in the Union to provide counseling services that his agency could not offer. Such assignments were made only to agencies where the program would be supervised by someone holding a master's degree in social work. The Union got around the credentials barrier only when it was able to hire a full-time staff member with an M.S.W.

In the 1960s, throughout the country, storefront recreation centers and other programs depending upon indigenous leadership enjoyed growing popularity. Did I have anything to do with this? I doubt it. I assume that the change grew out of the growing militance of slum people, which forced an increasing recognition that the old paternalistic strategies were not working. At best, my book may have provided some academic legitimacy for this trend, and it may have stimulated some rethinking among planners, teachers, and students of social work. Nevertheless, the underlying problem will not be resolved simply by placing indigenous leaders in charge of "outreach" programs if those positions offer no possibilities of rewarding good performance with advancement and job security.

In recent decades, as the general level of education has risen, it has become increasingly difficult for the non-college graduate to rise into management in private industry, but it still does happen now and then—even fairly often in some fields. In general, a college degree is all that is required for eligibility for management positions, and in many firms, graduate degrees confer no advantage on the degree holder in competition for most management jobs. Can it be that the credentials barrier is now much tougher in social work than in private industry?

What happened after 1940 to some of the chief characters in the book? Joseph Langone (George Ravello) has long since passed on, but his funeral parlor remains in the family in the North End, and one of his sons was a representative in the commonwealth legislature in 1980.

It took Ernest Pecci (Doc) a long time to find a secure place on the economic ladder. He had no steady job until the war boom got well under way. Then at last he caught on and was doing very well until the postwar cutback came. People were then laid off according to their seniority, and Pecci was out of work once more.

He finally did get a job in an electronics plant. At the time of my last visit (December 1953), I found that he had worked his way up to a position as assistant supervisor in the production planning department of the factory. Such a department is a nerve center for the factory, for it handles the scheduling of the orders through every department of the plant.

Pecci had achieved some success in attaining his position, but he tended to minimize his accomplishments. He explained, "On the technical side, I stink. The only place I really shine is where I have to go around and talk the foreman into running a new order ahead of the one he was planning to run. I can do that without getting him upset." So Pecci was applying some of the social skill he displayed in the North End in this new factory world. However, he was working in an industry of very advanced technical development; so his lack of knowledge in this field set a ceiling upon his advancement.

Pecci got married shortly after he got his first steady job during World War II. His wife was an attractive North End girl, a very intelligent and able person who had opened a small clothing store of her own.

I had one visit with Pecci about five years after the book was published. His reaction seemed a combination of pride and embarrassment. I asked him for the reaction of the members of his own gang. He said that Frank Luongo (Mike Giovanni) had seemed to like the book. Gillo's (Danny's) only comment was "Jesus, you're really a hell of a guy. If I was a dame, I'd marry you." The other members of the gang? So far as Pecci knew, they had never read it. The question had come up all right. One night on the corner, one of the fellows said to Pecci, "Say, I hear Bill Whyte's book is out. Maybe we should go up to the library and read it." Pecci steered them off. "No, you wouldn't be interested, just a lot of big words. That's for the professors."

On another occasion, Pecci was talking to the editor of the *Italian News*. The editor was thinking of publishing an article about the book. Pecci discouraged him, and no such notice appeared.

I assume that in his quiet way Pecci did everything he could to discourage local reading of the book for the possible embarrassment it might cause a number of individuals, including himself. For example, it could hardly be pleasant reading for the low-ranking members of the Bennetts to see it pointed out how low they ranked and what sort of difficulties they got into. Therefore, I have every sympathy with Pecci's efforts in limiting the circulation of the book.

Years later, I heard that Pecci had been promoted to head of production planning, but I heard nothing more of him until the 1960s, when I learned that he had died. I was sorry then that I had allowed myself to get out of touch with him, and yet there seemed to be a growing problem between us that led to an estrangement I still do not fully understand. I had tried to keep in touch through letters, but Pecci was even less conscientious as a letter writer than I. The last letter I received from him was a request that I henceforth not tell anyone who "Doc" was.

In the early years after the publication of the book, Pecci had accepted invitations to speak to classes at Harvard and Wellesley. I gather that he acquitted himself well on these occasions and was particularly effective with the Wellesley girls. Quite naturally, he got tired of this kind of thing, and I was glad to comply with his request.

On one of our visits in the Boston area, Kathleen and I had visited the Peccis in their suburban Medford home, and we seemed to get on well on that occasion, but when I was in Boston several years later, we failed to get together. We talked over the phone about meeting, but Pecci gave the impression that he had a lot of other things to do and was not eager to see me.

Perhaps Pecci had come to feel that I had gained fame and fortune through *Street Corner Society*, and he, who had provided the principle keys to that society, had not received his fair share of benefits. While a fair share would be impossible to determine, Pecci did in fact make some material gain out of our association. He had got himself on the then popular television program "The $64,000 Question." He was not one of the big winners, but he did make off with a Cadillac. While he never told me what he had written in order to get on the show, and the announcer made no mention of *Street Corner Society*, I suspect that Pecci must have built up that aspect of his life, because a prospective contestant had to find some way to make himself appear unusually interesting in order to get on the show.

Or perhaps the problem between us was simply that by the time I had last called, Pecci had left the street corner so far behind that he no longer had any interest in connecting up with old times.

Frank Luongo moved on from the North End to become a labor union leader. It began with a job in a rapidly expanding war industry. Frank had no sooner been hired than he began looking around to organize a union. Shortly after this, he was fired. He took his case to the appropriate government agency, charging that he had been fired for union activities. The company was ordered to put Frank back to work. He wrote me that when he reappeared on the job, the situation seemed to change suddenly and dramatically. The other workers had thought they had seen the last of him. Now that he had shown what could be done, they began signing up. For some months Frank was at the plant gate for half an hour before the shift came on and half an hour after his shift went home, distributing pledge cards. And he personally signed up fifteen hundred members. When the union was recognized, Frank became its vice-president. He also wrote a weekly column in the union paper under the heading Mr. CIO. The column was written in a colorful style and must have commanded a good deal of attention in the local.

At the next union election, Frank ran for president. He wrote me that his opponent was a man who had had very little to do with organizing the union, but he was a popular fellow—and he was an Irishman. Frank lost. Shortly after this time, the company began large-scale layoffs following the end of the war. Without a union office, Frank's seniority did not protect him, and he dropped out of his job.

We exchanged letters for several years after I left Boston, but then the correspondence lapsed. I lost track of Frank until many years later when a Cornell student dropped in to my office to tell me that he had met Frank in the course of some field work for a paper on union organizing. Frank then was an organizer for the Textile Workers Union and was working out of Stuyvesant, New York.

A year or so later, when I was planning to drive to Boston, I wrote to Frank to suggest that Kathleen and I stop off to meet him for lunch on the way back. He responded cordially, but when I telephoned him to make definite arrangements the morning of our planned meeting, I learned that he was in the hospital. We stopped at the hospital and visited with him and his wife for an hour or so. It was a gloomy occasion; Frank had advanced cancer and knew he would not have long to live.

We talked about old times, and then Frank filled me in on the intervening years, when he had been working regularly as a union organizer. Finally he told me that over those years, on a number of occasions, he had been approached by students or professors from universities for information about the union. He added, "I have had enough of that. I will never again do anything for anybody from college." I asked him why he felt that way.

"I have always taken time with them. I have gotten things out of the file for them and answered all their questions as well as I could. And I never asked anything in return except, I would say to them, 'When you get through, send me a copy of what you write, will you?' They would always say yes, they would be glad to do it, but I never yet have got anything back. So to hell with them."

I was glad I had remembered to send Frank a copy of *Street Corner Society*. Social researchers have not lost anything in Frank Luongo's rejection of future cooperation, since a few weeks after our meeting he was dead. I quote his last words to me in the hope that future researchers will try a little harder to keep their promises to people in the field even after they no longer need them.

What has happened to Christopher Ianella (Chick Morelli)? I was particularly concerned with that question, and yet I hesitated to seek the answer. I debated the question with myself. I finally decided that Chris could be the one individual I had hurt. I must find out what the book had done to him. I telephoned Chris to ask if I could see him. At first he missed my name, but then he replied cordially. Still, I was wondering what would happen when we sat down to talk.

I found that he had moved out of the North End, but, paradoxically enough, he still lived in the same ward. Pecci, the old corner boy, had moved to the suburbs, and Chris, the man who was on his way up, had stayed in the center of the city.

Chris introduced me to his wife, an attractive and pleasant girl, who neither came from the North End nor was of Italian extraction. We sat in the livingroom of an apartment that, with its furniture, books, curtains, and so on, looked distinctly middle class. For a few minutes we skirted about the subject that we all knew we were going to discuss. Then I asked Chris to tell me frankly his reactions to my book.

Chris began by saying that there were just two main criticisms as far as he was concerned. In the first place, he said that he did not think I distinguished his own way of speaking sufficiently from that of the corner boys when I quoted him. "You made me talk too rough, just like a gangster."

I expressed surprise at this, and here his wife joined in with the comment that she thought that I had made Chris look like a snob. Chris agreed that he had got that picture too. His wife pulled the book down from the shelf and reread the passage where I quote Pecci on the occasion of a political meeting during which Chris was on and off the stage seven times in order to take the tickets that he was going to sell for the candidate. They both laughed at this, and Chris commented that he would never do a thing like that anymore. She said that Chris had told her before they got married that he had once had a book written about him. But she added that he didn't give her the book to read until after they had been married.

Chris laughed at this, and then he went on to his second criticism. "Bill, everything you described about what we did is true all right, but you should have pointed out that we were just young then. That was a stage that we were going through. I've changed a lot since that time."

He expressed concern over the reactions of other people to my book. "You know, after the book was out a while, I ran into Pecci, and he was really upset about it. He said to me, 'Can you imagine that! After all I did for Bill Whyte, the things he put in the book about me. You know that thing about when I said you would step on the neck of your best friend just to get ahead. Well, now, maybe I said that, but I didn't really mean it. I was just sore at the time.'"

Chris seemed concerned about what the book had done to my relationship with Pecci. I did not tell him that Pecci had read every page of the original manuscript, nor did I give my interpretation that Pecci was simply going around repairing his fences after some of these intimate reactions had been exposed.

Chris assured me that he was not the hard character that the book seemed to make him. ("Really, I'm a soft touch.") And he gave me instances where he had helped out his friends at no advantage to himself.

As I was getting ready to leave, I asked Chris if he had anything more to say about the book.

"Well, I wonder if you couldn't have been more constructive, Bill. You think publishing something like this really does any good?"

I asked what he meant. He mentioned my pointing out (as he had told me himself) that he had difficulty with his *th* sound. I had also discussed the commotion the fellows sometimes caused in the theaters, the fact that they sometimes went to dances without ties, and so on—all points that make the North End look like a rather uncouth district. (I am unable to locate any references in the book to commotions in the theaters or men at dances without ties.)

"The trouble is, Bill, you caught the people with their hair down. It's a true picture, yes; but people feel it's a little too personal."

As he walked with me to the subway station, we got to talking about his political career. I had been astounded to hear that he had missed being elected to the city council by a scant three votes. The Chris Ianella whom I had known never could have come so close. Without expressing my surprise, I tried to get him to talk about this.

"You know, the funny thing is, Bill, I didn't get many votes from the North End. The people that you grow up with, it seems, are jealous of anybody that is getting ahead. Where I got my support was right around here where I live now. I know these fellows on the street corner, and I really fit with them."

As if to demonstrate for me, he nodded and waved cordially at several corner groups as we walked by. In a later visit I learned that Chris Ianella had at last been elected to office, and in 1980 he was president of the Boston City Council.

Chris left me with a good deal to think over. In the first place, it is hard to describe the sense of relief I felt after seeing him. Although it must have hurt him at first to read the book, he had been able to take it in stride, and he was now even able to laugh at himself as he had been in that earlier period. As I discussed these things later with Pecci, I began to wonder whether the book might even have helped Chris. It was Pecci who presented this theory. He argued that not many people have an opportunity to see themselves as other people see them. Perhaps the reading of the book enabled him to change his behavior. Certainly, Pecci argued, Chris had changed a good deal. He was still working hard to get ahead, but he seemed no longer the self-centered, insensitive person of earlier years. Chris certainly had to change in order to have any hopes of getting ahead in Democratic politics—and somehow, for reasons that I cannot now explain, Chris had decided that his future lay with the Democrats rather than with the Republicans, in whose direction he had seemed to be moving when I left the North End. So, at least, the book had not hurt Chris, and it seemed just possible that it had helped him.

I was also pleased to find that basically Chris accepted the book. This, of course, pleased me as a writer, but it also spoke well of Chris. I suspect that the man who can accept such a portrait of himself is also the man who can change the behavior described.

Chris's objections to the book seemed interesting. As to the way I had quoted him in the book, I felt on very firm ground. He did talk differently from the corner boys, but not quite as differently as he had imagined. If a quotation from him contains an ungrammatical expression or some typical corner-boy phrase, I am reasonably sure that that part of it is authentic. I was so sensitive to the differences between Chris and the corner boys that I would have been unlikely to imagine any expressions that made them appear more alike. The criticism seemed to say more about Chris's status and aspirations than it did about my research methods.

Perhaps, indeed, I should have pointed out that Chris and his friends were young and were just going through a stage of development. But youth, in itself, does not seem a full explanation. These men were not adolescents; they were at least in their mid-twenties. The important fact is that they had not yet secured any firm foothold in society. They were young men who had left home but who had not yet arrived anywhere. I am inclined to believe that this is an important factor in explaining the aggressiveness, the self-centeredness, and so on, that appear in Chris and some of his friends during that period. Later on, when Chris had found something of a place for himself, he could relax and be more concerned with other people. Is this just a phenomenon of social mobility out of the slums and into middle-class status? As I think back upon my own career, I can recall with a trace of embarrassment some of the things that I said and did in the early stages of my career, when I was struggling to gain a foothold on the academic ladder. It is easy to be modest and unassuming once you have achieved a fairly secure position and won a certain amount of recognition.

I had no quarrel with Chris's point that I had caught people with their hair down, and I could sympathize with the people who felt that way. If you are going to be interviewed for the newspaper, you put on your good suit and your best tie, make sure that the kitchen dishes are cleaned up, and in general take all the steps you associate with making a public appearance. You appear before the public in the role that you would like to play before the public. You cannot do this with a social researcher who comes in and lives with you. I do not see any way of getting around this difficulty. I suppose there must always be aspects of our reports that will give a certain amount of embarrassment to the people we have been studying. At least I was reassured to find that the reaction in Chris's case had not been nearly so serious as I had feared.

While we can only speculate about the impact of the book upon Pecci and Chris and many others, there is one man upon whom it has had a profound effect—and I was not always sure that the effect would be constructive. Working with me made Ralph Orlandella, a high school drop out, want to do social research. In this case, I can let Ralph tell his own story (see Appendix B).

15. An Unnatural History of the Book

Although I was drifting away from my earlier ambition to be a writer of fiction, I was determined to write *Street Corner Society* so that it would be read beyond the academic world. I first submitted the manuscript to Reynal and Hitchcock, a commercial publisher which had announced a competition for nonfiction manuscripts, based on scholarly research, but deserving broader readership. That was a near miss. I came in second to a book on philosophy, which I like to think has long since passed into oblivion.

With the encouragement of W. Lloyd Warner and Everett C. Hughes, I then submitted the book to the University of Chicago Press. A few weeks

later, I received the good news that the editor was happy with the manuscript and would publish the book. But then I got a letter from the business manager, who informed me that in order to make it a feasible publishing venture, I would have to cut the manuscript by one-third and put
up a $1300 subsidy, since the book was not going to sell many copies. For
a couple who had been living for two years on fellowships of $600 and
then $1500 (minus $300 tuition for each year), the $1300 was a formidable
challenge, but we managed to get the money together, largely from what
we had saved from the North End period. I was at first even more concerned about the revision, because I had already done considerable con-
densing before submitting the manuscript and did not see how I could reduce it further without cutting the heart out of it. However, as I look back
on it, I believe the discipline was good for me. I can no longer remember
anything that I cut out, and I am sure that the manuscript emerged as a
better book after the condensation.

During the same period, I was faced with the task of getting *Street Corner Society* through the Department of Sociology as my doctoral thesis. I
had arrived in Chicago to begin graduate work with the first draft of my
thesis in my trunk. That is not to say that the thesis derived no benefit
from my two years at the university. I did considerable revising and
rewriting during that period, and the lively intellectual environment of
the university made the book better than it otherwise could have been.
Still, my unorthodox beginning required some unorthodox maneuvers at
the end of my Chicago educational career. I took my field examinations
one week and underwent my thesis examination the following week—
though, according to the rules, the Ph.D. could not be awarded less than
nine months after passage of the field examination—which explains why
my Ph.D. was dated 1943 rather than 1942.

As is often the case, there were deep cleavages in the sociology department; so any student facing his thesis examination had to hope that with
the covert assistance and encouragement of the faction with which he
was allied, he would be able to withstand the attacks of the opposing faction. I was further handicapped because when I was coming up for the
ordeal, my chairman, W. Lloyd Warner, was on leave, and I had to hope
that Everett Hughes and Bill Whyte together could get me through.

At the time, Chicago had a requirement that all Ph.D. theses had to be
printed, and I was determined that I was going to publish a readable book
and a doctoral thesis at one and the same time. For this reason, I had refused to start the book with the traditional review of the literature on slum
districts or to conclude with a chapter in which I summarized my contribution to that literature, including the final obligatory sentence, "more research on this topic is needed." My reasons for this stance were not entirely literary. Fortunately for me, during the period when I was doing my

field work, I was unacquainted with the sociological literature on slum districts, as I had begun my study thinking of myself as a social anthropologist. During the two years at Chicago, I immersed myself in that sociological literature, and I became convinced that most of it was worthless and misleading. It seemed to me that it would detract from the task at hand if I were required to clear away the garbage before getting into my story.

As I expected, the sharpest attack came from Louis Wirth, who was himself the author of one of the better slum studies. He began by asking me to define a slum district. The purpose of his question was obvious. Whereas I had been arguing that the North End was actually highly organized, with many cohesive groupings, he didn't see how I could define a slum district without bringing in the concept of "social disorganization," which had been the central theme of previous slum studies.

I replied that a slum district was simply an urban area where there was a high concentration of low-income people living in dilapidated housing and under poor sanitary and health conditions. Wirth objected that this was not a sociological definition, but I refused to satisfy his conceptual appetite, replying simply that the conditions I stated were what had led me into the study of the North End and that I considered it an empirical problem to determine how people lived under those conditions.

Although not satisfied, Wirth was finally persuaded that he wasn't going to get the answer he desired, and he moved on to attack my effrontery in passing over without mention several generations of sociological literature. This provoked a lively interchange in which I attempted to demonstrate that I really did know that literature.

At this point, Everett Hughes intervened to lead us to a compromise. The department would accept the book as my thesis providing I wrote separately a review of the literature which made clear what I was adding to that literature. This supplementary material could then be printed (at my expense) and bound with the book in one copy, which, deposited in the university library, would make Bill Whyte's thesis fit into the traditions of the graduate school.

It later occurred to me that if I had to write a review of the literature, I might as well get some published articles out of this task (and indeed I did, as indicated in the references listed in Appendix C). When two of these articles were accepted for publication, I consulted again with Hughes. He persuaded the department to accept the published articles as my literature review and to abandon the formalistic requirement that these articles be bound with the book in the library copy.

Thus, the thesis defense ordeal had a happy ending, thanks largely to Hughes. I got the book published without the handicap of what I considered irrelevant material, and in addition, I launched myself upon an academic career with two articles as well as the book.

Initial reception of the book gave no indication that it might one day be considered "a sociological classic." The official journal of the American Sociological Society, the *American Sociological Review*, did not get around to reviewing the book. In the *American Journal of Sociology*, a distinguished criminologist, Edwin Sutherland, did give me a favorable review, but it was one which tended to place the book as just another good slum study.

At first, the book got a better reception outside of the academic world. Harry Hanson, a nationally syndicated columnist, devoted a full column to the book, ending with this statement: "Whyte offers fresh material on the ever important subject of American community life, presenting it eloquently from the human angle."

I was particularly pleased with the enthusiastic comments of Saul Alinsky, author of *Reveille for Radicals*, in the social-work periodical *Survey*. While acknowledging his prejudice against sociologists in general, he found *Street Corner Society* to be an impressively realistic analysis of the kind of slum districts in which he had been working as a community organizer.

The book was reviewed in a fair number of newspapers throughout the country, but there was one notable exception: Boston. Later I wrote to the editor to ask if there were not some way that he could get the Boston papers to review the book. He replied that if I would give him permission to write the book review editors of Boston papers and tell them that the book was about the North End of their city, he could guarantee me reviews in the Boston papers. After a bit of soul searching, I decided that this would be cheating. I had followed the sociological convention of disguising the location of my study, and it would not be fair to lift the veil at the very point where reactions to the book would hit closest to home.

At first, sales seemed to confirm the pessimistic prediction of the business manager of the press. The book was published in December 1943. By 1945 sales had declined to a trickle, and the book seemed about to fall into the remainder market.

My mid-1946 royalty check, reporting a tripling of sales over the previous year, came as a happy surprise. What had happened? In the first place, World War II veterans were flocking back into colleges and graduate schools, and their GI benefits provided generous allowances for the purchase of books. At the same time, many teachers of sociology were becoming dissatisfied with simply assigning text books for their courses and were requiring students to read research monographs.

Nevertheless, by the early 1950s, sales were in a steady decline, and once again the book appeared about to expire. Alex Morin, an editor at the press, told me that he had recently reread *Street Corner Society* in the hope of getting ideas for revisions that might justify a new edition and keep the book alive. This prompted me to think of writing the appendix on my field experiences, which appeared in the enlarged 1955 edition and which is included, along with later additions, in this edition. As director of Cornell's Social Science Research Center, I had been working with colleagues on the improvement of training in research methods for students of the behavioral sciences. As part of this enterprise, I was teaching a seminar on field methods in collaboration with Urie Bronfenbrenner, John Dean, and Steven A. Richardson. For this seminar, we wanted readings that would provide realistic descriptions and interpretations of the field research process as experienced by some of its leading practitioners. An exhaustive canvass of the field revealed practically nothing that we considered worth using.

It seemed as if the academic world had imposed a conspiracy of silence regarding the personal experiences of field workers. In most cases, the authors who had given any attention to their research methods had provided fragmentary information or had written what appeared to be a statement of the methods the field worker would have used if he had known what he was going to come out with when he had entered the field. It was impossible to find realistic accounts that revealed the errors and confusions and the personal involvements that a field worker must experience.

I decided to do my bit to fill this gap. In undertaking this task, it seemed to me important to be as honest about myself as I could possibly be. This meant not suppressing incidents that made me look foolish, like my abortive attempt to pick up a girl in a Scollay Square tavern, or my involvement in a federal crime (I voted four times in an election)—although in the latter case, several colleagues advised me against such a confession. I wrote as I did, not simply to cleanse my soul but, more importantly, to help future field workers understand that it is possible to make foolish errors and serious mistakes and still produce a valuable study.

The enlarged 1955 edition gave the book a new lease on life. In the 1960s, sales were again tapering off, but the publication of a paperback edition boosted them to a new high. By the late 1970s, *Street Corner Society* had sold over two hundred thousand copies, thus becoming, according to the press, the all-time best seller among its sociological monographs.

Even though sales were again dropping off in the late 1970s, I had no thought of a possible new edition of the book until the two-day celebration of my retirement, organized by my department in Cornell's New York State School of Industrial and Labor Relations. The events centered around presentations and discussions by seven former research assistants or associates in field projects: Angelo Ralph Orlandella, Margaret Chandler, Melvin Kohn, Chris Argyris, Leonard Sayles, George Strauss, and Joseph Blasi. While I shall always treasure the contributions of all these old friends, it was particularly the remarks of Margaret Chandler and Ralph Orlandella that set me to thinking of my research in a new perspective.

I had learned that beyond her research activities, Margaret Chandler had become an extraordinarily successful mediator of union-management conflicts in New Jersey. She claimed that the methods of interviewing and observation she had learned first in the study leading to *Human Relations in the Restaurant Industry* had provided her with the tools to penetrate the complex thoughts and feelings of the contending parties and thus to move them toward a resolution of the conflict.

Although I had given Orlandella no formal instruction in interviewing and observation, and I had certainly done nothing to increase his skill as a street-corner gang leader, he claimed that working with me had taught him methods of interviewing and observation and analysis of group structure that had served to win him leadership and management positions in his subsequent military and civilian career.

Previously I had thought of methods I was using primarily in terms of their utility for field research in the behavioral sciences. Thus, perhaps the best way for me to end my contribution to this book is by introducing Ralph Orlandella's statement of the practical implications of our field methods as he presented them to the enthusiastic audience at my retirement.

2 ✐

Introduction to Chapter 2

Ethnography was once the almost exclusive domain of anthropology. In studies dating from the end of the nineteenth century, American scholars went and lived in a remote culture for a substantial period of time. The following selection falls within this tradition of cultural anthropology. Alma Gottlieb, then a doctoral student at the University of Virginia, set out to do fieldwork for fifteen months among the Beng people in a tropical rain forest in a West African village. She had not secured the necessary governmental permission to do the research before she flew halfway across the world. In addition, since this group had never been studied by Western scholars, she could not learn the Beng language in advance of her trip. As with most classical anthropological studies, she would have to rely on a translator or informant and try to learn to communicate once there. Although field workers often work alone, in this instance Gottlieb was accompanied by her husband, Philip Graham, a fiction writer then working on his first book of short stories. Graham was between teaching jobs, and thinking that as a fiction writer he could "write anywhere," he "went along for the ride." The resulting collaboration, *Parallel Worlds: An Anthropologist and a Writer Encounter Africa,* won the Victor Turner Prize in Ethnographic Writing from the Society for Humanistic Anthropology.

Gottlieb had chosen the Beng for several reasons. Within the field of cultural anthropology, she was interested in religion, especially indigenous religions and women's lives. The Beng were attractive because they had not been studied seriously by any anthropologists. They were alleged to be a "matrilineal" society where females had a critical role in the passage of lineage. (This claim turned out to be only partly true.) In addition, few members had converted to Christianity or Islam, and most were reported to still practice an active traditional religion.

In the chapter preceding the one included in this volume, the authors describe in detail their first days in the capital city of the Cote d'Ivoire, where Gottlieb attempted to secure the permission she needed to study a Beng village. She was sent from one government agency to another and then back again, never able to see the right person or, if she did, to secure their permission. After several such encounters, she ultimately learned strategies for negotiating the system and obtained the necessary permission.

Her next task was to find a native speaker of Beng who might provide entry into a village where she could do her research. She finally located Kouakou Kouadio Pascal, a university student who willingly helped them by providing introductions to members of his family who lived in Beng villages and teaching them a few words of the language. Gottlieb and Graham bought a used car, kerosene lamps, many kinds of antibiotics, and other supplies and set out to search for Pascal's family. Once they were fully equipped, they headed for the village of Asagbe, where Pascal's uncle M. Kouassi André lived.

The couple wrote the book fourteen years after returning home; they coauthored it, but in an unusual way. Rather than blending their voices in a single narrative, they instead wrote alternating sections, shifting from the voice of the anthropologist (Gottlieb) to that of the writer (Graham) and back again. In so doing, they weave together two versions of the same story, giving the reader insights into their experiences that neither alone could have accomplished. In telling their versions of the story, they both address issues faced by all ethnographers and writers: how to tell a story honestly, fairly, and effectively while making decisions about what to include and what not to include in the narrative.

The following selection begins as Gottlieb and Graham arrive in the village of Asagbe. Gottlieb is engaged in her search for a suitable setting in which to do her research. For Gottlieb and Graham, this was the most difficult chapter of the book to write. In it they attempted, fourteen years later, to reconstruct their feelings of wonderment and confusion, to remember how their minds raced trying to capture every nuance and how they were overwhelmed by the sheer weight of sensory stimulation. In writing the book, they used Gottlieb's field notes, carbon copies of Graham's letters, and numerous photographs. However, Gottlieb's field notes for the period reported in this chapter were devoid of personal commentary. At the time, she believed that she must provide her dissertation advisors, the audience for whom she was self-consciously writing, with an objective description of what she was encountering. In an effort at being "professional," she edited herself out of her notes. For this chapter, then, they relied instead on their memories, photographs, and Graham's letters to friends and family in order to recapture the emotions they had experienced at the time. In these letters Graham described, in great detail, their reactions to individuals and events and to the world around them.

Their final product, reproduced here, is an excellent example of the ways in which anthropologists make decisions about how to conduct research. In particular, Gottlieb describes some common problems facing fieldworkers: frustration, anxiety, and uncertainty in the negotiation of entry into the chosen site. In so doing, she provides beginning field researchers with insights into the criteria she used in choosing an appropriate site for research. For his part, Graham ponders the philosophical implication of fiction, reality, and the art of storytelling in a setting radically different from his native one.

Glossary

Abidjan   capital city of Côte d'Ivoire

Asagbé	Large Beng village that Gottlieb and Graham used as a base of operations while choosing a smaller village in which Gottlieb would do her research
Baulé	one of Côte d'Ivoire's largest ethnic groups
Bouake	regional capital of the area where the Beng live
Didadi	the name of a dance, a word in the Jula language meaning "the best of the best"; also the name given by Gottlieb and Graham to their car
M'Bahiakro	town nearest to Bengland
Pagnes	brightly patterned, wraparound long skirts (from the French word for loincloth)
Pascal	Beng university student Gottlieb and Graham met in Abidjan and whose family they stayed with in Asagbé
PDCI	Parti Democratique de Côte d'Ivoire; the country's only political party
Préfet	a prefect; administrator of a department or region
Secrétaire	a village's representative to the PDCI
Sous-préfet	a subprefect; a mayor of a town

Choosing a Host
(November 6–
November 28, 1979)

ALMA GOTTLIEB AND PHILIP GRAHAM

Alma: Unpacking

The dirt road from M'Bahiakro was carved through a dense tangle of forest, and while Philip drove I unrolled an oversize map of the region; it flapped across my knees as I charted our course to Bengland. The map was clear enough, with its washes of green crisscrossed by a winding line for the narrow road that barely allowed oncoming trucks to whiz by, rattling our tiny Renault. But it showed only rivers and streams, main roads and footpaths, of the land we would soon inhabit. I needed a map to the invisible space, the unknown life, we were entering.

For I was about to become an anthropologist. True, I'd studied for years for this moment; but with little published information available about the Beng, I had no way of knowing whether my expectations would correspond to the villages I would soon see, the people I would soon meet. As I contemplated the question marks in our future, and my own failings—shyness, a stubborn streak—my anxieties multiplied. Would I be welcome, make friends, come to understand this new world? And how long would it take me to learn the language? Still, the churning in my stomach was from excitement, too: I was less than an hour away from another set of propositions about how the world worked.

We drove past a series of Baulé villages dotted with square, one-story houses of mud brick. The women, who carried babies on their backs or tended to cooking fires while their children played around them, wore long *pagnes,* the colors now faded to dull prints; the men chatted in groups, sporting old jeans and T-shirts worn from wear. I examined the map: after the last of the Baulé villages, it pictured a ten-mile stretch of forest before the first Beng village—perhaps another twenty minutes until we arrived. I looked out at the thick woods we were passing, then down at the squiggly lines of the map, then up again at the green mass, and I wondered if Beng people were walking along paths hidden in the forest around us.

Finally a road sign announced Bongalo—the first Beng village! Philip slowed the car and said, "I can't believe it. We're actually here."

But what was "here"? The square, mud brick buildings before us looked the same as those we'd just seen in the Baulé villages—though in the limited printed sources on the Beng, I'd read of enormous round houses with thatched roofs shaped like an inverted crown. And the people—they appeared no different from the Baulé villagers we'd just passed. My foreign eyes must have been missing subtle differences, I decided. Before long perhaps I'd come to know some of these people I now saw as strangers.

Soon we came to a second Beng village bisected by an intersection—here, the map indicated, we must turn left. After a mile through a mixture of forest and savanna, the road widened and became a street, with mud brick houses on either side: we were suddenly in Asagbé, the village where Pascal had been born. My heartbeat quickened as Philip braked slowly. Before we could think of what to do next, we were approached by a small crowd. These were Beng people, whose world I had come to study: a few young women with babies on their backs; a boy holding a homemade slingshot; an older woman with a turban around her head; a couple of young men in jeans and untucked shirts. They spoke quickly and animatedly to us, to each other. I strained to catch a familiar syllable, a common root with any of the languages I knew, but of course there was none. Would I ever learn to discern words, find a grammar, in that tangle of sounds?

I looked at the envelope Pascal had given us, then pronounced the name printed on it: *M. KOUASSI André*. Several people pointed across the road, and a few continued to flank the car as they led us slowly up the dirt boulevard. They pointed out a building of pale gray cement with a long concrete porch. A handsome man strode toward us.

"*Bonjour*," I began tentatively, unsure if the man understood French, "*nous cherchons M. Kouassi André*."

"*C'est moi*." He greeted us with a cautious handshake, surprise rising in his eyes.

"Ah," I said, "we're so happy to meet you. We saw your nephew Pascal in Abidjan, and he told us to look for you when we arrived." Philip and I introduced ourselves, and I handed him Pascal's sealed letter.

André studied the note carefully, taking in his relative's explanation of these unexpected visitors. Finally he looked up. "Welcome, welcome. You can stay with us—I hope you'll be comfortable in my home."

Our gratitude somehow left us mute for a few seconds—as if we'd been long awaited, this perfect stranger offered to take us in. Finally I managed, "Thank you, thank you very much," but it felt inadequate to the gift our new host had just bestowed upon us.

André said a few words in Beng to the crowd around us. Suddenly a pack of children ran to our car and started hauling out suitcases, typewriters, bags.

"Please, we can do that ourselves," Philip protested. But André insisted, admonishing the children to be careful. Uneasy, Philip and I whispered to each other in English. Was this special treatment, or was it standard practice for guests?

Soon a boy of about six appeared, his arms filled with two oversize bottles of beer. Our host gestured to the three wooden chairs ranged around a dark wooden table on the porch. "Come," he said firmly, and we sat down. Beside the bottles were two glasses, which André filled and set in front of us.

"What about you—won't you join us?" Philip asked.

"No, this is for you," André insisted, and so we slowly sipped the warm beer, all the while trying as politely as possible to wave away the flies that landed on the wet rims of our glasses. A growing group of women and children crowded the courtyard. A baby cried, and its mother bounced gently, her hands reaching around behind her to support the weight of the infant nestled cozily on her back in a sling made of *pagne* material. The child quieted to her mother's rocking. To my surprise, the baby's face was colored with bright lines and dots. I wondered about the meaning of this adornment, but I didn't dare ask as our audience stared at us intently, murmuring and giggling among themselves what must have been their own ethnographic observations. Were Philip and I creating a first impression we would cringe to hear about later?

When we finished André filled a glass for himself. He tilted it ever so slightly, intentionally spilling a few drops onto the cement floor—perhaps we'd been rude in not doing the same. Then André downed the beer in a few seconds. Another gaffe: we'd sipped our drinks rather than chugging them. My first minutes in a Beng village were starting to feel at once excruciating and exhilarating as I felt all my old patterns of polite behavior suspended—but still at a loss for what to substitute in their place.

André poured two more glasses.

"Won't you join us this time?" Philip asked.

"No, you go ahead," he answered, "I'll drink afterward."

Was turn taking the customary mode of drinking? Pondering what seemed like yet another mistake, I hesitated before taking my first sip. Should I let a drop or two of beer spill from my glass onto the porch floor? No, I'd better wait until I knew what it meant. But when would that be? We hadn't even managed to unpack our own car—how much harder it would be to unpack the significance of the new routines that were already claiming us.

Wordlessly we three downed another round of beer . . . and another . . . and another. A confirmed teetotaler, I couldn't imagine how we'd ever drain those two enormous bottles. And the vacant space that I thought conversation should fill was starting to feel awkward. Was André waiting for us to reveal more about ourselves, or was this a conventional drinking silence?

Finally, the bottles emptied, André broke the quiet and asked me about my research. I explained that I was an anthropology student here to study Beng culture, and André nodded. "I'm glad you've come. You can stay with us for the whole year—my house is large enough. Please be welcome."

Immediately I regretted that I hadn't explained our intentions more clearly: I'd already decided to settle in a smaller village, where I could more easily chart the connections between people's lives. With some regret, I explained my decision. Still, André's generous offer was tempting—who knew if another one would come along?

"Well, you can always reconsider," André said. "But now you should go and meet Pascal's parents. I'll have my son show you the way." He nodded to a boy with a rounded stomach peeking out below his short shirt; the child's intense gaze and smooth, light skin announced him as a miniature version of his father. Philip stood and reached for my hand: we were about to walk through our first Beng village.

Philip: Amwé and Kouadio

The boy beckoned to us with a shy smile, and we gestured back, indicating we were ready to follow. Thus, united by these attempts at a sign language, we three began our walk through the relentless brown of the village: the milk chocolate of single-story mud houses; the dark wooden stilts of granaries, their sloping thatched roofs seeming to flow with motion; and curving mud paths that wove throughout coffee-colored dirt courtyards. I was glad André's son led us so confidently through what—to me—appeared to be a maze.

Villagers gathered to gape at our strangeness, and in turn I was overwhelmed by the poverty and illness of our audience: malnourished children with thin limbs and distended bellies or large, herniated belly buttons; thin old men and women, their eyes clouded by cataracts; an enormous goiter distorting the neck of a young woman; and people of all ages with craterlike sores on their legs, poulticed only by leaves. Aware of being an alien, privileged presence, I wanted to vanish from the gazes of the curious villagers, disappear from this world that had never requested my arrival.

Finally our young escort stopped at a courtyard edged with mud brick buildings, their corrugated tin roofs shining in the late afternoon light. One small house had clearly seen better days: the thatch roof sagged in places, and parts of the mud walls were worn away, exposing the dark interior. Another, larger house was under construction but seemingly arrested midway, a hope gone sour: the walls uneven, no roof, and stacks of unused mud bricks that appeared to be melted into each other, perhaps from years of exposure to the rains. Was this unfinished home an example of the great sacrifices Pascal's family was making to support his university studies?

At the end of the courtyard sat a small group of older men, drinking and talking gaily. They grew quiet when one of them rose to greet us. Short and solid, he wore a Western-style raincoat and a torn woolen cap, though it was neither raining nor cold.

"*Bienvenu*," he said, smiling. "I'm Bwadi Kouakou, Pascal's father. Welcome to the village. I understand you've met my son."

This man had politely addressed us in French—shouldn't we respond in Beng? Alma and I glanced at each other, and I whispered, "You go first." This was, after all, her fieldwork.

"*Aba ... ka kwo!*" she managed, and the men in the courtyard roared with delight.

Bwadi Kouakou grinned and said, "Very good! But that's for the afternoon—it's evening now. We'll have to teach you those greetings."

Alma glanced down at her wristwatch. "It's only four," she murmured to me. Frowning, she shook the watch to check if it had broken. That would be a fitting reaction, I thought: our first day in the village, time stopped.

"Unless evening starts earlier for the Beng," she whispered, pleased with this sudden thought, but then she stopped: "*Damn*, I left my notebook at André's."

I stared at Alma's empty hands, surprised at her forgetfulness but relieved she was as overwhelmed as I.

Bwadi Kouakou was waiting patiently, and Alma knew the time had come to begin her formal speech. After introducing us, she began tentatively, "I'm a student of African culture, and I'm here to study your way of life. We'd like to live in a Beng village for about fourteen months."

"*Bon, bon,*" Bwadi Kouakou said, nodding. Alma paused expectantly—the *secrétaire* of Asagbé's first impressions of us would surely influence the other villagers' reactions. Just then a woman emerged from one of the smaller buildings, her smile almost toothless, her withered breasts dangling above a ragged, wraparound skirt that was tucked loosely into a knot at her waist. She shook our hands effusively, saying in Beng what we assumed were the evening greetings. Unable to reply, we smiled and nodded our heads encouragingly.

"Pascal," she said, then added something further in Beng.

"*Oui, oui,*" we replied, "we know Pascal."

She continued speaking in Beng excitedly, at first unaware that we couldn't understand her. Then, with some frustration, she pointed a long finger at herself and said, "*Maman.*"

Pascal's mother. We shook her hand again, hoping we hadn't insulted her.

"She's asking for news of Pascal," Bwadi Kouakou said.

Clearly, saying hello involved more than trying to memorize the right words. Chagrined that we hadn't mentioned Pascal earlier, Alma said how helpful he'd been to us, how well he spoke English. Bwadi Kouakou translated this to his wife, who shook our hands yet again. Suddenly a pair of frail metal folding chairs were produced. We were invited to sit, and a young man—who looked as though he might be Pascal's brother—addressed us: "The *secrétaire* says that you should join him and his friends in some palm wine."

"*Merci,*" we replied together. Did this mean he approved of Alma's speech?

The *secrétaire* nodded to the young man, who picked up a rectangular plastic container. I glanced at the faded label—the can had once held engine oil. He tipped the spout over a hollowed-out gourd and poured out a bubbly white liquid that, disappointingly, resembled watery milk: was this the magical drink of one of my favorite African novels, Amos Tutuola's *The Palm-Wine Drinkard?* That book's hero loved the concoction so much that he drank 150 kegs of it each day, then topped it off with another 75 kegs at night. Disconsolate when his palm-wine tapster died, he set off to recover the treasured employee from the Town of the Deads, and on his fantastical journey through the rain forest he saved a woman from a husband who was only a skull, discovered an entire village of creatures who looked like human beings but had artificial heads, and encountered a spirit who could kill a victim merely by blinking.

The young man handed me the gourd filled with palm wine. I lifted it to my lips, then stopped. Tipping the edge, I let a little spill to the ground, and the men around us laughed again.

Bwadi Kouakou clapped his hands. "*Voilà!* You're Beng already!"

"But what does spilling the drink mean?" Alma asked, annoying me— she was spoiling my performance. Yet she *had* to ask, I knew—with or without her notebook, Alma was an anthropologist.

"*C'est pour la Terre*"—For the Earth—he explained. "It's how we show our respect."

"The Earth?" Alma replied. While she and Bwadi Kouakou spoke, I took a cautious sip. My lips pursed at the excessive sweetness, which competed with an underlying bitterness—I couldn't imagine enduring any of the Palm-Wine Drinkard's torments for this unpromising stuff. In my mouth, at least, something was definitely lost in translation. I passed the gourd to Alma.

"*Bon,*" said Bwadi Kouakou, obviously pleased. "If you're going to live among us, you'll need Beng names." Of course—why not? In Beng eyes we were just one day old. In swift order I was dubbed Kouadio, and Alma became Amwé. We continued to pass around the gourd, and I repeated my name silently a few times, trying it on: Kouadio, Kouadio, Kouadio. Perhaps I was already under the growing influence of the palm wine, perhaps not, but Kouadio seemed to fit.

Alma: Very *Vlong Vlong*

We returned to our host's compound, and André chuckled appreciatively when we told him our new names. Then he called over his senior wife, Marie—a tall, stately woman who hurriedly whispered something to a young girl who I supposed was her daughter. She then came over and shook my hand warmly, both of hers enveloping my own.

"Amwé! Kouadio!" She laughed, delighted with the surprise of our sudden appearance and the incongruity of our newly minted Beng names. But there was little more to say: neither of us spoke the other's language. Our muteness stretched before us, an invisible valley over which we couldn't leap.

Perhaps sensing this, André joined in: "My second wife speaks French." He gestured to Maat, a slightly plump woman who sat nearby on a stool, tending to a cooking fire. Glancing up with curiosity to regard her improbable guests, she came over and welcomed us, *"Bonjour et bienvenu."* Delighted that we could speak together, I happily accepted her invitation to keep her company while she cooked.

On the dirt floor of her small, windowless kitchen, a round-bottomed pot sat on three large hearthstones; between them, three logs burned slowly. Inside the pot thick white chunks—yams, Maat told me—shook in the boiling water. Most of the smoke and steam escaped out the corrugated-tin door, but a few thin curls lingered, leaving a seasoned smell in the hot room. I asked for a knife and joined Maat in slicing okras into another large pot. Poor Philip, I thought—his least favorite vegetable. Maat added green berries to the pot and, to my chagrin, a *handful* of red peppers. Perhaps the berries would add a sweet touch to counter all those fierce chilies.

As Maat continued preparing the meal, she pointed out her children scrambling about the compound with happy energy.

"And your children. . . ?" she asked me.

"None yet," I said.

Maat nodded. *"Eki mi gba lenni."*

I reached for my notebook. "What does that mean?"

"May God give you children."

I thanked Maat, adding lamely that I hoped one day to be a mother, too. I didn't dare mention my techniques for family planning.

With a sigh of sympathy for me, Maat removed the white yams from the cooking pot and, stepping out the door, placed them in an enormous mortar made of a beautiful, mahoganylike wood. From a dark corner in the kitchen she fetched a shoulder-high pestle and then began to pound the chunks in a lovely rhythm—*kathunk* on the soft yams, *kathink* against the inner side of the mortar for a contrasting, hollower sound, *kathunk kathink, kathunk kathink.* I asked Maat if I could have a try.

"Sure." She laughed and handed me the heavy pestle. I managed to mash a few pieces, but I couldn't make that hollow sound or match its rhythms.

"That's very good!" Maat complimented me, but she gently took back the pestle: her hungry family couldn't wait indefinitely for their dinner. She resumed pounding until, miraculously, the yams transformed from a pasty mass into an elastic, round ball about the size of a small cantaloupe:

so this was the famed yam *foutou!* Maat completed the task, making two more white balls.

By now the sauce was cooked, and Maat apportioned it into a few colored enamel bowls, then divided the balls of *foutou* into matching plates. I watched silently as she carried out a pair of dishes, setting them on the ground in front of André, who sat on a low stool, chatting with some other men. A pail of water was passed around for hand washing, and the small group plunged into dinner. Why didn't the men wait for André's wives and children to join them? And why weren't these men eating with *their* families? Perplexed, I went into the house to fetch Philip. Ever the tidy one, he was unpacking our belongings and arranging them neatly in our new room.

"Hello, Amwé," he said.

I giggled. "It's dinnertime, but I'm not sure where to eat—actually, I'm not even sure *who* we should eat with. . . ."

"Oh, it can't be that complicated," Philip teased, following me out to the porch. We saw a set of pale blue bowls sitting on the table, two chairs ranged around it expectantly.

Maat walked over. *"Ka ta poblé."*

"Pardon?"

"Allez manger," Maat translated.

Ah, a good phrase to learn—Go eat! Obediently Philip and I sat down, but I was too disappointed to start right away. I'd hoped to dine with the family—but the family itself was divided. In front of the open doors to their adjacent kitchens, Maat and Marie crouched on the ground with their children, and the two groups started in on their separate dinners. I stared at the steaming plates in front of us. "I guess we should stay here by ourselves," I muttered to Philip.

We shot sidelong glances at André to observe how he lopped off a small piece of *foutou* with his thumb and forefinger, dipping it in the sauce. Then I tried, but my bit of yam plunged instantly into the slick sauce, and I cast about for it, hoping I had no audience. Unfortunately André caught sight of me doing battle with the fugitive chunk.

"The sauce is *vlong vlong*, eh?" he sympathized.

"Mmmm, very *vlong vlong*," I replied, chuckling silently. "Slippery" seemed a good word to learn on my first day: so far, the rules for all the day's encounters seemed, at best, *vlong vlong*. Eventually I fished out the doughy piece and popped it in my mouth. The peppery gumbo assaulted my taste buds, though it did little to mask the sharply bitter taste of the berries. I chewed the thick yam, then swallowed.

"Whew," I warned Philip quietly, "that's *hot!*"

"Hmmm," he said cautiously. Never a fan of spicy foods, he followed suit nervously. "My dear, you speak the truth," he gasped. Our eyes teared, our noses ran, with each bite of the fiery meal. A glass of water would be just the thing. I glanced around—why wasn't anyone drinking? Sighing, I dipped into the spicy roux again, sniffling and blotting my eyes with each bite. Soon André and his friends finished their meal, and they sipped from a gourdful of water. Ah—now was the time for drinking. I finished hurriedly so I could finally take a large swig of water.

After dinner Maat told me, *"Ta zro"*—Go wash up, she translated to my perplexed expression—and pointed across the courtyard to a tiny, roofless mud brick building; spanning the open doorway was a stick with a colorful *pagne* hanging over it. So this short structure was a bathhouse. Grateful, I walked over and found a bucket of warm water waiting. Then, under a vast black sky dotted by shimmering stars, I discovered the pleasures of a delicious outdoor pail bath. But this luxury was at my hostess's expense, for Maat must have carried the water some distance, perhaps from a pool or well deep in the forest. So I made sure to save Philip enough water in the bucket, which I left in the bathhouse. As I returned to the courtyard, I heard the sound of water splashing: Maat had emptied the pail! I cringed to think how Maat might interpret this new faux pas I'd just made.

Later that night Philip and I settled into the small guest room. In the corner was a straw mattress; our suitcases, cameras, typewriters, books, kerosene lamp—all now arranged carefully by Philip—occupied the remaining space.

"Well, this is it," Philip said as we lay in bed.

"What do you think?" I asked. "Can you handle it?"

"I have no idea, it's all so . . . I can't say, it's . . . overwhelming." Philip sighed.

"Do you think you'll be able to write about it?"

"Maybe." Philip paused. "Do you really think we'll learn the damn language?"

"We'd better," I answered quickly.

A sudden high-pitched animal cry interrupted us. Then the cry returned, this time longer and louder, again and again, until the shrill, gravelly scream seemed to fill the room around us.

"What's *that?*" I barely whispered.

"Shhhh, let's listen," Philip whispered back.

Slowly the screech receded; in moments it quieted to silence, and the room was again just four walls, no longer enclosed by our fear.

"Do you think it'll come back?" I asked.

"We'll know if it does," Philip said nervously, and we snuggled together into a worried sleep. My muscles ached, my mind was filled with images of mud brick houses, babies with brightly painted faces, gourds of palm wine tumbling over each other—perhaps, in the dark of the room, my dreams could make sense of them.

*   *   *

In the morning we stepped outside and found the family scattered about the compound—the children loitering by their mothers, who were stirring some kind of porridge over their fires, André packing coffee beans into a large burlap bag. We asked our host about last night's eerie concert. He pursed together his lips. "I'm not sure. . . ."

Philip tried his best imitation of the roar. The children all looked up and tittered.

"Oh, that!" André laughed. "It was just a *gbaya*, a tiny animal that lives in the trees—all they eat are fruits and leaves."

So we'd been afraid of something like a squirrel! The forest seemed one shade less dark and looming as I imagined those furry creatures scampering among the trees.

We passed the rest of the morning meeting neighbors, with André or Maat serving as translators. I felt immensely grateful for their efforts and guilty for the time they must have been taking from their own work. But by noon I was exhausted by all those dual-layered conversations—which made it seem as though the villagers' words were spoken from behind a scrim. I knew I needed to begin language lessons, but at the moment I knew of only one possible teacher. After lunch I said to André, "There's a young man who Pascal told us might be a good language tutor, maybe help me in my research. His name is Kona Kofi Jean. Do you know him?"

"Yes, he lives in the village of Bongalo."

"What's he like? Do you think he'd work with me?"

"*Ça, je ne sais pas,* he's the only one who can say," André said.

"Of course," I agreed. "I guess we'll go over to Bongalo to meet him."

"*Bon,* I'll come along, too," André offered graciously, and we all readied for the drive.

I was about to interview someone for a job, a role I'd never played before. Yet in the car I found myself suppressing the urge to prepare a list of questions—for if Jean didn't answer them to my satisfaction, then what? He was an applicant pool of one. Most likely there *were* other Beng who spoke French, were curious about their own culture, and could move to a new village for some fourteen months . . . but I had little idea how to find them.

In Bongalo a curious crowd gathered as André escorted us through the village. In front of a tiny, ramshackle house, André clapped his hands three times rapidly, said, "*Kaw kaw kaw,*" and entered. Philip and I followed a bit hesitantly. Inside the small room, a young man wearing old blue jeans and a striped shirt squatted on the dirt floor. Seeing us, he stood and greeted André in Beng; then, casting us an intense gaze, he greeted Philip and me in a French that was far better than that of most villagers we'd met, who'd clearly just picked up some phrases in the marketplace. At Jean's feet lay an open wooden suitcase of the sort we'd seen in the Abidjan *marchés*—piled neatly inside it were cigarette packs, gold-colored chain necklaces, boxes of matches, individually wrapped candies, schoolchildren's notebooks.

Jean shut the case, explaining apologetically that he'd been arranging the wares of his small business. "Please, have a seat," he said, offering us some wooden stools.

"We bring you greetings from Kouakou Kouadio Pascal," I began. Immediately Jean grasped our hands and thanked us. Then I told Jean that I was an American university student and a longtime admirer of African culture, and that Philip was a writer, now working on his second book, a collection of short stories.

"I've always admired America," Jean responded. "I listen to the Voice of America's French broadcasts twice a day on the radio."

"*Ah, bon,*" I said, encouraged by his cultural curiosity. "We've come to see you," I continued, "because I want to learn your language. I hope to study your rituals, your customs, and people's everyday lives. We'll be moving soon to a smaller village for my research," I added.

Abruptly Jean hopped up from his seat, muttering, "Excuse me a moment." I worried that I'd said something wrong. Jean rummaged around the room until he found a small stack of papers.

"Please, would you look at these?" he asked nervously. "They're some drawings I've done."

I accepted the sheets and marveled: in pale, colored pencil lines there was a detailed map of Jean's current village, another of his home village, complete with public plazas, chiefs' houses, main roads, and shaded-in trees—it seemed he'd made maps of all the Beng villages. "These are wonderful!" I said, passing them to Philip, a longtime map buff, and I saw that he, too, appreciated the observant eye behind those sketches.

I asked Jean a few questions—as much to get a sense of his French vocabulary as to hear his answers—and as we spoke I noticed Jean's wrinkled brow, a few worry lines around his mouth. He told us he'd converted to Islam some time ago—he no longer drank alcohol, and he prayed four times a day. This was an allegiance I hadn't anticipated.

"I myself am Jewish," I mentioned cautiously.

"Ah, one of the religions of the book," Jean responded immediately. "I have great respect for the Jewish people. But you're the first one I've met."

"*Ah, oui?*" I said, tickled by the exotic space I was occupying in Jean's mind. But I was also somewhat assuaged: with this ecumenical spirit, he'd probably be able to cope with my interest in another set of religious customs that he himself didn't practice. In short, Jean seemed qualified: he had an anthropological imagination, and his French was fine. I leaned forward and continued, "I need someone who can work with me as a language teacher, translator, and research assistant. When I spoke with Pascal, he suggested you. Would you be interested?"

Looking a little dazed, he stammered, "*Merci beaucoup,* it would be a great honor."

Had I really hired Jean, just like that? It seemed somehow too easy. Then, with the delicate help of André, I broached the question of a salary. I wanted to pay a fair wage—and then some—commensurate with Jean's skills. In the car ride over, André had suggested twice the rate customarily paid to day laborers; now I proposed that to Jean.

"*C'est bon,*" Jean agreed. "I'll pack up my business and move into Asagbé tonight with some relatives. Once you choose a smaller village, I'll move there with you."

Later that evening Jean joined us on André's porch. While the children lounged quietly around the courtyard near their mothers, who washed the dinner dishes in large basins set on the ground, I asked Jean about his life.

"I loved school, I worked hard, I always received the highest grades in my class," he began. "But my father didn't want me to continue—he wanted me to help him in his fields." Jean's face twisted into a bitter knot. "I started having terrible headaches. They were so bad I couldn't study anymore—I had to quit. I always wanted to go to the university, but now I'll never be able to. *Ah, mon père*"—he sighed—"*il m'a maltraité.* How could I return to the village and his farm after that? I refused. But without a high school degree, I couldn't get a job in town. That's how I became a trader."

"Oh, Jean, I'm so sorry," I said softly.

"And my father hasn't found a woman for me to marry—you know, *chez nous,* we almost always have arranged marriages. That's why I'm still single."

Contemplating what he had just confided to me, I realized that Jean was by no means the typical villager—whatever that was. Perhaps it was inevitable that I—far more marginal myself—had chosen him as my assistant. But Jean's liminality seemed to gnaw away at him. Was it arrogant to imagine that I might reverse the plunge his life had taken? I wondered if Jean himself expected as much from our collaboration.

"I'd like to hear more about you and Philippe," Jean said. We shared with him our family histories—Philip's Scottish Catholic background, my Eastern European immigrant roots. But it was late—some of the children had gone inside to bed; others were dozing on parents' laps. The next day we'd begin work.

*   *   *

In the late morning a letter arrived by bush taxi: Lisa had written us that the mayor of M'Bahiakro had returned from his relative's funeral. We decided to drive to town immediately. In the car I worried that the mayor might be annoyed because we'd gone to the village before obtaining his authorization. For his part, Jean fretted that his worn clothes weren't appropriate for meeting a high government official. With his first paycheck, he promised, he'd buy a new wardrobe for our work together. I told Jean this wasn't necessary, but he insisted, "Our work together is too important."

The town hall was a long white building with green shuttered windows. After a surprisingly short wait, the secretary pointed us to Monsieur Mory's office, an open doorway at the end of a hallway. Seated behind a desk was a tall man with a strong jawline. He looked up from a pile of papers. "*Bonsoir,* what may I do for you?"

"*Bonsoir, Monsieur le Sous-Préfet,*" I began, then introduced the three of us. I brought out my stamped papers and explained my research. "I'm very sorry we went up to Asagbé before seeing you," I concluded. "We didn't know when you'd return—"

"That's perfectly all right," he interrupted amiably, "you're here now, aren't you?" He glanced through my papers. "I'm very intrigued by anthropology. I'm from up north myself, and to tell you the truth," he said, leaning forward on his desk, "I know very little about these Beng people. You're probably aware that the constituency of this *sous-préfecture* is mostly Baulé."

I nodded. "Yes, quite a few anthropologists have worked with the Baulé—that's why I've come to live with the Beng, no one's done any research on their culture."

"Ah, that explains why I don't know much about them." Now the mayor turned to Jean. "Young man," he said a bit sternly, "you are in a most important position."

Jean sat straight on his seat, hands folded in his lap, and murmured, "*Oui, Monsieur le Sous-Préfet.*"

"This scholar has come from America to study your people—no one has ever done this before—and it's your job to ensure that she understands everything correctly. It's you who will translate for her; Americans will form their opinions and judgments about your people on the basis of your words. Speak wisely. Your country is counting on you."

"*Oui, Monsieur le Sous-Préfet,*" Jean repeated, his head bobbing.

Monsieur Mory went on in this patriotic vein for a while longer with Jean—I was touched, but also chagrined, by how much importance he was ascribing to my research. Soon the meeting was over. As we walked out to the car, Jean's hands fidgeted. The *sous-préfet*'s admonitions had clearly unsettled him.

Philip: "Thank You for Your Lie"

Each morning the solid sound and hollow echo of women pounding large wooden pestles into mortars rang through the air, that distinctive *thwonk-*

ing rhythm marking the new day like the pealing of communal bells. When Alma and I wandered sleepy-eyed onto the porch, the steaming pails of hot water for the morning bath and the smoke of cooking fires already mingled with the morning mist. Maat and Marie swept the dirt courtyard with hand-held brooms made of dried palm leaves, raising curling waves of dust before them. Watching these two co-wives perform their morning chores, I searched for hints of their true feelings for one another. But their easy formality together—very polite yet seemingly with little warmth—could have hid resentments as well as tenderness and resisted my curiosity.

After a breakfast of sweet corn porridge, with Jean's help we entered into the shifting puzzle of Beng greetings. Their complicated rules drew us into a pervasive social nicety, for whenever two people passed each other those elaborate exchanges started up, and even if by the end of the exchange they were sometimes twenty or thirty feet away, they still muttered the end of the greetings to themselves as they continued on their way.

Whenever hailed by a friendly villager, I made hesitant, fitful replies, calculating all the possible combinations I needed to match up, and with my accumulating, awkward silences I felt the need to speak faster. Yet one small mistake collapsed my confidence, and I was unsure of what to say next. Even if I *did* manage to reply correctly, the emboldened villager then chatted away rapidly to my stunned, silent face.

There was nowhere to hide our faltering abilities, for dozens of people surrounded us when we sat on André's front porch, conducting a running commentary in Beng on our peculiar ways. Sometimes the continuous gaze of all those eyes exhausted me—I couldn't see how I'd ever find the solitude necessary to write, but I would simply have to adjust to this aspect of my new life. I thought of a proverb Jean had recently taught us: "If I dislike one finger, should I cut it from my hand?"

Once, while Jean quizzed us on Beng verbs, I silently protested the numbing repetition by letting my eyes wander. Maat stood across the courtyard, pounding peanuts in a mortar for the evening's sauce, and sheep and chickens paced hungrily as close as they dared to the mortar. When a chicken darted forward at an untended morsel, Maat foiled its petty pillage with a well-timed kick.

I watched the villagers return home from their work in the fields, men with machetes in hand, women carrying large basins filled with firewood or yams on their heads. I had long grown used to the exceptional balancing skills of Ivoirians, but I gaped when I noticed a thin woman, her hair slightly graying, who walked past us with only an angular, pinkish stone perched on her head. She stared ahead intently, as if in a tunnel of her own making.

"Alma, look," I whispered.

She followed my gaze. "Jean, who is that?" she asked.

He glanced at the woman and quickly turned away. "I don't know," he said.

"Why is she walking with a stone on her head?"

"I don't know," he repeated, his normally animated face feigning indifference.

Now quite interested, Alma turned to Maat and asked, "Do you know that woman?"

"*Oui,*" Maat answered simply after a quick glance. "She is sick." Then she lifted her wooden pestle and returned to mashing peanuts.

Was Maat saying, as delicately as possible, that the woman was mad? In the embarrassed silence, Alma and I exchanged glances, and she asked no more questions, at least for the moment. We returned to our language lesson with an uncharacteristically subdued Jean. Of course he hadn't spent years honing an anthropological curiosity, as Alma had, yet I suspected that she was as disappointed as I over his uncooperative answers.

*   *   *

With the afternoon meal over, Alma and I washed our hands—stained an orange yellow from the palm-nut sauce—in a communal pail of water. "*E nini*"—Delicious—we called over to Marie, who'd prepared the meal. Then, silently, a boy appeared at André's porch. I dreaded the sight of this child—he was waiting to accompany us to Bwadi Kouakou's compound, where another lunch awaited us. Ever since our first day in the village, we ate first at André's home, then commuted to Bwadi Kouakou's for a second meal: two hosts honoring us. Of course Alma and I couldn't refuse, though we were always presented with more food than we could eat at each compound. So we began pacing our appetites, preparing for the afternoon's landslide of lunches, the evening's dueling dinners.

Pascal's mother was a good cook, but her co-wife, Kla, prepared terrible meals—the sauces watery and bitter, the *foutou* undercooked, pasty. Lately it had been Kla's turn to feed us. We sighed and set off. Jean, who accompanied us on these journeys across the village, set his face in silent suffering.

At Bwadi Kouakou's compound our host led us to one of the small mud houses, and we sat with him inside the entrance, away from the glare of the sun. Another circle of male guests was already gathered in the room, waiting to be served. Jean joined them. Then one of Kla's daughters appeared and set before us on the floor one bowl filled with a roundish ball of *foutou*, another filled with a thin green sauce—Kla's bitter specialty—well stocked with thick pieces of meat.

The meat was spoiled—its fetid smell filled the room.

"We can't eat this," I whispered to Alma.

"I know," Alma whispered back, her nose crinkled, "but how can we insult the *secrétaire?*"

"Ana poblé"—Let's eat—Bwadi Kouakou announced. He broke off a piece of *foutou* with his fingers, then scooped up a chunk of meat.

"What kind of meat is that?" Alma asked, stalling.

"Antelope," he replied, now chewing without complaint.

I turned to Alma and murmured, "Maybe it's not so bad." But the stench was nearly overpowering. My greatest urge was to leave the room as swiftly as possible and not, as I did now, reach down and pluck a bit of *foutou* from the ball, then dip it into the sauce and collect a piece of meat.

Slowly I raised it to my mouth. Eyes closed, I popped it in, then tried not to recoil. I kept chewing, unwilling to swallow. But I couldn't stall with this seemingly meditative mastication forever, so I gulped down the vile mess. Alma soaked up the sauce with her pinch of *foutou*, but she avoided the meat. Still, she had to stiffen her face to avoid grimacing— even the sauce was permeated with the putrid taste. She managed this tactic for a few minutes until Bwadi Kouakou said, "Don't be shy, eat some meat."

Her mouth a grim line, Alma followed our host's suggestion. "Oh my god," Alma said in English, her voice cheerfully disguising the meaning of her words, "this is absolutely horrible."

Following her example, I replied in a similarly happy tone, "You're right, it's quite monstrously bad. I think I'm going to throw up." We turned to Bwadi Kouakou, smiled, and lied: "*E nini.*"

Jean, sitting with the other circle of guests, cast a desperate look over to us, then bowed his head and continued to eat. So it wasn't just us. Then why was Bwadi Kouakou—and everyone else in the room—eating politely? Perhaps the *secrétaire* was too embarrassed to admit what his wife had served. And of course we, as guests, couldn't insult our host. So we all suffered through the meal, making a great pretense that nothing was amiss.

Finally we finished the ball of *foutou*, the last chunk of malodorous meat. "I thought that meal would never, ever end," I said in English, my voice now genuinely cheery. Suddenly Kla's daughter appeared and placed another bowl on the floor: seconds.

"Oh shit!" Alma gasped. Though Bwadi Kouakou didn't understand English, the tone of Alma's voice was clear. Shamed, Alma picked at this new ball of *foutou* and gathered up a few more slices of antelope, and I followed her lead reluctantly.

"Have more," our host urged us quietly as we slowed down, but I'd had enough. "*N kana*"—I'm full—I told him, and Alma said the same.

On our trek back to André's compound, Jean railed against Bwadi Kouakou's reluctance to criticize his wife's meal. "That meat should *never* have been served to anyone," he insisted, his arm sweeping dismissively in the air, "and certainly not to *guests!*" We nodded in agreement, and

Alma smiled slightly—Jean's vehemence eased her regret over her involuntary outburst.

The next morning I awoke to Alma's groaning; instantly awake, I turned over and saw my wife clutching her stomach, her face one large wince. One of us was finally sick—but which of the innumerable, exotic illnesses we'd fearfully anticipated did Alma have?

"Ooh, I just know it's from that meat," she gasped.

"Maybe," I replied, stroking her forehead, working hard at a pretense of calm. "But then how come I'm not sick, too?"

She had no answer. I paged through our medical text—with the less than comforting title *Where There Is No Doctor*—and found too many illnesses with symptoms resembling Alma's terrible cramps. Yet there *was* a doctor nearby, at the M'Bahiakro infirmary; Lisa had told us his name—Dr. Yiallo.

"I think it's time to go to M'Bahiakro," I said, and I helped her dress—she could barely move without sharp spasms.

On the trip down, Alma groaned in counterpoint to the rattling bumps in the road, and I drove as carefully as possible. When we finally entered the gates of the infirmary, I couldn't tell at first which of the long, single-story cement buildings bordering the vast courtyard contained the doctor. People wandered about the courtyard, but I wasn't sure if they were patients or visitors.

I parked the car under one of the large trees that formed a shady avenue. "Let's try over there," I said, pointing to one building where a long line waited outside a green shuttered door. There were Dr. Yiallo's patients for the morning: mothers carrying wailing infants on their backs, hunched old men, a young girl who hacked into a colored kerchief, a boy on crutches, another boy in a khaki school uniform who simply stared dully before him, and many more cases of stoic suffering. We stood at the end of the line, Alma's body bent from the pain. I held her by the arm, and slowly, over the course of a long, hot hour, we shuffled our way to the door. When we entered a dimly lit office the doctor rose from behind his desk. On the filing cabinets beside him loomed three large glass jars filled with alcohol and the thick, coiled bodies of snakes. The doctor's dark face filled with curiosity as he greeted us: though we'd come as patients, we were clearly a break in his busy day, a puzzle to be solved.

After Alma introduced us, Dr. Yiallo peppered her with questions about her research. Then he told us he was the only doctor for this entire complex, though there was a head nurse who sometimes doubled for him and occasionally even performed surgery. The doctor spoke so rapidly we could barely follow his words; I wondered if this breathtaking speed was the result of his trying to treat as many patients as possible in the course of a day. But Alma was a patient as well, and soon he asked her, now all business, why we were here to see him.

Alma described her pain, her suspicions about the spoiled meat.

"Amoebas, absolutely," he said, "though I'm sorry we don't have lab facilities here to confirm the diagnosis." He sighed, then swiftly scratched out a prescription.

We thanked him and left. Gaping at the line of new patients, now even longer, I was stunned by Dr. Yiallo's impossible, daily task. I wondered how many more times in the months to come we'd have to return to see him.

*   *   *

Sitting on a stool before a bowlful of one of Maat's violently spicy specialties, I made a brisk pinching motion with three fingers, reached for the ball of starchy *foutou*, and pulled away a pliant, sticky piece. I dipped it in the okra sauce and then deftly gobbled it up: my Beng mealtime mechanics were definitely improving. Yet while I ate with one hand, the other ached: across the base of my thumb and down to my wrist was a thin, pus-filled trench. Apparently some mysterious insect was responsible. None of the antibiotic ointments Dr. Yiallo had given me seemed to help.

After the meal we lounged about André's porch. Alma massaged her stomach cramps as inconspicuously as possible, while my hand continued its determined throbbing, and we cast each other grim smiles. Hoping for a distraction, I asked Jean if he would tell us a traditional Beng story. Realizing that Alma intended to tape his words, he agreed at once.

A small crowd gathered and grew. Jean began, emphasizing every word, his eye on the tape recorder, and André punctuated Jean's pauses with "*Hmm*," "*e-eh*," and "*yo*"—an appreciative commentary that seemed to speak for the entire audience. Alma and I understood nothing of what was said, and I found myself concentrating on the listeners' attentive faces, their obvious pleasure echoing Jean's words: they suddenly laughed—a burst of real glee—and then, when Jean began singing in a soft, high voice, the audience repeated the melody after him, an exchange repeated three times. I was surprised at how their impromptu chorus joined in so smoothly. It wasn't only the story they were listening to, I realized, but the *telling*, and this particular telling they obviously enjoyed.

Finally Jean said, "*E nyana*"—It's finished—and I was pleased that I understood at least this. The audience, by way of applause, chanted together, "*A oukwa*," and Jean thanked them for their appreciation. Then he translated their words—"Thank you for your lie."

"No, a story isn't a lie," I protested, prepared to defend my calling.

Jean and André nodded—out of politeness, not agreement. Cautioned by their response, I kept silent, too, suppressing a speech about the paradox of fiction: though invented, it expressed subtle truths not easily arrived at by other means. Labeling a story a lie denied fiction its essential power. But Alma and I were here to listen, not lecture. "Jean," I asked, "could you translate your lie for us?"

"Of course," he replied with a little laugh. The steadily growing audience waited patiently as he spoke—most villagers didn't speak French—and Alma and I reenacted in our minds the interplay of teller and listeners, the exuberant rhythms of performance.

"Here is one of my stories," he said. "There was this young man who lived with his mother. The mother slept in this room here, and the young man slept in that room there." With his finger he gestured in opposite directions.

"His mother gave him some advice: 'If at any time you see a pretty girl, forgive me for saying this, but don't tell her all your secrets, don't show her everything. It won't be good.' So she told him.

"The young man was a hunter, and he usually killed antelopes. One day, one of these antelopes was transformed into a pretty young woman, and she came to his house. They went into his room and made love." Here Jean imitated the sound of a shaking bed—*"Krukrukrukru."* The villagers on the porch broke into laughter, as they had earlier.

Jean paused, then continued. "Later, his mother told him: 'Hmmm, what I told you the other day, don't you forget it.'

"However, he ignored her. One night he told this woman, who was really an antelope, 'I'm a hunter, and I'm especially good at killing antelopes.'

"So it was like this: that night when they went to sleep, the antelope-woman plucked out his two eyeballs so he could never hunt again. She put them in her turban, and *whoosh*, she was transported to the forest. There she found her fellow antelopes: they were in the middle of a *lolon-dalé* dance, catching each other in their arms.

"She sang this song: 'Here are the eyes of Mamadou, the antelope killer.'" Again Jean sang that clear, soft melody, and again the audience sang back. Jean translated the lyrics: the dancing antelopes called out, "Give the eyes to me, so I can look at them."

He continued. "Okay. Since the young man had spoken like that to the antelope-woman, well, his mother, she knew some things, too. So *she* was immediately transformed into an antelope and appeared in the forest, *whoosh*. When she arrived, the eyes of her son were being thrown around, thrown around like this." Jean made a tossing motion.

"The mother-antelope joined the dance, and soon her son's eyes fell into her hands—first one, then the other. She put them in her turban and was transported back to the village. She had taken her son's eyes, and now she gave them back to him. She said, 'The other day I warned you about this, but you didn't listen. You must never do that again, never again.'

"Okay, it's finished," Jean said, and even though he hadn't told the story in Beng, the villagers chanted, *"A oukwa."* I refrained from joining in, still mulling over the message of Jean's story: did this eerie paranoia that cautioned against intimacy contain a Beng truth?

But the storytelling session wasn't over. It was André's turn to perform. "Here is one of *my* stories," he announced in Beng, and now it was Jean who supplied the *hmm*'s and *yo*'s. They leaned close to each other, André speaking as though they were alone, and again I found myself relishing the rhythms of the Beng language when spoken by an enthusiastic story-teller. Small children giggled throughout André's performance, and at one point the villagers roared gleefully. I couldn't wait for the translation.

When the crowd once more chanted, *"A oukwa,"* André turned to us and spoke in French. "Here's one of my stories: Mosquito used to be king, but he was big back then, as big as a person. One day, Arm and his companions started a journey on the road. Ear heard something: he heard the footsteps of their slave, who was running away in the forest. Then Eye saw him. Then Leg caught up with him. Then Arm grabbed him, like *this.*" Reaching out, André grasped an invisible person with his hand.

"Then all the parts of the body started to argue over who had really caught the slave. They argued until finally they said, 'Really, Mosquito is our king, so let's ask him to decide.'

"When they arrived there and told him of their argument, Mosquito said, 'The truth: who saw him?'

"Eye said, 'It was me, I saw him.'

"Then Mosquito said, 'Who heard his footsteps?'

"'It was me, I heard his footsteps,' Ear replied.

"Mosquito said, 'Who chased after him?'

"Leg spoke up: 'Me, I chased after him, and then Arm grabbed him.'

"So Mosquito said, 'In that case, the slave belongs to Arm.'

"Now the others still didn't agree, and they angrily announced: 'It's you who are king, but since you said the slave belongs to Arm, may you shrink and grow small.' Then Mosquito shrank." Here André pursed his lips and said, *"Kokloko!"*—apparently the sound of shrinkage—and his audience again howled delightedly.

"Now, Mosquito stayed teeny-tiny, and he wasn't at all content with this state of affairs. So he decided to apologize to Ear, who had first heard the slave. Mosquito wanted to be big once again. He flew up to Ear and tried to change his decision, but Arm said, 'That's not what you decided before, go away, that's not what you decided before!'" André slapped at the air near his ear, as people do to confound buzzing mosquitoes. Again, everyone hooted with pleasure.

"So, if you see that Mosquito comes buzzing in someone's Ear, that's why the Arm tries to swat it away. *E nyana.*"

"*A oukwa*," the crowd chanted. Thank you for your lie. Now I joined in too with the required appreciation, but I would never like that phrase. I wondered if someday I might stand among Beng villagers at night, telling a story in this unfamiliar language. And what story would I tell—one of my own or one I'd learned here?

Alma: A Difficult Village

Seated on André's porch, Jean, Philip, and I were working on a new set of "hello" phrases when a woman approached who, after greeting us briefly, asked me if I knew her. I couldn't remember her name, but I knew we'd met, so out of politeness I muttered, "Uh-huh."

My nervousness at being found out must have given me away, for immediately the woman asked me teasingly, "*Ngwo n si paw?*"—What's my name? I was mortified—my bluff had been called.

Another day, after being introduced to a man named Kwamé Kouassi, a distant synapse clicked: I recalled meeting someone else with the same first and last names. I asked Jean if that was unusual.

"Oh, no," he answered casually, "because lots of people are called by day names, and there are only seven, one for each day in the week."

"What?" I blurted out.

"Well, actually there are fourteen," he clarified, "seven for men and seven for women. Take my name: Kona is from my father, because he was born on *Mlan*—Wednesday. Kofi is my day name, because I was born on *Fwé*—Saturday. And Jean is my French name—I got that when I started school." So much information in a simple moniker. Now that I knew the system, it was easy to decode—or so I thought.

One Wednesday morning, on a break from a language lesson, I glanced up and noticed Maat and Marie returning from the fields. They walked along on the narrow path; each balanced a large basin on her head, some logs poking over the edge. When they reached their kitchens, Maat slowly, carefully helped Marie down with her heavy load, then Marie assisted Maat. Their movements were so deft, I was sure they must have helped each other in this task thousands of times before.

I walked over to the two women to try out my new "Welcome back to the village" greetings. They chuckled approval of my progress, then Maat mentioned that she was going over to visit a friend who'd given birth to a baby girl last night. Proud of my new knowledge, I asked if the infant was named Ajua, for *Jowole*—Tuesday. No, she corrected me: the baby was named Amenan, for *Mlan*—Wednesday.

"*Mais pourquoi?*" I asked, baffled. Maat explained patiently that since today was Wednesday, then the child must be called Amenan.

I was even more confused. "I thought you said she was born last night?"

"Yes, she was."

"But last night was Tuesday!"

"*Mais, non*"—Maat laughed—"for us, the day begins at dusk. Last night, it was already Wednesday."

Another morning, sitting on André's porch, I worked on constructing an alphabet for this language whose intimate pathways I was just beginning to sense: with the International Phonetic Alphabet as my guide, I asked Jean to pronounce a few select words over and over. This was important, for if we mispronounced a vowel, we might ask a visitor where she shaved from (*baw*) rather than where she came from (*bow*) or ask a hunter if he'd successfully followed his prey's run (*bey*) rather than its tracks (*beh*). The consonants presented no less of a challenge as Philip and I tried to produce little explosions: *kp*'s and *gb*'s that proclaimed irrefutably the alienness of this language. Now it was Jean's turn to drill us, coaxing those bursts of sound from our unwilling lips.

In the middle of this lesson a woman came by to say good morning to Maat. I was happy to give my mouth a rest and eavesdrop on their conversation, listening furtively for diphthongs that had no life in my own language. At well under five feet tall, Maat's very pregnant friend looked almost comically round, but something in her penetrating gaze—a sharp intelligence and curiosity—checked my urge to smile when the woman, done chatting, strode onto the porch to greet Philip and me.

"*Je m'appelle Amenan*," she said, surprising me—so far, Maat was the only woman in the village I'd met who spoke French. After our introductions Amenan asked me about my research.

"I'm here to study village life," I began. "I'm especially interested in women's experiences."

Amenan nodded. "*Oui, c'est très important de considérer les femmes.*"

I couldn't help glancing down at Amenan's large belly. "Actually, one of the things I hope to study is pregnancy and childbirth."

"Ah, that's something we women know much about!" She laughed, then spoke again, lowering her voice. "If you're pregnant, you shouldn't eat large plantains, only small ones—otherwise the baby will be too fat. And you can't eat the striped gazelle we call *kiya*, or the baby's skin will come out striped. Also, never eat the small mongoose we call *kangbo*, which has a long snout and teeth like a dog. If you do, your baby's mouth will be as long as the *kangbo*'s snout! Oh, and you mustn't eat the fish we call *kokofyofyo* that bites people in the water—otherwise your baby will grow up to bite people, too."

Before I could respond, Amenan said, "*Pardon*, I must return to my compound now, I hope we'll meet again." With that we parted, and I walked back to the table. I felt breathless from Amenan's unexpected flood of revelations—and disappointed that she'd vanished as quickly as she'd appeared.

Jean was examining our list of Beng vowels, so I turned to Philip. "My god," I said, "did you hear everything she told me? Too bad we're not staying in Asagbé. . . . " I stopped, caught up in regret—Amenan and I might not have a chance to resume our conversation.

"Mmmm. But I bet there'll be lots of others like her, wherever we move," Philip offered. I wanted to believe him.

*   *   *

Philip and I often stayed up late with our two host families, drinking and trading stories. When André asked skeptically about the lunar landings he'd heard reported on the radio, he listened politely to our answer, but we weren't sure he believed us; and Bwadi Kouakou was shocked on learning that Philip and I weren't related to each other—many Beng couples, he explained, are the grandchildren of two sisters, while most others are related in some other way.

Philip and I both felt so welcome in these two compounds that it was painful to contemplate leaving—but I was anxious to settle into my research site. How to choose the right village? I had certain requirements. A population of less than four hundred would allow me to know everyone personally, charting their genealogies to figure out exactly how everyone was interrelated. I also hoped for a village in which there were few Christians or Muslims, so I could concentrate on the traditional religion of the Beng. And Philip and I both wanted easy access to a decent road even in the rainy season, so that we could drive to town quickly in case of a medical emergency.

This list had seemed reasonable enough when I'd constructed it in consultation with my professors. But now that I was in Bengland, I wondered if any village actually met all these criteria. With Jean we made up a schedule of the smaller ones to visit. Tolégbé, Anzanzangbé, Siaregbé, Gbagbé, Ndogbé, Kosangbé—their names were hard to pronounce, the possible futures they represented even harder to imagine. For each of these villages housed people with their own family histories, and each villager would undoubtedly interpret an uninvited observer in his or her own way. What if I selected the wrong village?

When we arrived in Tolégbé, a crowd of children whooped and ran to inspect this rare vision of a car stopped at their small patch of roadside, though some of the smallest children ran in terror at the sight of us. A small group—some elders, some mothers with babies—ambled over to an enormous tree that dominated a cleared space, and someone offered us chairs. Philip and I tried out the morning greetings, and a few villagers exclaimed *"Yih!"*—a combination of appreciation and surprise. But my paltry attempts only depressed me—so far, saying hello marked the limits of my linguistic competence.

Jean whispered that now was the time to announce why we'd come to visit. Standing next to me, he seemed to relish the public role of translator; indeed, his rendition of my short speech that we'd practiced earlier seemed to have expanded significantly. Just how was Jean embellishing my thoughts?

Then the chief, an elderly man in a toga, announced to Jean that the villagers would be happy if we settled among them. The chief outlined a brief history of Tolégbé—it was a new village, the founders having left Asagbé to start their own village—and he mentioned that according to the last census, the population was ninety-two.

I'd already been told that this was the smallest village, but now I was disappointed to hear the exact figure, for the village was *too* tiny—not enough families, not enough social ties to chart. Before I could respond, a boy brought some bottles of beer, evidently on the chief's instructions. The older men formed a circle, and we shared the bottles, while Jean sat quietly a few feet away, abstaining from our drinking fest.

A child brought a red-and-black feathered rooster over to the chief, and the old man made a short speech, which Jean translated: "The elder is presenting you with this chicken as a sign of respect for you and your work."

Having already decided that I couldn't live in tiny Tolégbé, how could I accept this generous gift? Yet refusing the chicken would surely be a terrible insult. So after profuse thanks, Philip tucked the rooster under his arm, and we gave the squawking bird what must have been the first car ride of his life—and its last, for once in Asagbé we donated him to André's household for that night's dinner.

The next village, Siaregbé, promised to be a better candidate: it wasn't too small, and we'd heard that most of the residents still practiced the indigenous religion. But well before we reached the village we had to abandon our car because of the narrow dirt road that was pockmarked with huge, gaping craters every few yards—hardened remnants of the rainy season's puddles. As we trekked the rest of the way, we worried: what would happen if one of us became seriously ill or were bitten by a snake? By the time we arrived in Siaregbé we were exhausted and certain that this village would not be our home. We stayed long enough to be polite, then began trudging back to our car.

As Philip started up Didadi, Jean suggested we consider his hometown. I had to demur. While Dezigbé was the right size for my study, two-thirds of its inhabitants were Muslim. Jean continued to press me, but I worried about his motives: given his difficulties with his father, he must have yearned to return in triumph with a new, prestigious position. I wished I could help him, but it might be impossible for him to separate his personal problems from my research.

Out of courtesy to Jean, I agreed to visit the village. The residents were polite enough—even his father, a small, bearded old man with sharp features, put on a good front of civility. But I wasn't swayed; hoping Jean would forgive me, I eliminated Dezigbé from my list.

Over the next few days we continued to visit the other small villages—always leaving with a chicken in tow—but none seemed fitting for my study. Finally only one small village remained. Kosangbé was my last hope—and fortunately it sounded fine: situated on the main road, the size was just right, about 250 people. Even better, almost all the villagers were animists. With a mixture of hope and anxiety, I said to Jean, "I guess it's down to Kosangbé—we haven't been there yet."

Jean frowned. "Those people drink all day. I don't think you'd be happy."

André, sitting nearby, agreed and added, "They don't have much water: their pump is two miles away."

"Oh, really?" Philip asked, then turned to me. "Are you sure you want to bother?"

"But this is the last village on our list! It might not be so bad. Anyway," I said, now lowering my voice, "Jean could be calling them drunkards just because they're not Muslims and drink a gourdful of palm wine once in a while."

When we arrived at Kosangbé, Jean led us to the village's kapok tree, and the elders in the village assembled to meet us. After Jean's standard speech there was an awkward silence. Finally the elders spoke quietly, and the chief, a thick-set man with speckles of gray flecked through his beard, said, "We'll have to talk this over ourselves, and we'll let you know what we decide." In a few minutes the meeting concluded.

We walked back to Didadi, taken aback by our swift dismissal. In the car Philip said, "I guess we can cross that one off the list."

"Well, let's just wait to see if they'll accept us," I said cautiously.

Philip raised an eyebrow and kept on driving. Back in Asagbé, when I told our host of our less-than-enthusiastic welcome in Kosangbé, I also mentioned that I still hadn't given up on the village. André wrinkled his brows. "You know, there's no bus service there to M'Bahiakro. What if your car breaks down?"

Philip cleared his throat conspicuously. Then André's cousin Bertin, who'd been chatting in the courtyard, piped up with another problem: "It's a difficult village. They get into fights all the time." But coming from Bertin, I didn't find this objection particularly compelling, as Bertin was rather cantankerous himself.

* * *

While I was awaiting word from Kosangbé, my stomach cramps returned. After seeing Dr. Yiallo in M'Bahiakro, Jean suggested we pay a visit to Blaima, a Beng elder living in town. We found Blaima at home relaxing on a lawn chair while a throng of children played noisily around him in the courtyard. He welcomed us and, after offering us Tip Top sodas, asked how we were getting along in Asagbé.

"We love it, but it's just too large for my study," I explained. "I'm looking for a small village where I can study the traditional Beng religion."

"Have you thought of Kosangbé?" Blaima suggested. "That's the seat of our religion."

"Really? Quite a few people have warned us away. . . ." I stopped.

Blaima smiled mysteriously. "Well, in that case. . . "

But I'd heard all I needed. If Kosangbé was the *center* of indigenous religious practice, my mind was made up, for this easily explained the cautiousness of the villagers: if they were the most traditional Beng, of course they would be reluctant to accept outsiders. I would have to be delicate in my questions in the beginning and just ask about simple things, take a census, collect genealogies. Later I could broach more sensitive topics.

Back in the car, I tried out my decision on Philip. He stared intently at the road, hands hugging the steering wheel. Finally he said, "It would be nice if they wanted us there. Anyway, we've already settled into Asagbé, and André's family is great."

"I know, honey, but it's just too big."

"Then what about Tolégbé? Those people seemed *really* friendly. And we'd still be near Asagbé."

I shook my head. "Too small."

"Oh, maybe you're right—the people in Kosangbé might warm up to us." But Philip didn't seem swayed by his own logic.

I turned to Jean, who was on the backseat gazing out the window, and told him in French that my talk with Blaima had decided me on Kosangbé. "I still think you should try Dezigbé," he muttered, and was silent the rest of the ride.

That evening, on André's porch, I shared my news with our hosts. Marie said simply, *"Ka ka an dé."* André translated: We'll miss you. But other people who'd come to chat with the family trotted out the same objections to Kosangbé that I'd heard before—plus a couple of new ones: the village was divided, they could never agree on anything; the food supply wasn't adequate because the villagers never worked in the fields. So many people were passionately opposing my plan, yet each had a different reason! I had to admit it: my curiosity was more than piqued.

Later that night I composed a letter to San Yao, the chief of Kosangbé, writing that if he and the villagers were willing, we would very much like to live among them. In the morning a messenger biked over with the letter. I eagerly awaited the reply, but the next couple of days brought no return message.

"It's not a very good sign," Philip offered.

"Maybe people have been too busy in the fields to hold their meeting," I replied, trying to believe my own words.

"They gave you *two* chickens in Dezigbé," Jean reminded me.

After another few days of silence, we decided to drive to Kosangbé. The chief greeted us coolly. Soon several elders and a group of young mothers joined us under the large kapok tree; some children brought chairs and stools for the older men and women. Was my future about to be announced? Philip and I sat expectantly; Jean declined a seat.

San Yao addressed us with a short speech. We looked at Jean inquiringly. "The chief says that they've had a meeting about your letter," he translated, his even tone concealing his own reaction, "and he says the three of us may move into the village."

"Ah, *merci!*" I said. I smiled at Philip; he forced a smile back. Then we rose and shook the chief's hand. Though San Yao's unexpectedly firm grip encased my own, his curt welcome speech had done nothing to help me imagine how we might call this village home.

As I regarded the faces around us, wondering who among them might become my first friend, another man in the group, whose trim physique belied the wrinkles on his forehead, came up to introduce himself: he was Wamya Kona, the national government's party representative in the village. But unlike his Asagbé counterpart, Bwadi Kouakou, this *secrétaire* spoke no French. Flashing us a wry smile that I couldn't interpret, Kona addressed us through Jean: "You'll need a place to stay. My cousin Bandé Kouakou François is building a house. Perhaps you could live there."

A line of excited children followed us to the courtyard, where we found a short man sitting outside. François looked at us quizzically, then greeted us in French. What luck—to have a host we could talk with while learning Beng! I was inclined to like the house. François pointed it out—a long, mud brick structure facing the back of his own home. He unlocked the wooden door, and before us was a small but sunny room connected to an inner chamber of the same size.

"We could use the second room as the bedroom," I whispered to Philip, "and this outer room could be a kitchen." He nodded agreement.

"The house belongs to my younger brother, Kossum," François explained. "He's waiting for the harvest money to finish building it. If you want, as rent you could cement over the inner walls."

"Okay, let's take it," Philip whispered to me, and I nodded.

Now the *secrétaire* addressed Jean. "I have an extra room in my compound. You can stay there if you like."

So Jean, too, had just found a new home. But his acceptance barely forced its way through his tightly set lips. He'll just have to adjust, I thought, disappointed by his continued sulking. We all shook hands, then sealed the deal with a large bottle of Ivoirian beer. By now I'd reconciled myself to celebrating each meeting, each decision with alcohol. Even the smallest villages, I discovered, to my teetotaler's regret, had beer: a local middlewoman or -man bought cases from a Lebanese shop owner in M'Bahiakro who toured the area each week in a truck. After we emptied our glasses, Kona spoke through Jean: "I'll be your village father. When you need anything, come to me."

I turned to Philip and flashed him a tipsy smile: we'd been adopted! He returned my grin with a wink: he seemed to want to believe the "Hurrah!" in my eyes.

"How can we finish building Kossum's house?" I asked our new father through Jean.

"You'll need sand for the cement. We can gather it on the riverbank."

"That's very kind," Philip said, "but we can help, too."

"No, you're our guests," François broke in firmly.

Over the following week, there was no news of the sand. Via a messenger, we suggested to François that we fetch the sand ourselves. The return messenger brought us our new landlord's response: this was out of the question. If the villagers would neither fetch the sand nor allow us to do so, what *could* we do? Finally Bwadi Kouakou suggested we contact the *sous-préfet*. We did, and for a small fee he quickly arranged for a load of sand to be delivered to Kosangbé by the M'Bahiakro road crew. Now that we had the sand, the cement must be mixed and the inner walls of the entire house plastered. But no masons offered their services in Kosangbé. I didn't allow myself to examine too closely the Kosangbé villagers' continued stalling, but one thing was certain: it was taking longer and longer for my research to get under way.

Philip: Almost Moving In

No one wanted us to move to Kosangbé, least of all the people of that village. Even though they'd given us permission to live there, it seemed we were always unraveling the latest delay, always *almost* moving in. I still felt Alma had chosen poorly, and I repeatedly expressed my doubts— until I realized that these objections, like those of the Asagbé villagers, only increased her fascination with Kosangbé.

At the time I was reading Laurence Sterne's *Tristram Shandy*. I had brought to Africa a box of various great works of Western literature— books I had neglected over the years—believing that a remote village might be an ideal place to read them. Sterne's novel made an odd fit: Tristram, the procrastinating narrator, spun ambling digressions—small books in themselves—that reminded me of the mysterious postponements we encountered from the Kosangbé villagers. Near the end of the novel, Tristram provided charts depicting the dramatic curve of his narrative: demented loopy lines that resembled curled, abandoned shoelaces. In light of our continuing negotiations with Kosangbé, those convoluted lines seemed like photorealism.

Jean, also dissatisfied with Alma's choice of a village, grew sullen and less forthcoming, even about apparently innocuous details. But was this the only reason? Recently we'd overheard Jean tell André and a few visitors that he would soon be interviewed by the Voice of America, that through his work with Alma he would make the Beng famous around the world. I remembered that long speech the *sous-préfet* in M'Bahiakro gave Jean, telling him that Côte d'Ivoire was proud of him and counting on his good work. Alma and I began to worry that Jean was intent on presenting to the world a Chamber of Commerce view of Beng culture; if this were so, he might feel free to hide whatever didn't present the Beng in a positive light.

As the days passed, whenever Jean resisted Alma's questions she suspected he was hiding something. Once, at one of Asagbé's evening dances, we saw a single old man twirling among the young girls. Curious about this apparent anomaly, Alma pointed and said, "Jean, who's that?"

"He's a man," Jean replied tersely.

"Who is he?"

"He's an old man."

"I know that. But what's his name?"

"I don't know." Jean turned away from her, but she ignored this rudeness.

"Will you please find out?"

Reluctantly Jean ambled over to the man, then returned. "His name is Kouassi Kona."

Alma marked this down in her notebook, then looked up. "Why is he there alone among the girls?"

"He's dancing."

"I *know* that. Why?"

"Because he wants to."

Alma sighed. *Was* her curiosity so unreasonable? She looked over the crowd—there was no one else nearby who spoke French, no one else she could appeal to. She bit her lip and said no more. But her resentment was growing.

Another evening a group of girls gathered in front of André's courtyard to perform *lolondalé*, the same dance that Jean had mentioned in his story. The girls formed a tight circle, clapped their hands, and sang in an affecting, ragged harmony. Then the girl who led the song suddenly leapt backward, flinging herself into the waiting arms of the girls across from her—such playful trust!

Alma decided to record the sweet lilt of the children's voices, which delighted Jean. "The *lolondalé* songs are so sweet, the whole world should hear them!" I set a tape in our small machine and checked the batteries.

But before long a minor tussle broke out between two girls who'd come to watch, and as the dance continued they aimed a few insults at each other, setting off a minor ripple of nearby giggles. Suddenly Jean screamed at the two culprits, his arms waving wildly. They clutched each other momentarily, staring up at Jean in fear, and then they fled, joined by some of the dancers. *Lolondalé* was over. To my surprise, Alma—normally so patient—shouted at Jean for his interference. "Don't you *ever* interrupt again!" she hurled at him. Soon André appeared, trying to calm everyone, and we made our way to the porch for his mediation of the dispute.

"Those girls were swearing, they were spoiling the dance—I had to stop it! You were *recording* them!" Jean insisted.

"I'm an anthropologist, Jean," Alma said. "I have to observe *everything*, even arguments."

"But those girls will break the name of the Beng!"

"Jean, *everyone* swears, all over the world. The Beng would seem odd if they didn't."

Jean knew he couldn't win. After all, he was arguing—with a stubborn bravery—with his employer. Yet he sulked all evening, and the next morning as well, until he finally apologized. But it was tactical, grudging—he didn't agree with Alma's approach. Ashamed over her public anger, Alma let the subject drop, though it was clear that she and Jean wanted to present competing stories about the Beng. If she couldn't convince him, there were bound to be more disputes in the future.

* * *

A marriage had recently been arranged between Gaosu, a young man from Asagbé, and Afwé, a young woman who lived in Kosangbé. A large group of women from Gaosu's extended family would soon walk the five miles to Kosangbé and dance their thanks for this arranged marriage. We were invited to come along. I looked forward to the celebration: in Kosangbé we were invariably greeted with only perfunctory hospitality by the wary crowds who gathered to watch us; perhaps at this festive occasion we'd see another side of that reluctant village.

In the early afternoon the Asagbé women began the long walk to Afwé's village, and Alma and I drove ahead with a few women who'd asked us for a ride. We swiftly left the gently sloping terrain of the savanna and entered a forest thick and seething with green. Towering here and there above the dense mass were gigantic trees, their enormous bases fanning out like the flying buttresses of Gothic architecture, their trunks rising up to a huge crest of leaves. Perched here and there at the edge of the dirt road were magnificently large termitaries, some ten to fifteen feet tall, each rising from a broad, brown base to a thin, irregularly shaped spire.

We arrived at Kosangbé long before the rest of the engagement thanking party and waited at the village border, for none of our future neighbors seemed pleased to see us. Standing by our car, I looked back at the road we had driven down, hoping for any sign of the rest of the celebrants. The thick smell of long-haired goats—a smell unlike that of any other Beng village—filled the air. Bored, I watched small herds wander in and out of the compounds, I listened to their harsh bleats; I even examined the broad, dark scar on my hand—that oozing trench had finally healed.

When the Asagbé women finally arrived, they danced in a slow, swinging motion, waving fans and singing, as they formed a circle in an open space in the village. Their hosts gathered slowly to watch, an oddly quiet audience. If Afwé—the center of this grand event—was present in the crowd, even standing next to me, I didn't know. Would I soon learn the names of all these people, would Alma and I learn something of their lives, their personalities? Alma moved among the crowd, taking notes on the dance, and the villagers of Kosangbé eyed her furtively, perhaps seeing in her scribbling an inkling of what they could expect once we lived among them. But I couldn't read welcome in their gazes.

I was happy to return to Asagbé: I felt more at home there and was reluctant to leave. Still, I tried to convince myself that perhaps Alma was right—the Kosangbé villagers' initial resistance would surely ease once they saw that our desire to live among them was respectful, that Alma simply wished to understand and record their lives. Furthermore, she argued cannily, with our own two-room house, we'd be able to close the doors and be alone whenever we wanted. Here in André's compound, we had no choice but to be part of the constant flow of family and neighbors. Now, as I sat in a corner of the busy porch dimly lit by lamplight and tried to reawaken one of my unfinished stories, I thought that setting up our own small household would be—for me—a necessary anchor in this confusingly unfamiliar world.

Still, I *did* enjoy those friendly gatherings on the porch after dinner, always loud with gossip and advice. One evening I carried out of our room on a piece of cardboard the corpse of a spider I'd just killed, a corpse as wide as the span of my hand. Too often I would reach for a shoe, a book, or my eyeglasses and startle one of the nestling monsters; while it swiftly scuttled away I'd try to calm my staggering heart.

"What is that?" André asked as I flung the corpse to the edge of the dark courtyard.

"A spider."

"Did it bite you?"

"No," I replied, suddenly worried. "Do these spiders bite?"

"No," he said.

Alma, her anthropologist's antennae out, snatched up her notebook. "Then why did you ask, André?" she said.

"*Chez nous,*" he began, "we only kill insects that try to bite or sting us—because they have bad characters. Otherwise we leave them alone."

I understood the indirect criticism. By killing a harmless creature—though to me it was frightening—I myself exhibited bad character. Shamed, I vowed silently to restrain myself, and I was grateful for André's words. The lack of privacy in a family certainly had its advantages: even a casual exchange filled me with this new life we were entering, a novel of manners written in a foreign language.

*   *   *

I stood in the bathhouse and stared up at the stars covering the sky: bright clusters surrounding the wide, luminous path of the Milky Way. Lifting full cups of hot water from the pail, then letting that water pour down my hair and the length of my body, I listened to the distant sounds of the village: a children's song, the excited gab of two or three young women passing by, disembodied laughter, a baby's sharp wail. Entranced by the glimmering stars and the insect hum of the forest, I was suddenly aware of how cold the night air was—perhaps the cooling harmattan winds we'd heard about had arrived. I held my arms to my chest and felt a chill run through me, so I filled another cup with hot water, splashed it over my shoulders.

I still felt cold. I stood quietly and tried to feel the evening's thick heat against my face, yet I shivered, a small shudder I couldn't control. Malaria, I thought.

But how? I took my daily malaria pill religiously. I'd grown up fearing the disease, primarily because of an old film, *Monkey on My Back,* that I'd seen on television when I was a child. Made soon after World War II, the movie depicted the inexorable wreckage of a man's life, a man who'd contracted malaria in a mosquito-infested bomb crater on some battle-racked Pacific island. Given morphine for the disease, a growing addiction stalked the man after the war, tightening an increasingly unhappy fate around him.

I quickly finished my bath, returned to the porch. Alma sat with Maat, helping her chop okra.

"Alma, do you feel cool?"

"Cool?" She squinched her face in surprise. "It's boiling!"

"Well, I feel a little chilly."

Alma set down her knife and led me into our small room, where she began flipping through our medical text. I lay under a blanket but still felt shivers race through me. We decided to wait and see if I developed a fever.

Within two hours my blankets were soaked with sweat, so I popped six quinine pills—equivalent to a week's dose. Then we waited and worried until the fever—surprisingly quickly—subsided. In the morning I felt fine, and with a certain jaunty air I swallowed an additional six pills, as prescribed by the medical text. Was *this* malaria, so easily conquered? Already I was composing in my mind letters to friends, filled with contempt for my exotic illness.

Alma insisted on driving me down to the M'Bahiakro infirmary, and after Dr. Yiallo examined me he agreed that I'd likely contracted malaria. "But you are well now, so who can tell? There are so many different fevers here." He suggested I rest for a few days.

But how could I? The next day we received word that our mud house in Kosangbé had finally been cemented and was ready for our arrival. Now there was so much to do, to prepare for our move.

Alma: Sweeping a Room Good-Bye

Our last day in Asagbé we hauled our belongings out to the car. Still tired from his malaria attack, Philip seemed to grow weaker with each lugged suitcase, each carton of books. I insisted he rest while I finished packing.

"I'll check the room one last time," I said. Dust clung to the corners. Hurriedly I grabbed the palm-leaf broom Maat had loaned me and began sweeping out the room. Behind me, André's vehement voice filled my ears: "No, no, you mustn't!"

Turning around, I saw our host facing me, his hand now on the broom. "But why?"

"If you sweep out the room when you're about to leave, you'll never return to stay with us—and we want you to return."

"Oh, André, thank you for telling me," I replied, chagrined at my error. André nodded nonchalantly—no doubt he was inured by now to our mistakes.

We said our sad good-byes to our host and his family. Then Philip, Jean, and I started down the road to Kosangbé. Would our new neighbors share with me tidbits of knowledge such as the one André had just divulged? Or was André's remark a prediction that the people of Kosangbé would refuse to discuss their lives with me? It would be an intense year if what I most wanted to study our new hosts and hostesses most wanted to conceal.

3 ❧

Introduction to Chapter 3

As an undergraduate at a university in a large eastern city, Jay MacLeod established and directed a youth enrichment program at a nearby public housing project. While working with children in this community, he became interested in the educational and career aspirations of their older brothers. Thus began the research that led to his senior thesis and, ultimately, to the publication of *Ain't No Makin' It: Aspirations and Attainment in a Low-Income Neighborhood* (1987).

Although he had access to some of the young children and their families through the youth program, he needed to devise a way to make contact with the young men with whom he wanted to work. He discovered that the best place to meet and establish a relationship with them was on the basketball court. Through pick-up games and more organized contests, he eventually became acquainted with two groups of young men: the Hallway Hangers and the Brothers.

Except for one or two members, the Hallway Hangers were white and heavily involved with drugs, alcohol, and petty crime. Like the Lads described by Paul Willis in his classic work *Learning to Labor* (1977), they possessed a culture that was in opposition to mainstream values of achievement and success. They did not believe that school or any other social institution would help them escape from the life of poverty in which they were raised. Consequently, they did not attend school very often, and most were destined to drop out before graduation.

In contrast, the Brothers, who were mostly African American, bought into mainstream achievement ideology, believing that through hard work they would be able to overcome the obstacles posed by poverty and race and ultimately achieve success in American society. Unlike the Hallway Hangers, they did not develop an oppositional culture; instead, they adopted mainstream values and beliefs regarding occupational and social mobility. Partly because of this and also because they were black and did not drink or take drugs, the Brothers were frequently the target of abuse from the Hallway Hangers.

In the appendix to his book, reprinted here, MacLeod discusses in very frank detail the trials and tribulations of carrying out ethnographic research in a community very different from the one from which he came. This urban housing project, which he called Clarendon Heights, was quite a contrast from the lower-middle-class rural New Hampshire community in which MacLeod was born and raised. In making this transition, he needed to learn new ways of acting and relating to others. He faced problems balancing his life at the university with his work in the housing project. He learned quickly that the roles he adopted and the language he used while doing his research were inappropriate with his fellow students at the university.

Working with groups as diverse as the Hallway Hangers and Brothers posed additional dilemmas for MacLeod. He had to figure out ways of staying friendly with both groups in spite of their animosity toward each other. He describes in vivid detail a basketball game in which the two groups played against each other and he was forced to choose which team to play on. Luckily, the referee resolved this predicament for him by asking him to play for the Brothers since they had fewer players and were smaller and less able. That MacLeod was able to stay on good terms with both groups and collect the data necessary to complete his senior thesis was a delicate balancing act and remarkable achievement on his part.

Particularly in relation to the Hallway Hangers, MacLeod was dealing with a group that held values quite at odds with his own beliefs. Their use of drugs and alcohol, their involvement in petty crime, and their overt racism and sexism caused problems for him that he needed to overcome in order to carry out his research. Such conflicts of values are often discussed by researchers working in distant countries among groups whose culture is dramatically different from their own. What is notable in this case is that MacLeod did not have to travel far to encounter this clash of values. His examination of these issues provides a helpful guide for first-time researchers who work with cultures different from their own.

Eight years after completing this work and graduating from college, MacLeod was interested in learning what had become of the young men with whom he had worked. On his way to England to study to be an Anglican priest, he revisited Clarendon Heights and tracked down and interviewed the Hallway Hangers and Brothers. In the interim, the first edition of *Ain't No Makin' It* had been published and had done very well as a sociological text.

In the following section, MacLeod raises concerns about the work he did when he returned to Clarendon Heights. His interviews at times proved difficult (as when he and an informant were questioned by the police when they were seen conducting an interview in McLeod's car); some of the men he interviewed were by then dealing drugs. He questions the advisability of doing research based entirely on interviews, as compared to his earlier work in which he combined the interviews with participant observation. He examines the issue of relying exclusively on what people say, rather than being able to observe them interacting with others and thus see whether what they say about themselves matches what they do.

MacLeod found that none of the former members of the Hallway Hangers or the Brothers had succeeded in the job market. The Hallway Hangers's oppositional culture had all but disappeared, and several of them declared that they wished they had tried harder to succeed in school and the job market. The Brothers, though continuing to adhere to mainstream achievement ideology, were also struggling financially. No one in either group had attained stable employment; instead, they bounced around from one low-paying dead-end job with few or no benefits to another.

In the discussion of his findings from the first phase of his work, MacLeod takes to task major sociological theorists who deal with social reproduction, including Bowles and Gintis (1976) and Bourdieu and Passeron (1977). As mentioned earlier, the Brothers believed in mainstream achievement ideology whereas the Hallway Hangers actively rejected such aspirations and beliefs. MacLeod's finding that there is not a single, unitary response to issues of aspirations and achievement ideology among poor young men—as would be predicted by most theorists—offers an alternative and insightful way of thinking about these issues. Based on his work during both phases of the research, MacLeod argues for a radical change in our society, where wealth is distributed more equitably and the life chances of those at the bottom of the economic ladder are at least equal to the life chances of those at the top.

What is most remarkable about this work is that MacLeod accomplished much of it as a senior in college. We are fortunate that he shared with us how he went about doing his research. His appendix will serve as a model for other beginning researchers as they set about the task of learning about a particular group, culture, or institution.

On the Making of *Ain't No Makin' It*

JAY MACLEOD

Fieldwork: Doubts, Dilemmas, and Discoveries

Few sociologists who employ qualitative research methods discuss the mechanics of fieldwork in their published writings. A frank account of the actual process by which research was carried out might disabuse people of the notion that sociological insight comes from logical analysis of a systematically gathered, static body of evidence. If my own experience is at all typical, insight comes from an immersion in the data, a sifting and resifting of the evidence until a pattern makes itself known. My research methods were not applied objectively in a manner devoid of human limitations and values. Of course, I had access to books that describe the various methods used in sociological field research. But many of these statements on research methods, as Whyte argues in the appendix of *Street Corner Society*, "fail to note that the researcher, like his informants, is a social animal. He has a role to play, and he has his own personality needs that must be met in some degree if he is to function successfully."[1] If, as I would argue, the best fieldwork emerges when the sociologist is completely immersed in the community under study, it means that his or her personal life will be inseparably bound up with the research. What follows, then, is a personal account of my relationship with the Clarendon Heights community and the way I came to understand the aspirations of its teenager members.

Walking through Clarendon Heights for the first time in the spring of 1981, I felt uneasy and vulnerable. Entering another world where the rules would all be different, I was naturally apprehensive. I might have been closer in class background to the people of Clarendon Heights than the great bulk of my university classmates were, but neither my lower-middle-class origins nor my attendance at a regional high school in rural New Hampshire made me particularly "at home" in the project. Most important, I was a university student, a status that could breed resentment, for it implied an upward social trajectory to which these people do not have ready access. To undertake research under such conditions would have been inconceivable. But that spring sociological research was far from my mind. I was at the project with two other university students to begin the Clarendon Heights Youth Enrichment Program, with which I would be involved for the next four years. The youth program led to my interest in the aspirations of Clarendon Heights young people and also provided me with a role and an acceptance in the community without which the fieldwork would have been close to impossible.

Contrary to the expectations of the city's professional social workers, the youth program turned out to be a great success. We lived in the neighborhood during the summer months and established close relationships with the children in the program, their parents, and other project residents. Initial distance or coldness gradually gave way to trust and personal regard as the program's reputation and the rapport between counselors and community grew. Engaging nine boys aged eleven to thirteen in a varied mix of educational, cultural, and recreational activities, I gained more than acceptance by the project's residents—I also learned a great deal about their day-to-day problems and concerns. As my understanding of the community and sensitivity to the pulse of the neighborhood developed, so did my self-confidence and sense of belonging. Although class and racial differences could never be completely transcended, by September 1982 I counted among my closest friends many Clarendon Heights tenants.

It was during that second summer working in Clarendon Heights that my interest in the kids' aspirations really began to take shape. I was amazed that many of the twelve- and thirteen-year-old boys in my group did not even aspire to middle-class jobs (with the exception of professional athletics), but rather, when they verbalized aspirations at all, indicated a desire to work with sheet metal, in a machine tool factory, or in construction. The world of middle-class work was completely foreign to them, and as the significance of this fact impressed itself on me, I concerned myself more and more with their occupational aspirations. But at such a young age, these boys could not speak with much consistency or sophistication about their occupational hopes. To understand why aspirations were so low among Clarendon Heights youth, I would have to look to these boys' older brothers and sisters, to those in high school.

I say brothers and sisters because my study of aspirations should have included equal consideration of girls. That this study concentrates solely on boys puts it in the company of many other works in the male-dominated field of sociology that exclude half the population from research. But with class and racial barriers to overcome, I felt hard-pressed to understand the situation of the boys and would have been totally incapable of doing justice to the experience of girls because yet another barrier— gender—would have to be confronted. Already thus handicapped, I felt totally incapable of considering adolescent girls in Clarendon Heights, whose situation was so far beyond my own experience.

The boys presented enough problems. I'd had the least contact with Heights teenagers. I knew a few of the Hallway Hangers on a casual basis because Stoney, Steve, Slick, and Boo-Boo had younger siblings enrolled in the youth program. Still, no relationship extended much beyond the "Hey, how's it going?" stage, and although I was never hassled coming or going from doorway #13, I was still very much of an outsider as far as the Hallway Hangers were concerned. My previous involvement in the community, however, had gained me a small degree of acceptance. They knew that I had been around for more than a year, that I worked hard, and that I got along well with many of the tenants, all of which ensured that I would be considered different from the typical university student. Had I been seen in such a light, I'm not sure I ever would have been accepted by the group, for college students were not welcome in doorway #13. My work with the Clarendon Heights Youth Program, however, allowed me to get my foot in the door and paved the way for future acceptance by the Hallway Hangers.

The Brothers were not so difficult. I played a lot of basketball with the kids in my youth group; we had a team of sorts and used to practice a few hours each week during the day. In the evenings, I invariably could be found at the park a block from Clarendon Heights playing a game of pick-up basketball with the younger kids from the project. Many of the Brothers played, too, and I soon got to know them quite well. Some of them also had younger brothers and sisters in the youth program, so they were acquainted with me from the start. In addition, I had remained close to Mike, and my association with him helped me to befriend the others. For the Brothers my status as a college student was grounds for a measure of respect rather than suspicion. Nor did they seem to distance themselves from me because I was white. How they could endure the racist taunts of the Hallway Hangers and not come to resent whites in general is difficult to comprehend. It may be that I was insensitive to any covert racial strain between the Brothers and me, but I never felt its effects.

By November 1982 I had decided to write my undergraduate thesis on the aspirations of teenage boys in Clarendon Heights. I generally spent a few hours each week down at the project seeing the ten boys in my group anyway, but I began to increase my trips to Clarendon Heights in both duration and frequency. I also made more of an effort to speak to the older guys, particularly members of the Hallway Hangers. But I had an exceptionally heavy academic workload that semester; my real fieldwork did not begin until February 1983 when I enrolled in a course in sociological field methods.

The course introduced me to the mechanics of ethnographic fieldwork. From readings, discussion, and an experienced professor, I learned about the techniques of participant observation, oral history analysis, unstructured interviews, and unobtrusive measures. I realized that the real learning would take place through firsthand experience in the field, but discussion of methods and the examination of representative sociological work using qualitative methods served as a valuable introduction.

My initial research forays into Clarendon Heights were awkward and tentative. I wanted to determine the nature of the teenagers' aspirations and the factors that contribute to their formation. Sensing that there was a conflict between the achievement ideology promulgated in school and the experiences of the boys' families, I particularly was interested in how this tension was resolved. But although it was obvious that the Brothers and the Hallway Hangers experienced school in different ways, I had no idea of the extensive disparity in their outlooks. Most of my trips down to Clarendon Heights in February and March were spent as they always had been: in the company of the younger kids in the youth program helping with homework, talking with parents, and generally maintaining contact with the families to which I had grown close. I also was spending some time with the Brothers, casually asking them about their aspirations, their high school programs, and their family backgrounds. This was possible because I had struck up friendships with Mike's closest friends: Super, Derek, and Craig. But with the Hallway Hangers my acceptance was progressing much more slowly. Those I knew would return my greeting on the street, but I still was subject to the intimidating glares with which those outside the group are greeted when walking past doorway #13. There was also an element of fear involved. I knew of the fights that took place in and around doorway #13, the heavy drinking, the drugs, and the crime. I also knew of the abuse the Brothers suffered at the hands of the Hallway Hangers and realized that, in their eyes, I was to some extent associated with the Brothers. I was fascinated by the activity in doorway #13, but I needed an "in" with the Hallway Hangers if they were to be included in the study.

Basketball provided the opportunity I was looking for. The city's Social Services Department opened up the gym in the grammar school located just across the street from the Heights for a couple of hours on two weekday evenings. The Brothers were the first to take advantage of this opportunity for pick-up basketball, along with Hank White. Hank is a big muscular fellow, slightly older than most of the Hallway Hangers, who commands the respect or fear of everybody in the neighborhood. After his sophomore year in high school, Hank spent eighteen months in a maximum security prison for allegedly taking part in a rape behind the school building. With scars dotting his face, Hank conforms to the image of the stereotypical street "hood," and the manner with which he carries himself hardly dispels that impression. Nevertheless, he was the least racist of the Hallway Hangers, for in prison he had gotten to know and like a few blacks. He enjoyed playing basketball with the Brothers and was on good terms with all of them. We had seen each other around, but it wasn't until we were matched against one another on the basketball court one evening in early March that Hank took any real notice of me. Both of us are six feet tall, but Hank has the edge in strength and basketball ability. It was a good, hard game, and when it was over we walked back to the project together. It turned out he knew I was the student who ran the youth program. In parting, he grinned at me and told me to come back next week, "so I can kick your ass again."

Thus began my friendship with Hank. Only later would I discover that my new acquaintance was a convicted rapist, and by then I was prepared to believe the disavowals of his guilt. His apparent regard for me clearly influenced the light in which the other Hallway Hangers saw me and helped facilitate my acceptance by the group. If my team had won that evening, his friendliness may well have been enmity, and my status among his friends could have been of an entirely negative type. Still, basketball was turning out to be an important vehicle for gaining acceptance into the community.

The next week a number of the other Hallway Hangers turned up at the gym to play ball. Pick-up basketball, around Clarendon Heights at least, only vaguely resembles the game played at the college and professional level. Defense is almost nonexistent, passing is kept to a minimum, and flashy moves are at a premium. We had access to only half the gym, so we played cross-wise on a reduced court, a fortunate setup because none of us was in good shape. In fact, many of the Hallway Hangers would come in to play high or drunk or both. The games were nearly as verbal as they were physical. A constant chatter of good-natured kidding and self-congratulations could be heard from most players: "Gimme that fuckin' ball! I feel hot tonight. Bang! Get out of my face, Slick. I'll put those fucking fifteen footers in all day." Matched up against Hank again, I responded to his joking insults with abuse of my own, being ever so careful not to go too far. The Hallway Hangers present noticed my familiarity with Hank and treated me accordingly. I was making progress, but it was slow and not without its problems. Every step I gained was accompanied by apprehension and doubt. That night on the basketball court a vicious fight broke out between two people on the fringes of the Hallway Hangers. Everybody else seemed to take it in stride, but I was shaken by the bloody spectacle. I was entering a new world, and I wasn't certain I could handle the situations in which I might find myself. It was an exciting time, but it also provided moments of anxiety and consternation.

The next week, while waiting outside the gym with the Brothers, I was asked to play on a team they were putting together. I readily assented. I sensed that they were confused by my developing association with the Hallway Hangers and in a sense felt betrayed. That I could enjoy their company as well as those who openly and maliciously antagonized them was incomprehensible in their eyes. So I was anxious to reestablish my allegiance to the Brothers and saw participation on their team as a good way of doing so. That same evening, however, after the usual pick-up game, I was approached by Mark, one of Frankie's older brothers recently released from prison, who wanted me to play later that night for a Clarendon Heights team against another housing project across the city. I thought that there might be a league of some kind and, as I already was committed to a team, that I should forego the opportunity. But this was simply a one-time game he had arranged, and after checking with the Brothers, I consented.

About nine of us piled into two cars and sped, screeching around corners, three miles to a grammar school gym adjacent to Lipton Park Housing Development. We lost the game, and I played horrendously, but in terms of my project significant advances were made. There is nothing like a common adversary to solidify tenuous associations and dissolve differences. That night I felt in some sense part of the Hallway Hangers and was treated, in turn, simply as a member of the group. Of course, there were still barriers, and I obviously was different from the rest, a fact that was lost on nobody when they dropped me off at the university on the way home. Nevertheless, even while they jokingly derided me for my poor performances as I climbed out of the noisy, run-down Impala, I felt a sense of belonging that hitherto had eluded me.

Only a week later, however, the status I had managed to achieve in both groups was threatened. The Brothers challenged the Hallway Hangers and their older friends to a game of basketball. Although considerably younger and smaller than the white youths, the Brothers were generally more skilled on the court and, with Craig playing, promised to give the Hallway Hangers a good game. Knowing nothing of the situation, I walked into the gym to find the younger kids cleared off their half of the court. Instead of playing floor hockey or kickball, they were seated in the bleachers, which had been pulled out of the wall for the occasion. At one end of the full-length court the Brothers were shooting at a basket; at the other end the Hallway Hangers were warming up. I heard Super blurt out, "Oh yeah, here's Jay," but I also heard a voice from the other end bellow, "It's about fucking time, Jay; we thought we'd be playing without you." Both teams expected me to play for their side, and I had no idea what to do. To choose one team meant to alienate the other. My own inclination was to go with the Brothers. I remembered the contempt with which Juan had spoken of a white friend's neutrality when a fight had broken out at school between the Brothers and a gang of white kids. I had developed close friendships with Juan, Craig, Super, and Derek, and I didn't want to let them down. On the other hand, in terms of the dynamics of the fieldwork, I needed to move closer to the Hallway Hangers. Tying up my shoe laces, I frantically tried to think of a way out of the situation but came up short.

I walked out to the center of the court where a social service worker was waiting to referee the game. He seemed concerned about the possibility of the contest turning into a violent melee and looked none too happy about his own role. Trying to assume a noncommittal air, I sauntered over to the Brothers' side and took a few shots, then walked to the other end and did the same with the Hallway Hangers. The Hallway Hangers had Hank's older brother Robbie playing, a six-foot-four-inch hardened veteran of the army's special forces. I suggested that the Brothers could use me more, that with Robbie's playing for the Hallway Hangers the game might be a blowout anyway. The curt response was something to the effect that if I wanted to play with "the niggers," that was my prerogative. Before I could reply, the referee shouted for me to play with the Brothers to even up the sides, and, hoping this intervention would mitigate the damage done, I trotted over to play with the Brothers.

The game was close and very rough, with several near-fights and nasty verbal exchanges sparked off by elbows flying under the backboards. We were much smaller than the Hallway Hangers and somewhat intimidated, but with Craig playing we undoubtedly had the most skillful player on the court. I made one lucky play early on that probably did more to establish my credibility among teenagers in the neighborhood than any other single event. With Hank coasting in for an easy lay-up, I caught him from behind and somehow managed to block his shot, flinging the ball clear across the gym. The crowd, about fifty or sixty kids from the neighborhood, roared with surprise, for such ignominy seldom befell Hank. The Brothers whooped with glee, slapping me on the back, and Hank's own teammates bombarded him with wisecracks. I couldn't suppress a grin, and Hank, taking it well, just sheepishly grinned back. Fortunately, the referee had whistled for a foul, which enabled Hank to maintain some "face." We ended up losing the game by one point, not least because I missed a foul shot in the last minute, but although bitterly disappointed, the Brothers had shown a much bigger and older team that they would not back down to them. The significance of events in the gym extended well beyond its walls, which is why such games between the two groups were contested with intensity and vigor.

At game's end, I made a point of walking back to the Heights with the Hallway Hangers, despite the questions it must have raised in the Brothers' minds as to where my loyalties really lay. As far as both groups were concerned, there was no middle ground between them. Each wondered which side I was on; my attempt to sit on the fence, I began to realize, was going to be a difficult balancing job. There would be other instances, like the basketball game, where a choice would have to be made. It was an uncomfortable position, one that plagued me throughout the research, but I derived some comfort from the fact that at least it indicated I was getting on with the fieldwork.

The research, in fact, made some significant advances that night. I hung around with the Hallway Hangers outside doorway #13 while they smoked cigarettes and talked about the game. Frankie began to insult the Brothers in no uncertain terms, glancing at me to gauge my reaction. Sensing he was trying to find out where I stood, I let it all slide, neither agreeing with him nor defending the Brothers. Finally, apparently satisfied, he said that it was a good thing I had played for the Brothers, for it had evened up the teams. In fact, it hadn't made that much of a difference, but Frankie wanted to believe that it was the sole white player on the opposition who had made the game a close one. In any case, it became clear that although my playing for the Brothers had jeopardized my standing with the Hallway Hangers, I was to emerge relatively unscathed. Soon Frankie and the others were laughing about the confusion a white player on the other team had caused, about how they had nearly passed the ball to me several times, and about the look on Hank's face when I had blocked his shot.

When I boarded the bus heading for the university, I was surprised to find Frankie right by me. Heading to see a girlfriend, he took the seat next to me and struck up a conversation. When we passed Lincoln High School, he pointed to a window in the school and noted that inside was his classroom. "What subject?" I asked, in response to which Frankie launched into a fascinating description of the Adjustment Class and his teacher Jimmy Sullivan. He told me he hoped to graduate in June, that he'd be the first of his mother's six sons to do so. After describing his brother's experiences in prison, Frankie related in a candid and poignant tone the vulnerability he felt in his role at the Heights. "I gotta get away. I gotta do somethin'. If I don't, I'm gonna be fucked; I know it. I ain't ready for fucking prison, man." I only had seen Frankie's hard exterior, and this quite unexpected glimpse of his feelings took me by surprise. In time, I became used to some of the toughest individuals confiding in me things they rarely could reveal to their peers. This particular episode with Frankie created a small bond between the two of us that had crucial implications for my fieldwork. My friendship with Hank was important, but he spent relatively little time actually hanging in the neighborhood with the Hallway Hangers. Frankie, on the other hand, was a fixture in doorway #13 and the undisputed leader of the group. I knew from other ethnographies that good rapport with one key member is often sufficient to gain entree to even the most closed group. William Foote Whyte's sponsorship by Doc allowed him access to the Norton Street gang,[2] and Elijah Anderson's relationship with Herman opened crucial doors to the social world of streetcorner men.[3] With Frankie's friendship, my entree into the Hallway Hangers' peer group was ensured.

I remember quite distinctly the first time I actually hung in doorway #13. Of course, I'd gone into that particular stairwell countless times, for one of the boys in my youth group lived in the entryway. Even then I felt uncomfortable making my way up the dark, littered stairway through the teenagers sitting sprawled on the steps and leaning against the walls laughing, drinking beer, and smoking marijuana. Walking in with Frankie, however, was entirely different. Everybody looked up when we came in, but when Frankie initiated a conversation with me, they all, as if on cue, continued on as if I weren't there. No one questioned my presence, and I found it not at all difficult to participate in the discussions. Frankie was collecting money to buy a half pound of marijuana, Chris was peddling cocaine, and at one point someone I'd never seen before came in wanting to buy some heroin but was turned away empty-handed. My presence seemed to have no effect; it was business as usual in doorway #13.

I knew then that I had crossed an important boundary. In the weeks that followed I was amazed at how quickly I came to feel accepted by the Hallway Hangers and comfortable hanging with them in Clarendon Heights. Despite the fact that my home was in rural New Hampshire and that I was a college student, neither of which I concealed from the Hallway Hangers, I was young (looking even less than my twenty-one years), and I was white. Those two characteristics and Frankie's friendship apparently were enough to satisfy the Hallway Hangers. Without consciously intending to do so, I began to fit in in other ways. My speech became rough and punctuated more often with obscenities; I began to carry myself with an air of cocky nonchalance and, I fear, machismo; and I found myself walking in a slow, shuffling gait that admitted a slight swagger. These were not, on the conscious level at least, mere affectations but were rather the unstudied products of my increasing involvement with the Hallway Hangers. To a large degree I was unaware of these changes; they were pointed out to me by fellow students involved in the youth program.

The world of Clarendon Heights and the world of the university were at odds with each other in almost every conceivable way. To stand with one foot in each often proved a difficult posture. It was only a ten-minute bus ride from the dark squalid confines of doorway #13 to the richly decorated college dining hall with its high ceiling and ostentatious gold chandeliers. I remember turning up for dinner directly from the Heights and unthinkingly greeting one of my upper-class friends with, "Hey Howard, what the fuck you been up to?" His startled look reminded me of where I was, and I hurriedly added, "I mean, how's your work going?" The dichotomy between the university and Clarendon Heights and the different standards of behavior expected of me in each were not sources of constant angst, but I found it somewhat difficult to adjust to the constant role changes. That I talked, walked, and acted differently on campus than I did in Clarendon Heights did not seem inconsistent, affected, or artificial to me at the time. I behaved in the way that seemed natural to me, but as Whyte points out in describing his fieldwork, what was natural at the project was bound to be different from what was natural on the college campus.[4]

In Clarendon Heights I found myself playing a number of roles, and the conflicts among these caused me the greatest consternation. In the first place, I was Jay MacLeod, human being with personal needs, including that of maintaining a certain level of self-respect. The Hallway Hangers' racism angered me a great deal, and the feeling was especially pronounced because of my proximity to the Brothers. The deep emotional scars left on the victims of racial prejudice were only too apparent. So naturally I often had the inclination to confront the racism of the Hallway

Hangers, to tell them, in their terms, to "fuck off." But as a researcher I was striving to understand the boys, not change them. Challenging their racism also would be of no great help in facilitating my acceptance by the Hallway Hangers. Thus, I generally kept my mouth shut, neither questioning their racist views or defending the Brothers against bigoted remarks, an exception being the conversation that is used to introduce the Brothers in Chapter 3.

If my roles as a person and as an ethnographer sometimes conflicted, then my role as director of the youth program complicated the picture further. What did the mothers of kids in the program think of me hanging in doorway #13 with Frankie and Hank and company? This was especially serious because by that time I was associated very closely with the youth program. I was seen not just as a counselor but as the major force behind its inception and continued existence. To invite disapproval was to invite condemnation of the program. I was particularly sensitive to this issue because the youth program was still my main priority in Clarendon Heights. I tried to minimize my visibility when associating with the Hallway Hangers, a feat not particularly difficult because they preferred to stay out of view of the police. Still, when lingering outside with the Hallway Hangers, especially if they were "partying," I stepped away from the group or otherwise tried to distance myself when a mother approached. Not surprisingly, this was not a very effective maneuver, and the problem was never resolved completely.

Late one Friday night, after a great deal of alcohol and drugs had been consumed and the noise level in the hallway reflected the decreased inhibitions of the group, a mother whom I knew quite well threw open her door and yelled at everyone "to shut the hell up." Noticing me, she shook her head uncomprehendingly and went back to bed more than a little bewildered. To ease the conflict between these two roles as much as possible, I simply kept up contact with the children's parents so they could see for themselves that I was undergoing no drastic character change. Although never confronted by any of the mothers about my association with the Hallway Hangers, I sensed that it was an issue for them and that it was discussed behind my back.

However, I was able to use this role conflict to my advantage in one respect. One of the stickiest issues with which I was confronted was whether or not to join in with the drinking and use of drugs in doorway #13. As the activity in the hallway revolved to a large degree around the consumption of beer, marijuana, and other intoxicants, I could fit in most easily by doing the same. Still, I was inclined to abstain for a number of reasons. First, both are illegal in the hallway because it is public property, and I had no desire to be arrested. I already had seen Stoney arrested in doorway #13 for possession of mescaline, and a number of older youths also had been apprehended for various drug offenses. Second, I needed to be alert and perceptive in order to observe, understand, and unobtrusively participate in the dynamics of the social relations. I had enough trouble participating in the discussions and writing up accurate field notes when I was completely sober. Third, drug and alcohol use would have hurt my credibility with the children in the youth program and with their parents. This last reservation was the only one I could express to the Hallway Hangers, but they understood and accepted it completely. Although I sometimes had a shot of Peppermint Schnapps or whiskey and smoked an occasional joint, I generally abstained from using intoxicants.

Other facets of the Hallway Hangers' subculture raised few problems. I learned to take and deal out playful verbal abuse; although my wit was never as sharp as Slick's or Frankie's, my capping ability certainly improved in time. I also became comfortable with the physical jostling and sparring sessions that took place in doorway #13, although I was more careful than the others to make sure they didn't erupt into serious bouts. My strongest asset was my athletic ability, but it probably was exaggerated by my sobriety, whereas the Hallway Hangers often were impaired in one way or another. In addition to basketball, we used to play football on the hardtop area between the project's buildings. The favorite sport of white youths in the Heights, however, was street hockey, and even individuals well into their twenties got involved in the neighborhood games. Once I rediscovered a long-abandoned affinity for goalie, I strapped on Jinks's old pads and attempted to turn away the shots Shorty, Chris, Stoney, and the others would blast at the homemade goal we set up against doorway #13.

Another element of the Hallway Hangers' subculture with which I had difficulty, however, was the blatant sexism. Involved tales of sexual conquest were relatively rare; the Hallway Hangers generally didn't discuss the intricacies of their sexual lives. Still, it was quite obvious that they saw the woman's role in their relationships as purely instrumental. Women were stripped of all identity except for that bound up with their sexuality, and even that was severely restricted; the Hallway Hangers always spoke about their own experience, never about their partners' experiences. Women were reduced to the level of commodities, and the discussions in doorway #13 sometimes consisted of consumers exchanging information. "Yeah, fuckin' right, Tracy'll go down on you, man. She's got that nice long tongue, too." Because of the discomfort these conversations caused me, I avoided or ignored them whenever possible. This was a serious mistake. An analysis of the gender relations of the Hallway Hangers could have been a valuable addition to the study, but with very few field notes on the subject, I was in no position to put forth any sort of argument. I managed to stomach the racial prejudice of the Hallway Hangers and in striving to understand their racism came to see its cultural, political, and theoretical significance. Put off by their sexism, I missed an opportunity to understand it.

My fieldwork with the Brothers did not pose nearly as many complications. Neither my status as a student nor my white skin seemed to be grounds for their distrust, and with the help of my long-standing relationship with Mike, I had little difficulty gaining acceptance by the group. But with his involvement in school athletics, Mike began to spend less and less time with the Brothers during the week, and I was often the sole white person in a group of eight or nine blacks, an anomalous position that was especially pronounced when we went into black neighborhoods to play basketball. I tried to fit in by subtly affecting some of the culturally distinctive language and behavior of black youths. It wasn't until I greeted a working-class black friend at the university with "Yo Steve, what up?" and received a sharp, searching glance that I finally realized how unauthentic and artificial these mannerisms were. I dropped the pretensions and found that the Brothers were happy to accept me as I was. Although I naturally picked up some of their lingo, I felt more comfortable with the honest posture of an outsider to black culture. My ignorance of soul and funk music became something of a joke in the group, and they found my absolute inability to pick up even the most basic breakdancing moves greatly amusing.

The Brothers were interested in university life, both the educational and social sides; after a discussion of their attitudes toward Lincoln High School I invariably was called upon to relate my own college experiences. On a couple of occasions I invited them to productions sponsored by the university black students' association—plays and movies—and they seemed to enjoy and appreciate these outings. Personal friendships with each of the Brothers were much more easily and naturally established than with the Hallway Hangers and were less subject to the vicissitudes of status delineations within the group. Whereas the respect I was accorded by many of the Hallway Hangers was based initially on my friendship with Frankie, with the Brothers I was able to establish a series of distinct one-to-one relationships. Spending time with the Brothers may have been less exciting than hanging in doorway #13, but it was certainly more relaxing and pleasurable. The only strain between me and the Brothers arose because of my continued association with the Hallway Hangers. Although I was never confronted directly on this issue by the Brothers (as I was by the Hallway Hangers), they began to recount with increased frequency stories of physical and verbal abuse at the hands of the Hallway Hangers. The implication of the stories and their searching glances was clear; although the Brothers never stated it directly, they wanted to know why I was spending so much time with the Hallway

Hangers. Fortunately, it wasn't long before they were provided with an answer.

By April, having established a level of trust with both the Brothers and the Hallway Hangers, I felt ready to go beyond the unobtrusive research techniques I had thus far adopted. Hitherto I had been content to elicit as much information from the youths as I could under the guise of curiosity. I knew in which high school program each of the Brothers was enrolled and had an idea of the occupational aspirations of each boy. But for the Hallway Hangers, who were less tolerant of my questions, I had very sketchy data. I needed to explain to both groups the proposed study, my role as researcher, and their role as subjects. This I did in a casual way before initiating a conversation on their aspirations. I simply explained that to graduate from college, I must write a lengthy paper and that instead of doing a lot of research in a library, "I'm gonna write it on you guys down here and what kinds of jobs you want to go into after school and stuff like that." In general, they seemed happy to be the subjects of my research and patiently answered my questions, which became gradually more direct, pointed, and frequent.

Actually, I probably should have explained my project to them much earlier, but I wanted to be considered "okay" before springing on the youths my academic interest in them. I also was reluctant to be forthright about my research intentions because I was afraid some of the Brothers whom I'd befriended would see our relationship as based on academic necessity rather than personal affinity. This wasn't the case, although there was certainly an element of truth in it, which is doubtless why it bothered me. Neither the Brothers nor the Hallway Hangers, however, seemed as sensitive to this issue as I was. Although my researcher status added a new dimension to my relationship with each youth, all seemed willing to accept and distinguish between my academic agenda and my personal regard.

The revelation of my scholarly interest in the boys had one very important positive ramification. It gave me a special position in both groups, a niche that justified my continued presence but set me apart from the others. Whereas previously neither the Brothers nor the Hallway Hangers could understand my association with the other group, my involvement with both became much more explicable once I revealed in full my intentions. As Frankie explained to a fringe member of the Hallway Hangers who confronted me as I emerged from Super's apartment, "No man, see, to do his shit right for his studies he's got to check out the fuckin' niggers, too." Likewise, the Brothers had more tolerance for the time I spent with the Hallway Hangers. Although simultaneous affiliation with both peer groups still caused problems for which there was no solution and with which I found myself constantly burdened, the situation improved significantly.

This position of being at once of and yet apart from the group had other positive implications, especially for my standing with the Hallway Hangers. There are many things that go along with membership in that subculture of which I wanted no part: the violence, the excessive consumption of alcohol and drugs, and the strident racism and sexism. Had I completely integrated myself into the group, I would have been expected to partake of all of the above. Fortunately, the unwritten rules that govern the behavior of the Hallway Hangers did not always apply to me. Had I been vociferously insulted by another member, for instance, I would not be confronted necessarily with the only two options normally open to an individual in that situation: fight or lose a great deal of social standing in the group. For this special status within the group I was thankful.

I was not, however, totally free of the group's status delineations. The fact that I spent a good deal of time with the Hallway Hangers talking, joking, exchanging insults, and playing sports meant that I could not stay entirely outside the group's pecking order, even if my position in it was very fluid. My friendships with Hank and, especially, Frankie must have troubled those who received less attention from them when I was present. I wanted to excel in some of the things that matter to the Hallway Hangers in order to gain their respect, but attempting to do so necessarily threatened the status of others in the group. It was the same situation I faced on the basketball court that first evening with Hank: I wanted to play well, but I didn't want to imperil his status on the court. Hanging in doorway #13, I learned to be acutely aware of status demarcations and the threat I posed to the standing of other individuals. I would try to placate those whose positions suffered at my expense by self-disparagement and by consciously drawing attention to their superiority over me. I'm certain that I was not as sensitive to these situations as I could have been, but I did come to realize the importance of minimizing the degree to which I could be regarded as a threat by other members of the group. The success of my project depended on good relations not just with Frankie and Slick, but with Shorty, Chris, Boo-Boo, Stoney, Steve, and Jinks as well.

Once I told the youths of my sociological interest in them, I set about gathering information more aggressively. I was intent on amassing material on their attitudes toward school and subsequent employment, but I was still very much at the reconnaissance stage; these unstructured interviews were a preliminary ground survey. Still, my conversations with boys from both groups often were quite lengthy and covered a great many topics. Taping the discussions or taking notes, obviously, was out of the question, so I was forced to rely on my memory. After a conversation with one of the boys, I'd hop on the bus and return to my dorm room immediately, preferably without speaking to anyone, and promptly write up the interview. At first, I made summary notes of the interview, remembering as much of what was said as I could and putting it in paragraph format. I was able to recall more, however, when I tried to reconstruct the interview word for word and wrote it up in script form with each question and answer. The more interviews I conducted and recorded, the better my concentration and memory became, until I could recall most of what was said in a thirty-minute discussion. Writing up the interview as soon as possible with no distractions was crucial. I remember having an excellent discussion with Super, Mokey, and Craig on the way to play basketball at the Salvation Army gym. But after playing two hours of ball, conversing on the way back to the Heights, and finally returning to my room to write up the interview, I had forgotten a great deal of it. Writing up interviews was extraordinarily tedious, especially because after conducting a good interview one wants to relax, but the importance of good field notes was impressed upon me by my professor and was indeed borne out by my own experience.

The requirements for my field methods course spurred me to conduct as many unstructured interviews as I could, for by mid-May I had to produce a paper on my project. By that time I had managed to conduct interviews with fourteen boys, eleven of whom would end up in the final study. I had information on all seven of the Brothers, but only on Chris, Boo-Boo, Stoney, and Frankie of the Hallway Hangers. Except in the cases of Mike and Frankie, the material was very thin, often including not much more than their high school programs, their attitudes toward school, and their expressed aspirations or expectations.

To gain a measure of understanding of the high school curriculum I obtained a detailed course catalogue and conducted an interview with Karen Wallace, the school's career counselor. That I was compelled to examine and organize the data I had collected and search it for patterns and findings at that stage of the research was fortunate. Fieldwork is an organic process that should include a nearly continuous analysis and reorganization of the material into patterns and models that in turn guide the fieldwork in new directions. Writing the final paper for the class forced me to consolidate my research, and although a detailed picture of the social landscape did not emerge, I did gain a vantage point from which to formulate a strategy for exploring in greater depth the terrain staked out for study.

That strategy included fieldwork in the Lincoln School: observation in the classroom and semiformal interviews with teachers, guidance counselors, and administrators. I also planned to interview as many of the Hallway Hangers' and Brothers' parents to whom I could gain access as possible, a number I estimated at about one-half the total. Most important, I decided to conduct semiformal, in-depth interviews with all of the boys. My research demanded detailed data on each boy's family background and their experiences in and approaches to school and work, information I could elicit most effectively in private discussions relatively free of distraction. I was unable to construct with sufficient depth a portrait of each individual by piecing together the bits and pieces of data I collected on the street, no matter how much time I spent with each group; I needed to sit down and talk with each boy for an hour or so to gather simple data, such as family members' occupational histories, as well as to probe intricate issues like the degree to which each had internalized the achievement ideology. To this end, I drew up an interview guide, a list of issues that I wanted addressed in each discussion. I did not always stick to the guide, but having it before me in abbreviated form prevented me from missing crucial questions when the conversation got too intriguing. The guide also jogged my memory when I wrote up the discussion.

Unfortunately, the interview guide lay dormant for nearly two months, and much of the ethnographic strategy never saw the light of day at all. I simply was too busy with the youth program during the spring and summer to concentrate on the research. I failed to do any substantive fieldwork in the high school aside from conducting interviews with Bruce Davis and Jimmy Sullivan, and in Clarendon Heights I only managed to undertake interviews with Derek and Chris. But in September 1983 my work got a big boost.

Instead of returning to a university dormitory, I moved into a recently vacated, rent-controlled apartment in a large tenement building directly across the street from Clarendon Heights. It was a run-down, cockroach-infested dwelling, but it was large, cheap, and gave me a much-needed base where people could find me and I could conduct interviews. This move enhanced my research in vital ways. Spending time with the Brothers and the Hallway Hangers was no longer a commuting hassle but rather a break from studying, a way to relax and enjoy myself. Living so near Clarendon Heights, despite my continued status as a full-time student, also gave me a better feeling for the rhythm of the community and further reduced the degree to which I was an outsider, both in their eyes and in mine. Although my residence in the neighborhood was not free of complications, it marked a positive new development in my research and in my relationship with the entire community.

I began interviewing individuals in the apartment in October. Each interview would last approximately an hour, and I found that even if I made extensive notes it was difficult to recall with precision all that had been said. Finally, I decided that the formality of a tape recorder would be no worse than the formality of the interview guide. I tried it a few times, and although it certainly made people self-conscious at the beginning of the interview and probably deterred some of the Hallway Hangers from being as frank as they might have been about their criminal exploits, the benefits seemed to outweigh the disadvantages. Transcribing the tapes, however, was just as tedious as writing up the discussions from memory, for it generally took at least four or five hours and sometimes up to seven.

Both the Brothers and the Hallway Hangers regarded these interviews as a favor to me. The Brothers generally were more accommodating; I had little difficulty cajoling them up to my apartment for the required session. The Hallway Hangers were more elusive. Theirs is a world in which something is very seldom had for nothing, and they saw quite clearly that there was nothing in this project for them. I was the one meeting an academic requirement for a college degree, a principal attainment in my own pursuit of "success." In a year's time I would be studying on a scholarship in Oxford, England; most of the Hallway Hangers would be back in doorway #13, in the armed forces, or in prison. To be fair, I had contributed to the community through the youth program, as the Hallway Hangers were well aware. They didn't see me as "using" them. However, they did sense an imbalance in the relationship, and when I requested an hour of their time to level a barrage of personal questions at them, many of the Hallway Hangers vaguely expected something in return.

It soon became clear, however, that I had very little to give. I couldn't help the Hallway Hangers with their academic work as I did with the Brothers because those who were still in school very seldom did any. I did assist Slick when he was struggling to finish the work required for his G.E.D., and some of the Hallway Hangers would approach me about legal or personal problems with the often mistaken hope that I could be of some help. More often, however, the requests were less innocent.

Like all the people aged twenty or so who spent any time in doorway #13, I was asked to buy beer for the Hallway Hangers. These requests put me in a difficult position. I wanted to be of some use to the Hallway Hangers, but, well aware of the debilitating role of alcohol in their lives, I didn't want to buy them beer. Moreover, although the risk of police detection was not particularly high, other Clarendon Heights tenants easily might discover what I was doing. Nevertheless, I did make a couple of trips to the local package store for the Hallway Hangers. Those two trips attest, I think, to the unease I felt about the one-way nature of my involvement with the Hallway Hangers, to my desire to maintain my standing in the group, and, of course, to their powers of persuasion and manipulation. One of the biggest mistakes one can make in the company of the Hallway Hangers is to appear hesitant or uncertain; after I decided that buying beer for them was ethically dubious and pragmatically stupid, I answered their subsequent requests with an adamant "no" and was frank and honest in dealing with their appeals and protests.

Despite the fact that there continued to be much take and little give in my relationship with the Hallway Hangers, I did manage to get them all up to my apartment for a taped interview that autumn. In the end, sensing how important it was to me, the Hallway Hangers did the interviews as a personal favor. Some of them consented immediately, and we did the interview as soon as we had some common time free. Getting some of the others up to my apartment in front of the tape recorder was a significant achievement. Stoney, for example, is a very private person. Rather than undergo the weekly ordeal of having to talk about his "drug problem" with a counselor at the city's drug clinic, Stoney opted for a three-month stint in the county jail. In trying to gauge the influence his mother has on him, I asked in the actual interview if they had ever discussed his performance in school. "I didn't talk to her that much. I'm not the type of person who opens up and talks to people. That's why it took you so long to get me up here. I go to the drug clinic, and the lady just asks me questions. I hate it. I just ask her back why she wants to ask me this for. I'm not into it. I'm just doing this for a favor to you."

Once up in the apartment, many of the Hallway Hangers actually seemed to enjoy the interview. Boo-Boo and Frankie both stated that it was good to discuss and examine their feelings and thoughts. I was impressed by the honesty and thoughtfulness with which the Hallway Hangers answered my often probing questions. The Brothers were no less candid, but I had expected the Hallway Hangers to be less forthright and honest. Only Shorty refused to take the interview seriously and maintained a level of distance and invulnerability throughout the session.

Chris and Jinks came up to the apartment together. As Chris already had been interviewed, Jinks and I left him in the kitchen and went into the small room I used as a study where we talked for nearly ninety minutes. We emerged to find Chris sitting at the kitchen table smoking a joint. On the table was a mound of marijuana, probably a half pound, which Chris was rolling mechanically into thin joints at an amazing pace. Chris must have seen the look of surprise on my face because he immediately offered up a couple of joints to placate me. Jinks and I had a good laugh but were interrupted by the doorbell. My mirth faded quickly as I figured that with my luck the police were onto Chris and had picked this opportune moment to make the arrest. Fortunately, it was only Craig and Super inviting me to play ball in the park. I declined and quickly shut the door before they could catch a glimpse of Chris and Jinks or a whiff of the joint. I sat in the study and began to transcribe the tape while in the kitchen Chris rolled his joints and Jinks smoked.

I conducted a number of discussions with more than one individual, but one really stands out in importance for the amount of information it produced. On a cold afternoon in December I managed to assemble Frankie, Slick, Shorty, Chris, and Jinks in my apartment. The discussion, which lasted more than an hour and a half, began this way:

FRANKIE: Okay, man, ask us a fucking question, that's the deal.

JM: I wanna know what each of you wants to do, now and . . .

CHRIS: I wanna get laid right now (*laughter*).

JM: Everyone tell me what they wanna be doing in twenty years.

SHORTY: Hey, you can't get no education around here unless if you're fucking rich, y'know? You can't get no education. Twenty years from now
Chris'll prob'ly be in some fucking gay joint, whatever (*laughter*). And
we'll prob'ly be in prison or dead (*laughter*). You can't get no education
around here.

JM: How's that though? Frankie, you were saying the other day that this city
has one of the best school systems around (*all laugh except Frankie*).

FRANKIE: Lincoln is the best fucking school system going, but we're all just
fucking burnouts. We don't give a fuck.

SHORTY: I ain't a fucking burnout, man.

JINKS: (*sarcastically*) You're all reformed and shit, right?

SHORTY: Shut up, potato head.

I had very little control of the interview and wasn't able to cover all of
the ground that I'd hoped to, but the material that emerged as the conversation swept along from subject to subject was very rich and poignant.
Disagreements and conflicts between individuals, some of which I actively probed, produced some fervid and well-argued viewpoints that
never would have emerged from an individual interview. It took me an
entire day to transcribe the discussion, and I never had time to conduct
another one, but the yield from this group interview was very impressive.
Although the ethnographer must weigh the impact of the dynamics of the
discussion on its content, this added task should not deter researchers
from cultivating this fertile area more thoroughly than I did.

By November, time constraints were cutting into more than my capac-
ity to conduct group interviews. I had to scrap my plans to do any kind of
extensive fieldwork in the school. Although I had interviewed only half
the subjects in the study, I already had accumulated more than three hundred pages of field notes and interview transcriptions. I desperately
wanted to interview as many of the youths' parents as I could, for I saw
that as crucial to the study. In fact, I still see it as crucial to the study, but I
simply did not have the time to conduct interviews with more than two
mothers—Stoney's and Mokey's. Chapter 3 consequently is incomplete,
and I think the study as a whole suffers from the limitations on my research into each boy's family. Another important item on my fieldwork
agenda that I never was able to carry out and that would have been quite
enjoyable was hanging at Pop's, the little store where the Hallway Hangers and their friends congregated during the school day. These casualties
of my research strategy were the unfortunate results of my full-time student status and of the community work with which I continued to be involved in Clarendon Heights.

After I moved into the apartment, I found myself entwined in the lives of many families to a degree I hadn't experienced before. Youngsters in the youth program would stop by to say hello or to ask for help with their schoolwork, as did the Brothers. During this period I became very close friends with Billy, the former member of the Hallway Hangers who had won a scholarship to college as a high school junior the previous spring. Billy was struggling with the academic workload of the Fundamental School, having recently switched from Occupational Education, so I ended up spending about ten hours a week assisting him with homework, advising him about college admissions, and generally just hacking around. I also became a regular tutor to an eighth grader who had been in my youth group the previous three summers. He really was struggling in school, both academically and with respect to discipline, and at his mother's urging I met with his teachers, but to no particular avail. In none of these roles did I consider myself a social worker. I was simply a friend, and I probably got more out of these relationships in terms of personal satisfaction and fulfillment than they got from me. Sometimes the rewards were more tangible: A Haitian family to which I'd grown particularly close used to cook me a delicious West Indian meal about once a week, brought to my apartment wrapped in dish towels by nine-year-old Mark, fourteen-year-old Kerlain, or sixteen-year-old Rhodes.

Despite the fact that I never was viewed as a social worker, except perhaps as a very unorthodox and informal one, I was approached more and more often by people with serious problems. I stopped by to see Freddie Piniella, a tough little twelve-year-old kid whom I'd known for three years. He wasn't home, but his mother was. Mrs. Piniella always had maintained a cool distance from me, but suddenly she began to relate in a subdued, beaten tone her daughter Vicki's predicament. Vicki was a resilient fourteen-year-old girl whose violent temper, exceptionally loud voice, and strong frame made her at once an object of grudging admiration and resentment by her peers. Mrs. Piniella had found out that morning that Vicki was pregnant, well past her first trimester. She would need to have an abortion, but Mrs. Piniella had less than eighty dollars in the bank, and the cost of terminating such a late pregnancy was more than five hundred dollars. Mrs. Piniella, a part-time custodial worker at the university, was on welfare, but the state would under no circumstances, not even rape, fund abortions. I agreed to try finding a hospital or clinic that would carry out the operation at a reduced cost, but none of the places I contacted would do so for a pregnancy beyond the third month. Nor could Planned Parenthood or any other agency direct me to a hospital that would.

I returned the next day to report this news, only to hear from her very depressed mother that Vicki, it turned out, had gonorrhea as well. Eventually a social worker attached to the local health clinic located a hospital that would accept a reduced payment on a monthly basis, and Vicki had the abortion and was treated for venereal disease. I don't know how Vicki managed to cope with the strain of the whole experience, but I spoke with her the next week, and she seemed very composed. Her plight had quite an effect on me and pointed up the dichotomy between Clarendon Heights and the university more starkly than ever. It was an ironic contrast to learn of her predicament and then to hear the consternation my student friends were expressing about their upcoming midterm exams.

One morning in mid-December I was awakened by the door buzzer at four o'clock. It was a very cold Super who had left home two days earlier after being beaten by his father. I found a blanket, and he slept on my couch. Later that morning we tried to decide what to do. Super was adamant in his refusal even to consider going home and trying to reach some sort of reconciliation with his parents. He had come that night from his uncle's apartment on the other side of the city, but reported that his uncle had a severe drinking problem and was prone to violent outbursts. With nowhere else to go, Super urged me to find a place for him in a home for runaways. So together we embarked on a very circuitous, time-consuming, and frustrating exploration of the social service bureaucracy. No shelter for teenagers would accept Super without a referral from a social worker, but the city's Social Services Department would not assign him one. Instead, they insisted on tracking down his family's social worker, a process that took four days. We finally got the woman's name and phoned her office repeatedly, but she must have been exceedingly busy because we never heard back from her. I called the high school, and Super finally managed to get one of the youth workers attached to the school to secure him a place in a teenage runaway home. By that time, however, all the beds were full, and he was put on a waiting list. Finally, after more than a week with me, Super moved into a youth home for ten days before returning to his family in Clarendon Heights. I always had assumed that the stories I'd heard from residents about the inefficiency and ineptitude of the social services bureaucracy were exaggerated. Now I was not so sure, although the problem clearly lay not with the social workers themselves; the problem was too little funding and too much work. It was, however, especially frustrating to be asked by those who could not deal effectively with Super's situation whether I was aware that it was against the law to harbor a runaway.

During the year I spent conducting research in Clarendon Heights I often was troubled by legal issues. By spending time with the Hallway Hangers in doorway #13 I quite clearly ran the risk of arrest, but this was not especially distressing. Had I been corralled in one of the periodic police raids of the hallway, the charges against me would have been minimal, if any were brought at all. Although being in the presence of those smoking marijuana was illegal, possession of narcotics, especially with intent to sell, is what the police were generally after. Still, I saw people arrested in Clarendon Heights for simply having a beer in their hand, so I had to contend with the possibility of arrest. Had that happened, I certainly would have had a lot of explaining to do: to kids in the youth program and their parents, to the Brothers, to university officials, and to my parents.

A greater cause for concern was my unprotected legal status as a researcher. Whereas lawyers, journalists, doctors, and clergy can withhold information to protect their clients, for academic researchers there is no clearcut right of confidentiality. If any law enforcement official came to know about my study, my field notes could be used as evidence, and I could be put on the witness stand and questioned. In such a situation I would have two options: incriminate my friends or perjure myself. To avoid such a dilemma, my field methods professor urged me to explain to the youths that I preferred not to hear about their criminal exploits or at least not to record their accounts in my notes. But I found the criminal activity of the Hallway Hangers very interesting and also quite relevant to the study. Besides, my legal position was no different from their own. The Hallway Hangers had all the information I did, undoubtedly more, and they had no legal coverage, nor were they particularly worried about it. I was a more likely source for the district attorney because as a university student I was presumably less concerned about indicting my friends than I would be about lying under oath. Not wanting to draw attention to this fact and risk losing the trust of the Hallway Hangers, I made no effort to remain ignorant of potentially incriminating information, although I destroyed or erased all the interview tapes and was exceptionally careful with my field notes.

In fact, one absolutely hallowed rule among the Hallway Hangers and a large proportion of the project's older residents was not to "rat" to the police. As an ethnographer I wasn't interested in passing an ethical judgment on this maxim. I was there to understand as much as I could, and selective noncooperation with the police seemed to make sense as a means of self-protection for a certain segment of the community. When I saw two young men who recently had been released from prison arrested while they sat quietly drinking bottles of beer on the steps of doorway #13 and realized that the "offense" would mean up to six months in prison for them as a violation of parole, I began to appreciate people's reluctance to cooperate with the police.

My own subscription to this maxim was put to a very serious test in mid-October. Paddy, a Green Berets veteran on the fringes of the Hallway Hangers, shot his girlfriend Doreen, and I was the sole witness. Doreen, whom I knew well, wasn't critically wounded; the bullet pierced her arm and lodged in her breast, and after undergoing surgery she recovered rapidly and was out of the hospital in a few days. The details of the incident and subsequent events are too involved to relate here, so I'll concentrate on the issues I had to face as a citizen, as a researcher, and as a member of the Clarendon Heights community.

I was questioned by the police at the scene of the crime first as a suspect and then as a witness. I hadn't actually seen the shooting itself, but I had overhead the preceding altercation from within my apartment and knew what had happened. My first inclination was to relate everything, but I checked myself and repeatedly told the officers only what I'd seen after hearing the shot and running out into the street, thereby leaving out the key incriminating material I had heard. Doreen, it turned out, also refused to incriminate Paddy, but the police were nevertheless quite confident that he had committed the crime. He was arrested, but when Doreen refused to bring criminal charges, it looked as though the case might be dropped. Instead, the state decided to press charges, and I soon received a letter from an assistant district attorney asking me to phone him.

I was faced with a serious problem. Do I tell the whole truth, incriminate Paddy, and see justice done the American way? I had a number of doubts about this course, not all of them pragmatic, such as my physical well-being, my standing in the community, and the future of the study. Practically speaking, to "finger" Paddy would have had disastrous consequences, and I think most people under the circumstances would have balked at full cooperation with the authorities. I also happen to think that withholding information was not only expedient but also morally justifiable. Such an opinion may be pure self-delusion, as most people to whom I've related the incident seem to think, but from my position I couldn't help feeling that way.

As a member of the Clarendon Heights community and more particularly as a trusted associate of the Hallway Hangers, I felt in some ways that it was incumbent upon me to subscribe to their behavioral codes. There were obviously limits to this adherence; other duties or commitments (e.g., to justice) could override this allegiance to the group's rules of conduct, but I definitely felt in some sense drawn to respect the code of silence.

There were, of course, competing impulses. Paddy had shot and could easily have killed Doreen, and no community wants to tolerate that sort of behavior. Yet they were both very high and very drunk, and a violent argument had precipitated the incident. In addition, the shooting was not completely intentional (she was shot through a closed door), and Paddy immediately had repented of his action, rushing her amid hysterical tears to the hospital. Moreover, Doreen herself had lied in order to protect Paddy, and the two of them were back living together within a matter of days. But although I was conscious of these circumstances, they failed to diminish my conviction that Paddy should be punished.

Still, having spent the bulk of the previous summer researching prison life as part of a project undertaken by the kids in my youth group, and having tutored inmates at a state prison, I knew only too well what kind of impact a stint behind bars was likely to have on Paddy. In the end, this proved decisive. I was unwilling to jeopardize all that I had gained in Clarendon Heights in order to put Paddy in prison when he was likely to come out a much more dangerous person.

I decided to say nothing about the argument that preceded the shooting. When the trial finally took place in midwinter after a number of postponements, Paddy was found guilty despite my incomplete testimony, so all my speculation turned out to be academic. Convicted of illegal possession of a firearm, illegal discharge of a firearm, and assault with a deadly weapon, Paddy was sentenced to serve two years in a state prison. I didn't feel good about my role in the proceedings, especially refraining from providing information under oath, but neither did I lose sleep over the incident. Bourgeois morality has diminished relevance in a place like Clarendon Heights where the dictates of practical necessity often leave very little "moral" ground on which to stand.

During the fall of 1983 I felt myself drawn into the community as I had never been before, into its political and social life and into the web of personal, economic, and social problems that plague its residents. At the university, I had a full academic schedule, a work-study job, and a large extracurricular load. It was a very busy time, and I also found it emotionally draining, especially in trying to reconcile the two lives I led: the one on the university campus and the other on the streets of Clarendon Heights.

It was, of course, this study that bridged the two worlds. One of the most challenging (and rewarding) aspects of an ethnographic study is the synthesis the sociologist must create between a perceived intellectual tradition and the data daily emerging from the fieldwork. Without a theoretical framework to make some sense of the overwhelming quantity and variety of empirical material, the researcher would be swimming in a sea of field notes, each new interview tossing him or her in a different direction. By the same token, there is all too much theoretical abstraction with no experiential grounding whatsoever coming from scholars who are locked in their academic offices. This book began with a review of reproduction theory and, after the ethnographic material was laid out, moved on to a reconsideration of the theoretical perspective. That is the way this intellectual enterprise was actually carried out, although the progression was not nearly so linear. Since the beginning of the fieldwork in spring 1983 I had been studying the theoretical literature. The thinking of Bowles and Gintis, Bourdieu, Bernstein, and especially Willis (I didn't read

Giroux until long afterward) informed my own thinking at every stage of the research. My empirical data and the theoretical perspective were held in a kind of dialectical tension, and I found myself moving back and forth between the two until my own ideas coalesced.

The emergence of my ideas was a slow, circuitous process; I had expected to have problems analyzing the data, but the earlier stage of simply organizing the empirical material proved more difficult than I had foreseen. By January 1984 I had in excess of five hundred pages of field notes. By March I had to turn this mass of data into a senior honors thesis. I knew the analytical and theoretical sections would prove intellectually taxing, but I didn't realize how difficult it would be to organize my notes into the basically descriptive chapters on the peer group, family, work, and school.

I failed to make theoretical notes throughout the months of research. I had plenty of notes depicting events and conversations, but kept no record of my more abstract sense of the observed phenomena. By November, the ideas that make up the backbone of Chapter 7 were beginning to emerge, albeit in a rough and rudimentary form. I was especially cognizant of these ideas in carrying out the remaining interviews and strove to collect information that would help determine the validity of my fresh theoretical discernments. The entire research period, in fact, involved a nearly constant appraisal and reappraisal of abstract ideas I thought could help me make sense of the data. But, ludicrously, I kept no written record of the development of these ideas. I would mentally cultivate and modify my views in line with the empirical material, but I should have noted after every interview how the new data had forced revisions in or had affirmed my previous thinking. Had I kept such notes, the stage between the end of my fieldwork and the beginning of the actual writing would have been considerably less hectic and would have filled me with much less dread.

I remember spending days reading through my field notes again and again, sifting through the material trying to come up with an organizational framework. I began keeping a record of all new insights, some of which would come to me at the most bizarre times and places, often touched off by a chance incident or a stray comment. In order to get some sort of grasp on the data, I developed a one-page index for each youth, on which I recorded information that struck me as particularly relevant or important. Perhaps the most useful organizing tool I employed was a huge chart that contained for each individual information on the following specifications: race, peer group, high school grade level, school program, expressed aspiration, acceptance of achievement ideology, faith in the efficacy of schooling, father in the household, employment of father, employment of mother, educational attainments of parents, duration of tenancy in public housing, duration of tenancy in Clarendon Heights, and whether the subject smokes cigarettes, drinks alcohol, smokes marijuana, or has been arrested. Once the data had been systematically laid out, patterns began to emerge.

Such patterns gave form and further meaning to the lives of these boys and helped me measure the relative significance of the various structural and cultural factors that shape aspirations. Ultimately, however, it was on the basketball court with the Brothers or in doorway #13 with the Hallway Hangers that I gained whatever understanding I eventually achieved.

Second Harvest: Notes on the 1991 Field Experience

The fieldwork for the original study took place when I transformed a work site into a research venue in 1983. Having directed a youth program in Clarendon Heights, I was trusted by its teenage tenants, who agreed to help with my undergraduate thesis. When I returned eight years later to undertake research for the revised edition, Clarendon Heights had changed, and so had I. Moreover, the thesis had turned into a successful sociology textbook. I had maintained contact with some of the young men over the years, but many relationships had lapsed. Having taken up residence elsewhere, I no longer had a base in the community.

Thus I crossed the street to Clarendon Heights in July 1991 nearly as nervous as when I first arrived ten years earlier. I needn't have worried. "Hey Jay," Steve rang out, "what the fuck brings you back to the Ponderosa?" I was coming *back*. My history in Clarendon Heights meant that its residents were even more affable, accommodating, and forthcoming this time than they had been in the 1980s. The anecdotal account that follows gives a brief sketch of my field experience in 1991.

Although the Brothers and the Hallway Hangers had scattered, tracking them down proved less troublesome than I expected. Several lived nearby and seemed glad to see me. They were excited about being the subjects of a book and pledged to help me with an updated edition. Mostly, they wanted to know how many millions of dollars I'd made on the book, why I'd spent four years in a Mississippi backwater as a community organizer, and why I was shortly returning to a place even more obscure—England. Informed of my intention to become an Anglican priest, a disclosure that instantly kills conversations in sociology circles, these guys were apt to ask about discounts for christenings, weddings, and funerals. The Brothers and the Hallway Hangers also pressed me for details about my wife.

In turn, I pressed each of them for an interview to discover how they had fared in the eight years since I'd done the original research. Most of the interviews were undertaken in the back of a neighborhood bar and restaurant that a friend of mine owns about a mile from Clarendon Heights. I spoke with others in their homes, at their work sites, and in my car. With their permission I recorded most of the interviews on microcassettes. Only Super was understandably dubious. I started slowly in that interview, and as his wariness eased he forgot about the recorder and spoke with surprising candor about his drug dealing.

Boo-Boo also spoke frankly about his criminal activities. This interview was done in my car because Boo-Boo was living several miles from Clarendon Heights. We decided to drive around while we talked, a dumb idea. Doing an interview while wheeling around a city will result in a bad interview, an accident, or both. I pulled into a suburban shopping center and parked the car as we talked on. After describing his night-deposit robberies, Boo-Boo told of being confronted by a pistol-waving partner over a crack sale gone sour. Suddenly, there came a knock on my car window. In the same instant several police cruisers converged on our car. I looked up into the grim face of a policeman who motioned with one hand for me to roll down the window, the other hand on his holster. I looked helplessly at Boo-Boo as I eased down my window. The other cops stayed in their cruisers. Bidden to get my license and registration and to get out of the car, I surreptitiously turned off the tape recorder and did as I was told. Shoppers stopped and stared. I was stunned. I figured that with all Boo-Boo's violent drug troubles in Raymond, there was bound to be a warrant out for his arrest. So I vowed neither to divulge Boo-Boo's identity nor to let on about the book. I showed the police officer my license. He asked me what we were doing.

> JM: Just talking.
> PO: Just talking, huh?
> JM: Yessir.
> PO: You come all the way up from Mississippi to have a little chat? Who's your partner?
> JM: Actually, I'm shortly off to England where I'll be training to be a priest.
> PO: Uh-huh. Who's your partner?
> JM: I'm not sure of his name.

This wasn't exactly convincing, so I explained that I studied at a nearby university years ago, ran a youth project in a poor neighborhood, and was close to Boo-Boo's sister Shelly. Because Boo-Boo is struggling with some traumatic personal problems, Shelly asked me to speak with him. As she is only his stepsister, I don't know his last name. It suddenly dawned on me that except for the last bit, this was quite true, and I stopped on a note of triumph. The officer showed rather less enthusiasm for the story. So I fumbled about in my wallet, hoping against all hope that I'd kept an old college ID, the only one with a decent photo. I found it, saved by my vanity. As the policeman turned the ID over in his hand, it seemed to dawn on him that my car trunk might not be full of heroin or assault weapons. Disappointed, he waved the other cruisers away but continued to question me closely. Pressed about Boo-Boo's identity and address, and about what we were doing, I ducked and drifted and parried weakly. I kept imagining the cop would reach into the front seat, pick up the tape recorder, and play back Boo-Boo's detailed disclosure of his criminal career.

Eventually the police officer called to his partner, who had been interrogating Boo-Boo, and they retired to their car. They seemed to spend ages on the radio, confirming our identities, checking my license and car registration, and comparing our stories. Then he returned to give me back my license and apologize for the half-hour inconvenience. He invited me to consider how suspicious we looked sitting outside a supermarket in a car with Mississippi plates. Instead of berating him for flouting police procedure and our civil liberties, I nodded meekly and he let us go. Evidently they didn't compare our stories too closely, for when I sank into the seat beside Boo-Boo and asked what he'd said, he replied, "Nuthin' really. Just our names, where I live, what we're doing, y'know, having an interview. He was real interested in your book."

As we drove away and resumed the interview (not such a dumb idea after all), Boo-Boo apologized for the incident as if it were his fault.

> BOO-BOO: I'm sorry about that whole thing. You can't even sit in a car talking to me cuz I'm black. Shoot, these cops are so prejudiced around here.

Juan suggested I interview him as we drove to pick up his girlfriend. The drive took only fifteen minutes but he assured me she would be late. She was waiting at the curb when we drove up. Subsequently I struggled to set a time to speak with him. In the end, I went to Jim's Tow and caught him at work. I put in a tape, and Juan and I chatted as he painted a fender and then tinkered with an engine. When other employees began to pause as they passed by, I stuffed the small recorder into my pocket, thinking it would still pick up our conversation. That tape wasn't easy to transcribe. Juan's voice had been muffled even with the recorder perched on the car.

Slick's tape was also difficult to transcribe. I'd spent a few evenings hanging around his apartment, mostly playing with his baby son while he and Denise argued in an adjacent room. Without saying so, Slick seemed wary of doing an interview. The intervening seven years hadn't gone as he'd hoped. He was the proud father of two children. But he also had a difficult job, a girlfriend strung out on crack, and a rundown home. I stopped by one evening and the living room was full. Slick had just returned home from the construction site and was showering. Denise had three friends over, and there were three toddlers scrambling about on the floor. One child reached up and pulled a bottle of beer off a table. The women screamed, the babies shrieked, and Slick came in to suggest that we go out to do that interview. I knew that this was an escape from domestic duties and household chaos; I also knew that Denise was not pleased. But I jumped at the opportunity and lost little time in taking Slick to a cafeteria for dinner. "Turn the tape on," Slick commanded shortly after we sat down, "I don't give a fuck if people think I'm an FBI rat." We had an excellent talk over a good meal. Only later did I discover how easily voices are drowned out by background music and meal-time clatter.

The interviews done in prison were not tape-recorded. It shouldn't have been difficult to visit Stoney and Chris in prison, but it was. Stoney was in Carlisle State Prison twenty miles away. I called ahead to inquire about attire and was told not to wear jeans. I arrived fifteen minutes early, filled out the paperwork, placed the content of my pockets along with my belt and wristwatch into a locker, and presented myself at the desk. "Sorry, you can't come in with that T-shirt on." I protested to no avail. Since it was a plain T-shirt, she explained, I could easily be confused with the prisoners. Shaking with anger, I extracted a promise that if I returned with a different shirt within half an hour, they would let me in. I ran back to the parking lot, jumped in my car, and raced into the surrounding countryside. Smack in the middle of a rural region, I sped along dusty lanes for fifteen frustrating minutes until I came upon a general store. They had one shirt, a massive T-shirt emblazoned with the cartoon character Roger Rabbit, protesting "I was framed." I bought it.

Back at the visitors' desk, I was told this time that no T-shirts whatsoever could be worn into the prison complex. Fairly bursting with rage, I demanded to see the supervisor and was eventually let in because he found my story and my shirt so funny. I took off my shoes, strode through the metal detector, stopped to be frisked, and stepped into the steel trap. Finally I was ushered into the visitors' room where I sat for thirty minutes. Eventually, a guard came up to tell me that Stoney had been moved that afternoon to Grassmoor Prison thirty miles away.

A few days later I turned up at Grassmoor and was told that Stoney was off the premises for a physical. I waited in the parking lot for an hour until a prison van drove up and Stoney and two other inmates climbed out, accompanied by two guards. Pleased to finally have Stoney in my sights, I waved like an idiot and received several searching stares. Then recognition broke over Stoney's face and he came to greet me. He had minimum-security status because of severe overcrowding in the state prison system, and so we went out in the yard and talked at a picnic table. He brought me up to date on his parents, brothers, girlfriend, ex-girlfriend, and children. He asked about Clarendon Heights, about each of the Hallway Hangers, and about me. I've always been close to Stoney's mother and brothers, but never had Stoney and I talked so easily. I felt less distance between us than ever before, and yet in an hour's time he would walk back to his cell and I would drive away in my car. And I wanted something first. I had come to interview Stoney, not just to visit him. Much as I hated to broach the issue directly, I knew better than to dance around it. I explained uneasily that the study had become a textbook and that I hoped to interview him for the revised edition. The subtext was plain: "Yes, Stoney, you're a friend, but first and foremost, you're an object of research. Otherwise, I wouldn't be here." Stoney was aware of the underlying message, I'm sure. But he graciously put me at ease and proceeded to pour his heart out for ninety minutes.

After the interview, Stoney led me around the prison and showed me a photo of his girlfriend. In the lounge area, we were surrounded by vending machines. He explained that prisoners had to pay for decent food, for clothes laundering, for most everything. Given only two dollars per day for his work in the prison kitchen, Stoney found this difficult. I offered him some money. He refused but then relented. Since it was against prison regulations and even a $5 bill would arouse suspicion, I tried to break up $20 as best I could. It wasn't easy making various vending machines spew out quarters by the handful and then sneaking the booty into Stoney's socks!

I failed to learn my lesson when I visited Chris at Broadbottom State Prison. Broadbottom is part of a large farm complex, a crumbling Victorian structure where prisoners still slop out their cells. I arrived late and hurriedly dumped all my belongings into a basket at the desk, filled out a form, stepped through the metal detector, submitted to a search, and was herded with the other visitors into a small cafeteria. Every time a prisoner was brought into the room, I examined him closely. I hadn't seen Chris for several years and wasn't certain I would recognize him, or vice versa. When they did bring him in, I knew him straightaway, but he needed reminding who I was. He was surprised to see me. No one else had driven the two hours from Clarendon Heights to see him. Without his saying so, it was obvious that the first thing he wanted was some food. Everyone around us was shuttling back and forth to various vending machines, munching on candy bars, and downing cold drinks. Chris looked at them hungrily and I apologized profusely. Thinking the rules were the same as at Grassmoor, I had turned in my money with the rest of my things at the front desk. I had made lots of money on *Ain't No Makin' It*, and here I was without a couple of quarters to buy Chris a coke.

In spite of this disastrous start, the interview went well from my point of view. Chris described in detached but vivid detail how his life had taken one disastrous turn after another. He'd alienated everyone, he told me. Having spent two hours with his mother the previous week, I knew this was no exaggeration. He had no money to buy deodorant or other essentials like socks and raised his foot above the table to prove the point. Before leaving, I promised to call his girlfriend, to visit his mother, to receive his collect call a week later, and to send him a $20 mail order the next day. As we got up, Chris flashed me his old grin and said, "I know you're gettin' rich off me, Jay, with this book."

The issue of my financial gain bubbled up in several interviews, sometimes at my instigation, sometimes at theirs, and it was always there, simmering beneath the surface. Sometimes I felt like a manipulative, exploitative bastard. It's not just the money. It's also the power, privilege, and prestige this book has brought me. To the Brothers and the Hallway Hangers it has brought nothing outside of the satisfaction that their lives have had passing significance for several thousand college students. Most of them took pleasure in their anonymous notoriety. Some didn't. Mike didn't want to be part of the second edition. He had kept in touch with me in Mississippi. He had also called several times and talked of flying down with Craig. Once, on a trip up north, I showed him the book and gave him a copy. A few months later, I asked him what he thought. "Man, I just flipped through and looked at the stuff about me. I couldn't make any sense of that shit." When I returned to Clarendon Heights to research the revised edition, he said to leave him out of it. "I don't want everyone knowing my business, my personal stuff. I know you change the names and everything, but still." In the end, he relented only as a personal favor to me and because I eventually pushed the right button. Whereas with most of the young men the money I made from the book embarrassed me, this is what Mike respected. He was always railing at me for squandering a university degree to work for a pittance as a community worker. When I said that I needed his input for the revised edition to be a success, Mike came 'round to being included.

Having just spent four years in rural Mississippi, I was sensitive to the issue of "using" the young men for my own ends. In impoverished Holmes County, articles and books were there to be written, but I just could not generate the requisite analytical and social distance to turn my friends there into research subjects. Instead, I helped teenagers do their own fieldwork. Kids much like the Brothers ended up publishing two volumes of oral history interviews. They spent countless hours doing research, honing their questioning techniques, conducting interviews, transcribing tapes, editing their texts, preparing the manuscripts for publication, and promoting their book. Basically, they democratized the research process by converting it from a scholar's lone enterprise into an empowering learning process. Having masterminded this little revolution, I rode north and charged back into Clarendon Heights—as the lone researcher.

In 1983 I had been a youth worker in Clarendon Heights for several years. In 1991, however, I was just breezing through to satisfy my own research agenda. And yet writing this book is a way of giving something back to Clarendon Heights for all it has given to me. By striving to understand the young male world of Clarendon Heights on its own terms and then trying to translate and interpret that world for the wider culture, I like to think I have rendered a service to both. The outlook reflected in *Ain't No Makin' It* grew out of my work in the youth enrichment program. I saw many things on the streets that I could not fathom during those first summers in Clarendon Heights. When I looked closely and tried to suspend the biases, values, and assumptions I had imported from my own rural, white middle-class social world, I was driven to the fairly radical conclusions of this book. And so my political commitment, whether it is played out in Clarendon Heights, Holmes County, or Chesterfield, England, becomes another way of repaying the community for the privileged access it gave me.

Not much of this would wash with the Hallway Hangers. They know I owe them personally, and I was repeatedly asked for loans during the months of fieldwork in 1991. I gave Shorty $10 late one night. The money went straight into Super's pocket. "Thanks, Jay," Shorty said, grinning as he walked away to smoke the crack crystals. In 1983 I wouldn't even buy the Hallway Hangers booze. Now I was subsidizing a far deadlier addiction. I stood there feeling angry, guilty, and confused. That's fieldwork: It generates personal and intellectual satisfaction but also worry, ambiguity, and uncertainty.

I lent money to nearly all of the Hallway Hangers. At the time I knew these were gifts, and evidently they did too. Slick made out well. On the eve of my departure to England, I sold him my beloved '69 Chevrolet Impala with its beautifully rebuilt engine. Slick bought it for $1,300 so basically it was a gift. He paid me $500 in cash and signed a contract to send me the rest in monthly installments. I'm still waiting for the first one.

Many of the young men seemed to appreciate the opportunity to talk about their lives. At the end of a long interview during which the Jack Daniel's flowed freely, I asked Jinks if he had anything else to add.

JINKS: I pretty much said what I gots to say. I hope it helps you out.
JM: I feel really privileged and lucky in a way that from way back people like yourself were willing to take me in, in a way. I mean, I'd worked down here for four years.
JINKS: Uh-huh.
JM: So you knew I wasn't a narc and that I cared about the place, cuz you'd seen me with the kids, but I felt privileged then and even more so now comin' back, cuz I haven't seen people for a long time. And yet people are willing to sit down and talk about fairly personal things. Umm, so I appreciate that.
JINKS: Hey, well, as I say, y'know, there are not too many people out there who you can sit down an' you can get stuff off your chest with. Y'know, a

lot of times you don't want to talk to someone you're spendin' all the time
in the world with. You'd rather talk to someone impartial, someone who
you know it's gonna stay with. Y'know, cuz I keep a lot, I do, I keep a lot
of shit in my system. An' then when the time comes, I let it out. Instead of
letting it out when it comes, when it bothers me, I just absorb it all.

JM: When do you get a chance to talk about it?

JINKS: A lot of times I don't. A lot of times I don't.

Frankie, Shorty, Boo-Boo, and Stoney were also grateful to slip out of their
street front and to speak candidly about their lives.

I was depressed to discover how poorly many of the young men had
fared in the eight years since my original research. The Brothers especially had been shortchanged. Intellectually, this outcome confirmed the
social reproduction thesis of the first edition. Emotionally, I was drained,
disheartened, and disconcerted by their plight. As I listened to the men
relate their experiences, my head was pulled in one direction and my
heart in another. It was bizarre to feel simultaneously dispirited and vin-
dicated by the poor employment prospects of the men, particularly the
Brothers.

The interviews with the Brothers were more difficult for another reason. Whereas the Hallway Hangers had little stake in keeping up appearances, the Brothers' commitment to the American Dream meant that their
relationship with me was more complex. The research relationship between a successful, white university graduate and a struggling, black
high school graduate is inextricably bound up with the phenomena
under analysis: class, race, education, opportunity, and marginality. In a
sense, the subjects are inscribed in the object: The interview itself is a
miniature realization of the broader topic under investigation. Friendship
or not, there was a tendency for the Brothers to want to "look good" in
my eyes and for the book. They may have been disposed, for example, to
distance themselves from the twofold stigmata of race and poverty and to
display their mastery of the dominant discourse of individual achievement. "No, we're not gonna use race and all the rest as an excuse." The
crucial issue is whether their abiding belief in school and their dismissal
of racism were trotted out for me as a white intruder, or whether the
Brothers express these convictions among themselves.[5]

In 1983 I might have suspected that the Brothers' oft-stated belief in
equality of opportunity was a symbolic gloss put on their experience for
my benefit, had I not witnessed the practical outworkings of this belief in
their everyday lives and conversations. Then I could corroborate their
stories by firsthand observation; the new material relies on their word.
Whereas an ethnography based on interviews *and* participant observation
can compare a person's stated attitudes with his behavior, interviews
alone have to be accepted at face value. Because every interview is partly

an exercise in self-justification, then, my heavy reliance on interviews in Part Two is problematic. Lest this admission raise doubts about the data, let me say that I have complete faith in the candor and honesty of the interview material. When I suspected I was being fed less than the truth, I probed the issue and gently pushed the person to come clean. Invariably he did. If I was still unsure, I admitted as much in the text. In discussing Super's account of how the police planted drugs on him, for example, I allow that he "may be portraying his entry into the street economy in the best possible light." I am satisfied with the interview data, but the reader is required to trust my judgment.

To be sure, I was a participant observer as well as an interviewer in 1991. I spent countless hours hanging around with the Hallway Hangers and the Brothers, but often in their households and in neighborhood bars rather than on the streets. I stayed with Steve for a couple of weeks in Clarendon Heights. Given his hard exterior and often thoughtless behavior, I was surprised by his generosity as a host. It did me good to move back into Clarendon Heights, even for such a short time. It's so easy to forget the frustrations of project life: for example, the futility of keeping counters and cupboards clean when you're overrun by cockroaches anyway. One night I was awakened by a clamor in the living room. Steve was shouting, and I heard furniture shifting and things falling to the floor. I jumped out of bed and steeled myself for a fight as I peered through the doorway. There were Steve and his younger brother, hockey sticks in hand, chasing a rat around the room. Steve stunned the animal with a slapshot against the wall, picked it up by the tail, and flung it out the window to the street below. They collapsed in laughter. "Welcome to the Ritz," chortled Steve as I went back to bed. I moved out of Steve's place a few days later, the ever-present prerogative reserved for a researcher rather than a resident.

In late September 1991 I headed for Lincoln, England, to train for the Anglican priesthood. The contrast between Clarendon Heights and Lincoln Cathedral could not be sharper. In a moment of blind faith, I signed a contract with Westview Press to finish the revised edition by March 1992. I stole away from the library, lecture hall, and college chapel to transcribe the interviews and then to wrestle with 800 pages of transcripts and field notes that refused to be reduced to three new chapters. My wife, Sally Asher, and I devised all sorts of schemes to come to grips with the data. I highlighted the interviews using a complex color-coded scheme. Sally created a one-page index on each youth with crucial information. I developed intricate outlines, made reams of notes, created subject indexes, and distilled whole interviews down to a single sheet of paper. Reading the texts of the chapters now, I find it all seems so simple and straightforward. It wasn't.

Still struggling as 1993 loomed, I asked the Bishop of Derby to postpone my ordination so that I could go home and finish the book that summer. I lived with my parents and commuted to Dartmouth College's library. Suddenly surrounded by more than theological tomes, I read far too widely and intensely. Important discoveries were the works of Philippe Bourgois and Loïc Wacquant. In addition, I gained access to census data for Clarendon Heights and the surrounding city. I agonized over how to present the new material, made several false starts, and went back to England to start my ministerial post in Chesterfield less than half finished with the book.

This past year and a half has been crazy. Immersed in a poor parish in a declining mining and industrial town, I met plenty of indigenous hallway hangers. I began working with disaffected teenagers in addition to my full regimen of visiting, counseling, praying, funerals, baptisms, and Sunday services. But still I had the unfinished manuscript hanging over my head. I snatched bits of time in between my ministerial duties to work on it. My sermons began to sound like sociology essays and the book began to preach. Meanwhile, the patience of Dean Birkenkamp, my Westview editor, was wearing thin. I also wore out friends within and without the ranks of academia with drafts of chapters for their comments. Now, finally, with 1995 upon us, I print this file for what I trust is the last time.

I hope this book does justice to the young lives of the Brothers and the Hallway Hangers. I hope it provokes further study and sparks a critical attitude toward the American socioeconomic system. Most of all, I hope it spurs readers to struggle for a society that doesn't trample on the aspirations of its people.

Notes

1. William Foote Whyte, *Street Corner Society* (Chicago: University of Chicago Press, 1943), p. 279.

2. Ibid.

3. Elijah Anderson, *A Place on the Corner* (Chicago: University of Chicago Press, 1978).

4. Whyte, *Street Corner Society*, p. 304.

5. I am indebted to Loïc Wacquant for making these points in correspondence with me.

4 ~ઌ

Introduction to Chapter 4

Almost all fieldworkers complain of loneliness and isolation. Ethnographic research taxes the soul. It requires one to forge new paths with strangers. In the beginning, one is virtually always ill at ease; fieldworkers complain of feeling unsure of the pathway and long for the intellectual and social companionship that some are able to share with spouses and children but rarely with a collaborator or colleague.

Janet Theophano and Karen Curtis broke with tradition. They worked as part of a research team studying the relationship between food and ethnicity in an Italian-American community. Theophano, a doctoral student in folklore at the University of Pennsylvania, had experience doing ethnographic work in another Italian-American community. Curtis, a doctoral student in anthropology at Temple University, had previously lived in the community under study and had contacts among the Italian-Americans who lived there.

Previous research by social scientists on the relationship between food and ethnicity put forward a view that there was a stable and direct relationship between the two. Focusing on a single item of food, such as the use of matzoh ball soup among Jews or of spaghetti and meatballs among Italians, these earlier researchers assumed that food use among particular groups remained stable over time and was, in fact, resistant to change. Theophano and Curtis began with a more differentiated view of food and its use by the women with whom they worked. For one thing, rather than looking at a single food item, they looked at the entire system of food use in the community. Additionally, they examined the ways in which the women, both within a single age group and across generations, established and maintained relationships through the use of food. In so doing, they accounted for continuity and stability in the food system while at the same time noting the innovations that brought about cultural change.

Rather than split up the four families that were going to be the focus of the study, they decided instead to study all four together, going to the homes on alternate days, writing duplicate copies of their field notes using carbon paper (in the days before easy availability of copy machines) and sharing them with each other. Thus, they were able to bring their different perspectives and identities to the project and to enhance each other's insights and understandings. Their joint work created a deep and lasting friendship between them. They talked for hours while in the field about the families and what they were learning. In the process, they helped each other through this unknown professional rite of passage. As a result, their team approach solved some common problems in ethnographic work. However, it created other difficulties.

Theophano, married and with a twelve-year-old son, was treated differently by family members than Curtis, who was unmarried. (Some fairly mundane yet puzzling behavior occurred. For example, Curtis was served elaborate dishes; Theophano got leftovers.) By contrasting the ways in which the women they studied interacted with them, they were able to gain more insight into women's roles than either could have acquired alone. They had not anticipated the relationship between marital status, guest status, and food preparation; thus, their research demonstrates the benefit of having collaboration between researchers from different as well as similar backgrounds. It also shows the serendipitous nature of field research, the ways in which a study can take unexpected turns and be refocused by unanticipated factors.

Despite learning more about the families working as a team than they would have individually, their team research experience also engendered unexpected difficulties. Most researchers experience the emotional turbulence of fieldwork alone. In team work, sibling-like rivalry can erupt. In the following chapter, Theophano and Curtis discuss the strong emotions they experienced toward each other, their informants, and the work itself. For example, during the course of the study, one of the women discussed some issues with Theophano and specifically asked that she not share them with Curtis. Theophano was placed in the position of deciding between her loyalty to her research colleague and her pledge of confidentiality to her informant. Such clashes are inevitable in a team approach to ethnographic work; individuals will forge different relationships with persons in the field. Jealousy, spoken or unspoken, will emerge.

As Theophano and Curtis show, other problems arose in regard to the work itself. Because their study focused on food, they found themselves eating different sorts of food and larger quantities of it than they ordinarily would have in their everyday lives. The weight they gained was an unanticipated consequence of their research. They would sometimes dread going to their research settings, facing yet another meal and many more calories.

Also affecting the congenial collaborative nature of the project was the requirement that they each produce a unique piece of research and analysis. The conduct of independent research and the writing of a dissertation serve as a rite of passage into the cloistered world of academia. In the face of concerns raised by faculty advisors regarding this issue, they struggled to maintain a piece of the project that was their own. Thus, another probable tension in any collaborative relationship concerns the meaning of "original research" for a doctoral thesis for which so much data collection and thinking are woven together.

In the chapter that follows, written expressly for this volume and long after the original fieldwork, Theophano and Curtis provide a frank and compelling account of the complicated nature of doing collaborative research. Their intensive work led to strong bonds with some of the women involved in the study—bonds that have continued now for fifteen years. As such, these women have become more than just informants and objects of study; they are now friends, almost kin. Although this does not always happen in field research, it is often yet another of the consequences of being involved so intimately in the lives of others.

Reflections on a Tale Told Twice

JANET THEOPHANO AND KAREN CURTIS

The format of this chapter is unusual in that we address each other rather than you, the reader. We chose this format in part because it follows the pattern of our shared field work notes, which we wrote to each other, and in part because we came to understand our experience more fully through the dialogue.

Who's Who?

Janet

As I begin writing about our fieldwork experiences now I encounter some of the difficulties I had while we were doing the fieldwork years ago. I try to imagine how we will weave together our separate and distinct voices to create a single, blended one. This was the crux of the issue for the two of us: How were we to combine our perspectives to create a unified vision of the culture and community yet maintain our distinct identities? And yet why did we feel the need to create a unified vision of the community? As young researchers we were struggling to find and develop our unique voices. In time, the differences between us would help us to learn more about the community. Yet maintaining our individual perspectives was important for another reason as well: We each needed to develop an idea independently and write it up as our final task in our passage from novices to full-fledged members of the academy. After all, this, too, was part of our goal.

We had been colleagues for five years in the earlier phase of the food study and were graduate students nearing completion of our coursework for the Ph.D. You were in urban anthropology; I was studying folklore. We had both interviewed families, you in Maryton, I in Westfield. At the time of this research project, you were an unmarried woman with no children. I was married with one child. This status distinction was later to prove useful in the field. It helped us to learn more and understand the ways in which women's domains of activity were not only gendered but ranked. We saw the ethnographic phase of the research upon which we were about to embark as an opportunity both to collect data for the team project and a means to fund our individual dissertation research. The research was supported by the Russell Sage Foundation, and as doctoral students we were going to work with a world renowned anthropologist. Since we were both ethnographers it was a perfect arrangement. Well, not *quite* perfect.

The Project

Karen

I had lived in Maryton for several years prior to this phase of the research and had become friends with a prominent woman in the community, Marcella Fiore. Largely through her efforts, we were able to stay with several families (in addition to Marcella's) during this period of research. We participated in and observed a wide gamut of domestic interaction: shopping, cooking activity, meals, clean-up, visiting, and other exchange and gift-giving occurrences. We also had the opportunity to help prepare for and to observe occasions such as holidays and life-cycle events.

Originally conceived of as an interdisciplinary effort to study a food system comprehensively, the research had earlier included interviews, geographic surveys, participant recorded information, demographic analysis, life histories, and a biomedical substudy. In addition to conducting interviews, each of us had been involved in carrying out several of the other methodologies.

The first and final months of our research were in Marcella Fiore's home. At the time, she was recently separated from her husband; her household consisted of herself and two of her three daughters. However, she was often visited by her third daughter and grandson, and not infrequently by her large family and friendship network. Marcella was a member of an entrepreneurial family whose social and business ties were vast. Her job as information broker for a local government agency—staffing a county information center, a position gained through political ties—strengthened and widened her unusually large network. Not the least of her talents is her expertise in the kitchen and her deserved reputation for generosity and hospitality. Her prominence in the social and political life of the community is based on her history in the community and her continued involvement in both daily and festive food exchange and negotiation.

We were eager to regularly participate in daily and ritual life in this community. Our earlier work had left us with gaps in our understanding of the role food played in demonstrating ethnicity. Interviews provided us with general patterns and ideal conceptions of the food system, but diaries and record keeping seemed to diverge almost totally from the patterns derived from the interviews. And though we were looking forward to working together, our independent needs created tensions between us that in retrospect could have impeded our fieldwork.

Our relationship with the principal investigator on the project was the source of some of this tension. Paradoxically, she promoted the goals of team research to us while regularly warning us about the dangers of shared data and joint interpretation.

The Differences Between Us

Karen

Not only was there tension between the principal investigator and us, but you and I were experiencing discomfort because of our different styles and temperaments. We approached this task from seemingly divergent vantage points: ethnicity, religion, familial and personal history, personality, familiarity with the community, communicative style, and disciplinary/theoretical emphases. I am of northern European Protestant heritage; you are the child of German and Czech Jews who left their homelands during World War II. My three brothers and I grew up in many different U.S. communities, and our parents divorced when I was a young adult. You were born in England and grew up in various sections of Philadelphia, as the only child of a widow several times over. I had lived in Italy and worked in Maryton and was familiar with the community. You had lived and worked in Westfield. I tend to be quiet, especially at first, whereas you are gregarious and outgoing. At the time, my studies had emphasized social science perspectives on urban problems and your work centered on symbolic and interactional approaches.

Potential Sources of Conflict

Janet

We had been cautioned by the principal investigator to be sure that portions of our work remain distinct and identifiable as belonging to one or the other of us. After all, if we were going to write our dissertations from the jointly collected data, we had to be certain that our individual work did not overlap. The hallmark of a thesis is that it is a piece of original research. Careful, girls! It's pretty hard not to duplicate one another's work when you are sharing every thought with a coworker. It's tough to be a team player when you are trying to carve out a niche for yourself in an environment that does not permit, let alone encourage, teamwork. With this tension we proceeded to plan and to work as collaborators. Hence one of our dilemmas: how to continue to work as a team while preserving some aspect of our work as idiosyncratic—mine and yours. After all, someone had to "own" these data.

Teamwork may be touted as an excellent way to accomplish objectives, but it is unacceptable as a way to be recognized and rewarded in the Academy. Traditional knowledge is encapsulated in bounded domains called disciplines, and the work that is acceptable to these rather conservative fields of knowledge is work that is done *alone*.

Did this affect the way in which we approached our task? One might expect that this would have engendered very different renderings of the same situations—in order to preserve our unique way of looking and interpreting. In fact, the opposite seems to have happened. Instead of hoarding our data or withholding some information for ourselves we wrote both to ourselves and our individual theses and to each other and our cooperative effort. Why did we do that?

Ultimately I suppose we aligned with each other—seeing the Academy as the Other, the institution we were both struggling to be accepted into. At some level, this may have prompted a wish to reduce the tension we felt as we dealt with the task of teamwork in a situation that required a singular rite of passage.

There were other potential sources of conflict as well. Other human desires and needs were called out in the field. We were jealous of one another and competitive. We wanted to be liked but more than that. Each of us wanted to be the favorite. I was afraid that you would be closer to the families than I because you had lived in Maryton. Worse, sometimes I felt myself an outsider altogether. You never seemed aware of my anxiety. I never told you. You seemed above all my petty concerns.

From the beginning, you were much more familiar with the first family with whom we stayed. We began with Marcella Fiore, a neighbor of yours during the time you lived in Maryton, whom you had interviewed in the earlier phase of the research. Marcella was your friend and contact. I had met her only once and briefly before we began our work. I felt that I could not become as close to her as you were; this made me feel a little uncomfortable. I also was not as familiar with the town as you and here again felt at a loss. Had we worked in a community with which I was familiar I may not have felt as ill-prepared as I did working in "your" community. Perhaps this was "your tribe" and I the interloper. This conflict had occurred even among prominent anthropologists.

I have to wonder whether the tension we were experiencing was also felt by the families with whom we worked. It is conceivable that they felt and understood our need to be recognized as equals. They must have responded to that. Their constant reference to both of us, even if the other was not there, must have been their signal that there would be parity. They also monitored us to be sure we were sharing information. If you asked for the ingredients of a dish you were served on Sunday (your day in the field) and the dish had been made on Saturday (my day) they would say, "Janet had written it."

We were treated as equals by the families—given the same foods (more or less), told the same stories, and invited to the same events. These acts of equity assuaged the anxiety that one of us was privy to more. I realize now that parity is an important value in this community; and in their efforts to treat us impartially, to give us the same food, invite us to the same parties, the women also told us the same stories. On alternate days, the days on which one of us was in the field, the same story told to the other the day before would be told again. Clearly it was not simply our construction, independently and jointly produced; it was their rendering of the events twice, once to each of us, that also served to help both of us describe an event in the same way.

The women with whom we worked, with one important exception, wouldn't play favorites. Everywhere we went it was made clear we were "the girls." Undifferentiated, we eventually were named KarenJanet or JanetKaren making clear our equivalency, our total undifferentiatedness. Like it or not we were leveled, equalized; we were one person.

Our early fear of rejection in favor of the other was soon dispelled. In its place was near annihilation and invisibility as individuals. Or so we thought. One thing is clear: The women with whom we worked repeatedly made efforts to treat us impartially—despite the differences in our status and roles, despite the difference in our personalities. And together we constructed a vision of this community without conflict about what we saw.

A Shared Vision: How We Did It

Janet

In order to share our data and to work not simply as two individuals in the field but as a tightly knit precision drill team we decided to write field notes *in duplicate* (this was in the days before lap tops and even affordable computers or accessible copiers) with carbon paper. You handwrote your notes; I typed mine. Here is an entry from your field notes on day one at Marcella's:

> I got there at 8:00 AM—Marcella said 'I haven't even washed my face yet'. Marcella left for work at 9 AM (she is supposed to be there at 9:00) walks to work (about 4 blocks).

Through your parenthetical notes on the first page, you taught me about the details of Marcella's life—that she was supposed to be at work by nine o'clock and that her office was four blocks away. These were details with which you were familiar from your residency in Maryton and I was not. Perhaps you were not writing them for me at all, perhaps they were only memory prods. Aside from the parenthetical notes, the tone of our field notes is rather similar—almost as if we began in a single voice. Is that possible? From my field notes on the same day January 2:

> Arrived at Marcella's at 8:15. Karen was already here having coffee. We sat around til about 8:50. Marcella had her usual breakfast, cleaning and cleaning and preparing for us while she talked. As she was dressing to leave, Jill [her youngest daughter] came down, a towel wrapped around her head and in her bathrobe. She had a small glass of o.j. and a cigarette. We talked. . . . Karen and I worked until Marcella came home at 11:50.

My first day's notes are much more brief than yours. This may have been because I was still unfamiliar with the place and the people. I could not figure out what to focus on, so I focused on the food. My field notes are broken into eating events and not much more. In contrast, you wrote nine pages including substantial background information, such as the times at which members of the family had to be at work and who was related to whom. You recounted every detail to help me learn. Soon you would not bother with these asides; it would be expected that I was also familiar with the schedules and rhythms of the women's everyday lives.

Slowly I began adding to the collection of "raw" descriptive data my own embellished observations and comments on what was happening in the household. Over the next week, the amount of detail in our field notes varied. I began incorporating details about the weather, clothing, and other textural features of daily life, thereby adding a dimension that you omitted. By January 9 my field notes are richer and replete with their own parenthetical asides. For example, neither of us accepted or liked Robert, the fiancé of Marcella's oldest daughter, Roxanne. He often made comments that were, by our standards, rude and inappropriate. Marcella was hurt by them. Because you and I shared this feeling, we would comment to one another about the outrageousness of his remarks, usually marking these comments within parentheses to be clear that these asides were off the record.

The following is an excerpt from my field notes of January 8, in which I am describing Robert's malevolent and ungracious behavior toward Marcella, about whom we were soon very protective, and the meal she had prepared for him and Roxanne.

> Robert came in around 5:00 PM. First thing he said was he didn't like the salad. Marcella asked him if he wanted regular lettuce. "No," he said. "I just wanted to let you know for next time.". . . Then Marcella served him stew from the stove. Roxanne asked him if he liked it. "It's allright," he said. He had wanted fried chicken. When Marcella told him that Jill had made the meatloaf he said, "Ugh!" He looked at the trifle which Marcella had prepared. (He didn't eat it.) (Karen—I can't go on with this. Robert "acted"/pretended he was angry. He looked at it in mock disgust. But in truth he couldn't eat it.)

From the same day's notes I see that I have begun to incorporate my opinions and beliefs about their behavior and assume a familiarity with it that was premature and unsubstantiated.

> I took Marcella to Bingo where *I am sure* (emphasis added) she ate more cakes.

Equity

Karen

We created a shared vision of the community through the discourse carried out in our field notes, which we wrote to and for each other. In addition to reporting on a day's events and what we were told about previous days and future plans, we used the field notes to propose and discuss points of analysis. This is remarkable not only because of our divergent backgrounds and the cautions about shared data expressed by the project leader but also because at the time (1970–1980) there was only a meager literature on fieldwork of any sort to guide our efforts. However, there were instances when one of us had information that the other did not, and particularly in the first months of fieldwork, we were careful to convey in our notes that each of us was "carrying her weight" and that we each brought special talents and experience to our team effort.

We were helped in the construction of a shared vision by the women and their impartial treatment of us. The practice of the "twice-told tale"—conveyed to each of us in turn—was explicitly recognized by community members. I have noted numerous occasions when a family member asked me whether you had told me about something that had occurred when I was not present or began a report to you with the assurance that I had been told previously.

Later, in the last weeks of fieldwork, the principle of equitable treatment was extended and demonstrated through task assignment and in conversation. In March we returned to Marcella's home and began to play a more active role in preparing for her daughter's bridal shower and wedding. During this time we were less observers than participants—it was assumed that we would take on many responsibilities for shopping, cooking, cleaning, doing errands, and other needed tasks. Fulfilling this obligation meant many fieldwork days that did not end until 11 P.M. or midnight. We were now members of Marcella's female social network, making decisions about and carrying out the ritual activities central to the community's social life.

This connection was based in part on our several months of continual association, in part on affection, and in part on the seemingly overwhelming preparation necessary to "produce" such an event as a large wedding. Marcella noted this change in status in a conversation with a neighbor: "They were only supposed to be here for meals and then leave but they like me so much that they stay and help me." She also changed the regular seating arrangement and had each of us sit next to her (where one of her daughters or her grandson usually sat), rather than across from her or at the foot of the table as we had in earlier months.

We were assigned the same tasks on a list of "things to do before the wedding" and seen as a resource in organizing time and personnel in preparation for the celebratory events. This list was sometimes referred to in lieu of the "twice-told" instructions and thus served as an additional source for our joint interpretation of community life. Marcella referred to us collectively as "my girls" and in direct conversation as KarenJanet (when speaking to you) or JanetKaren (when speaking to me), thus giving priority to the absent party, merging our identities and seeing us as one interchangeable person. We are still referred to this way in Marcella's home. The melding is now so complete that when I was visiting Marcella recently, one of her daughters—the one who was not living at home during the fieldwork period—reported to someone who called that JanetKaren/KarenJanet was there and when asked, "which one?" did not know "which one" I was. While visiting a couple of years earlier, I was queried by the same daughter about the details of Jewish holiday observance, with the presumption that you and I, whom she saw as one person, shared your religious tradition.

At the outset, we realized that our differing statuses and responsibilities would affect the ease or difficulty of accomplishing fieldwork. We were unaware of how these differences would become integral to our interaction in the community. These differences became a vehicle for learning about the definitions of gender roles and domains in the community. We devised a schedule for fieldwork in which our time spent in the community was shared. We alternated days, shared field notes, and participated jointly in festive events. We became aware of the different conceptions we as researchers and they as participants held initially through the ways in which food and particular types of foods were offered to each of us. We might not have discovered the importance with which the community viewed our contrasting statuses had we not been focused on food-related activity and women's domains.

Early in our research, a puzzling situation emerged as we alternated field days in Marcella's home. I was consistently offered freshly prepared foods as the main course for the meals I shared with Marcella and her family, whereas you more often shared leftovers from previous meals. This disparity in the kinds of foods we were offered contradicted a verbal commitment to impartiality—that we would taste the same foods and be treated equitably. Through questioning and observation, we discovered that because you were identified through maternal status, you were expected to eat the leftover foods that mothers eat; in contrast, I was seen as a daughter and provided with newly prepared foods at each meal.

Have Child, Will Travel

Janet

My role as wife and mother of a twelve-year-old boy did nothing if not complicate my life in the field and the frequent meals I was expected to eat. I would go to dinner at one of the family's houses and then rush home to prepare and eat dinner with my own family. This I did so as not to disrupt the patterns of my family life and the important role I accorded to families' eating together. So every other night I would eat two or more evening meals. The written accounts of doing fieldwork close to home rarely describe the difficulties of balancing work and family when work demands all of your time. My husband, an accountant, was not willing or able to re-arrange his demanding schedule to become the primary caretaker of our son. His busy season coincided with the months we were in the field.

My son, Damien, was too old to be with me constantly and too young to be on his own, so I would bring him with me whenever I could or had to. I remember one evening a severe thunderstorm darkened the sky and crackled with light and sound; I needed to go to Maryton for dinner. Damien did not want me to leave. So I brought him along.

I had to do this often. However, it was a useful way to learn more about child care and child socialization in the community of Maryton, and the women welcomed my son into their homes. They fed and cared for him and worried about him and my husband. My son enjoyed these visits to their homes, savoring the delicious cooking and the fuss they made over him. He'd bring along some homework or watch TV while I observed and questioned. A quiet child, he was rarely impatient and did not dis-tract me. The women commented on how well behaved he was. The boys in the Fiore and Felice families actually looked forward to his visits. Often, I would discuss my concerns about Damien's progress in school and his interest in getting a motorbike (about which I disapproved) with these mothers. My expressed worries led to conversations about raising boys and raising girls, the differences between them and the rewards and difficulties of each. Damien's eating peculiarities even affected Marcella's cooking. A budding vegetarian, he declined to eat red meat. She began making turkey in place of the traditional beef meatballs when Damien was coming for dinner.

Most often the mothers worried about who was feeding my family while I was "watching them eat." This created some tension for me in my roles as competent fieldworker and good mother. I felt judged. I thought I was being criticized by the women because I was not a good mother and I worried about whether you felt I was holding up my end of our collabora-tion by bringing Damien along. I reassured the women that when I left after their dinner (anywhere between 7:30 and 9:30 most evenings) I went home and cooked for my husband and my son. Often, I would prepare some food earlier in the day, return home to heat it up and eat with my son and perhaps again when his father returned at the end of his long day.

Maybe the women did judge, but they also tried to help me. This pre-cipitated their gifts of food and leftovers. To ensure that my burden would be lightened, they often sent me on my way with packages of food for my family. I worried that this might be too much of an expense for them. None of the families we stayed with could afford to be so generous although they were remarkably so.

You also received gifts of food and care packages. Yet these presents represented a different kind of concern and nurturing. Because you were not married and had no children you had the status of "child," a not fully mature member of the community. They thought you needed care. And they gave it to you. Both of us received gifts because we had become fictive members of the family and also so as not to show partiality in treatment; each of us benefited from their generosity and concern. But the benevolence had different meanings. We learned this because of our differential status. Mothers ate leftovers. Children were not expected to. I learned this only after feeling for some time that you were being given the best and freshest food while I was fed leftovers from the day before.

I read your field notes day after day and not unlike sibling rivalry, I imagined that the women we were observing liked you better than me. That's why you got the best food, I thought. You would write about the fresh cold-cut sandwiches you were served on your days in the field; in contrast, my lunches consisted of leftover salad and last night's dinner. One day, while I was having lunch with Marcella, her youngest daughter, Jill, stopped by for something to eat. Immediately Marcella got up from the table and began preparing her daughter a sandwich of freshly made foods. Something clicked. Comparing their treatment of you with their daughters and mine with the other married women, we realized that it was not our personalities that distinguished us but our statuses as women. They did like me, after all. But I was expected to behave differently from you. This was an important revelation. You had the status of a child and needed care; I had the status of a married woman and needed support. It was this difference between us that resulted in a fuller and deeper view of women's lives, roles, and statuses and the meanings these held for them. With two of us in the field and my son tagging along occasionally, we were able to discover a more complete picture of women's roles. We developed an understanding of the phases of women's lives and expectations about appropriate gender behavior within the community. Neither of us could have learned that alone.

An Ethical Dilemma and Near Crisis

Janet

There were other indications of this status distinction including the secret of marital conflict I was asked to keep from you during our month with Anne and the Cooper family. February was a difficult month; it was the month we spent with Anne and her family. It proved to be the most difficult month of fieldwork. I developed a friendship easily with Anne. You did not. Marital discord in the family, which Anne asked me to keep a secret from you, created more tension between us. I felt that I was ethically bound not to disclose anything my informant wanted private. Yet I was torn between my loyalty to you and our shared project and Anne's right to privacy. Anne was worried that your friendship with Marcella might affect your ability to keep this secret. Above all, she was afraid to reveal to you, a "child," (this is a direct quote of Anne's from my notes) some of the realities of marriage. I kept several weeks of field notes, written in duplicate as were the others, and I did not give them to you until I was given permission to reveal the story. I told you in my field notes only that there was something I could not tell you and that I was withholding the notes until I was permitted to disclose the secret. You responded without overt emotion. You only recently told me that you had been upset and deeply hurt by this and had kept an entire set of field notes from me during this time as well. Retaliation? I wouldn't blame you. I don't know if I would have ever shared those notes with you if Anne had not consented. We managed somehow to continue our collaboration during this superficially collegial period. I don't know how. With this blatant exception, which was not a variant of a story told to us but a glaring omission of the premise that all stories would be told twice in the same way, a near crisis in trust had been created and averted.

How I Felt

Karen

I had not previously met Anne and knew her only as Jerry's mother. Marcella's youngest daughter, Jill, had dated Jerry throughout high school and would later marry him. The differences in our personality styles—you outgoing and me quiet—and Anne's more fixed view of appropriate gender roles and consequent evaluation of my life-style as deficient made you more comfortable (than me) in this household. You took the lead and became the "filter" through which we created a joint interpretation. I knew or had network connections to the other two families who participated in our study, the Weavers and the Felices. However, by this point, we had each been the "leader" in one household and were equalized in our roles as researchers although the status distinctions remained.

Anne Cooper's position in the community is different than Marcella's. Anne's focus is on familial ties rather than on an extensive friendship network. And unlike Marcella, she suffered in her youth the insecurities of poverty and segregation in common with many Italian immigrants to Maryton. The youngest of four siblings, she married a non-Italian, as had her sister. Anne lived a few blocks from Marcella's house with her daughter and younger son. Her eldest son had married and lived nearby with his wife and daughter, who were frequent visitors in her home. Although Anne had separated from her husband a number of years earlier, her children all worked in her husband's family auto and truck repair business. It is through her friendship with Marcella that Anne participates in many community activities, for she limits her own social sphere to her immediate and extended family and a few friends.

In January, in Marcella's home, I was on very familiar ground. I had known Marcella for five years, had been in her home many times, and had met many of the members of her family and friendship network. I was familiar with Maryton's history of chain migration from a town in Calabria, had collected Marcella's family history, and had begun to trace her social network. You were new to this situation, and I now see how I emphasized this difference between us in our field notes, by giving you explicit prompts (and even corrections on network ties and community activities). When we moved to Anne Cooper's home in February, I was less comfortable.

I felt like the newcomer, and if you worried that "they" didn't like you in Marcella's household, I was sure that the Coopers didn't like me. In this household my experiences in Maryton and Italy were not an advantage. Almost from the beginning of the month, and even while we were still at Marcella's, you and Anne were friendly. Since I had not known her before, I was quiet as I am in new situations, and perhaps Anne saw me as aloof. As I reread our field notes for that month, some of the feelings I experienced at that time welled up again. I felt excluded by Anne and you and inadequate in Anne's eyes.

As we both knew by the end of the month, Anne had been sharing confidences with you about a family crisis, and you, at her request, did not share that information with me, either in your field notes or in conversation at the time. You were treated differently in other ways as well. I see from your notes a number of times when you, Anne, and Anne's daughter engaged in playful behavior—joking, dancing, trying on clothes— which were not experiences I shared in. They were much more serious with me. Anne's son, perhaps because of his relationship with Marcella's daughter, joked and was more friendly. Many of Anne's conversations with you were about current affiliations, plans, and activities, whereas those she had with me were oriented toward the past and focused on her experiences as the child of immigrants.

While we were at Marcella's, you typed your field notes with a carbon copy to me, and I handwrote mine with a carbon copy to you. We exchanged them several times a week, a practice demonstrated by our regular comments on each other's notes. In the Cooper household, your field notes were handwritten, and, although we continued alternate fieldwork days, I received photocopies of your notes irregularly during the first weeks of the month, which contributed to my sense of exclusion. Not until the third week did you resume our earlier practice of recording and exchange.

In the following week, the family situation that had been troubling Anne all month came to a crisis. I was told of it then because I had been at the house at a critical time. At that point, I wrote several pages of "confidential" field notes and noted that Anne told me you already knew all of this but that she hadn't told me because I was "such good friends with Marcella," a clear statement of the double alliance structure—you and Anne on one hand and Marcella and I on the other. Marcella and Anne regularly compared their bodies, their homes, their marriages, their children and grandchildren, and their preferences in an ongoing but contained competition. Despite the crisis and the strained allegiances to Marcella's and Anne's families (the situation involved a member of each household), I was relieved to learn that at least some of the exclusion and distance I felt was due to perceptions about my relationship with Marcella rather than my personality and status.

In reaction to your withholding of information, I did not share my "confidential" field notes with you. I was also protecting the privacy of the participants (as were you) since I did not know who might read our "regular" field notes. Neither of us refers to these events in our field notes until several weeks later, and those allusions are in "shorthand." However, in the aftermath of this crisis situation, we both explicitly wrote to each other in our field notes, commenting on confusing sequences of events, participant explanations of the purpose of fieldwork, and analytic concepts, perhaps in an attempt to reactivate the bond between us. This was noticed by at least one member of the Cooper household (Anne's son) who repeatedly asked me whether you had "told me" about his trip to another state. You had. However, your relationship with Anne continued to be more intimate than mine; for example, about a month later, in field notes from a brief visit with Anne, you wrote, "We talked about Marcella's daughter's wedding [which would take place in the next month] and some other things which I cannot tell about yet. When I can I will." It seems to me that this statement acknowledges the strain created by the earlier lack of communication as well as the ongoing difference in our relationships with Anne.

Reconciliation

Karen

It was a relief to move on to the Felice household, where I was once again known from my earlier residence in Maryton. Bernadette and Thomas treated us differently but not unequally. There was more overt recognition of and conversation about the differences between us in this household, but there were also shared perceptions and aspirations and we were, over time, assigned jointly to the role of member of the extended female network.

The Felice family, unlike any of the others, had come to Maryton only after their marriage. They were raised in other Italian neighborhoods in the metropolitan area. Bernadette and Thomas, their three teenaged children, and an exchange student lived in another section of Maryton, near one of Marcella's brothers, apart from the rest of the Italian-American community. Although Thomas, the proprietor of an auto repair business, had developed a local business network, the Felices remained conspicuously peripheral to the social life of the community. Because male and female roles are so sharply defined in this household, the sharing of domestic responsibilities was not possible and prevented Bernadette's participation in a full-time professional life (for which she had trained). We had many conversations about the lack of fit between our behavior and aspirations and the gender roles expected by Thomas and to a lesser extent Bernadette.

Bernadette talked frequently with both of us concerning her ambivalence about her family responsibilities, although she shared some specific complaints (and satisfactions) about childrearing with you as the mother of a son close in age to her own son. Thomas chided both of us about our professional aspirations, which he saw as inappropriate, although his eldest daughter shared such aspirations (and later became a lawyer). Bernadette often asked me questions about the social life of long-term Italian-American Maryton residents with whom I was acquainted, including the other households in our study. During our second week with the Felices, she said "I wish I had grown up in Maryton. Everyone knows everyone else and is related. It's friendly." This was contrasted with her own family's circumstances of residential separation from close relatives.

Because we were closer in age to Bernadette and Thomas than we were to either Marcella or Anne, we shared generational cohort experiences with them, in contrast to the first two homes where we fell in between the householder and children's generational cohorts. This is not to say that we and the Felices agreed about the meaning and desirability of our generation's experiences, but that they linked us to each other and were a common topic of conversation and sometimes joking. We were also seen as somewhat "ethnic" and therefore similar to them, although in my case, through experience rather than birth. Your heritage as a European Jew married to a Greek-American and (to a lesser extent) my experiences in Italy and Maryton were viewed as providing a connection.

For several reasons, the bond between you and me was strengthened during our experience with this family. We were similar to each other but different from the family members in our class, education, religion, and status as researchers. Class differences were discussed openly, and the benefits of higher education were often questioned. Although you and I did not share religious traditions, we were clearly not informed about the details of practicing Catholicism. The research was also taken much more seriously in this household, as indicated by meticulous meal preparation, intake, and shopping record keeping in our absence. In the final analysis, we were treated as known, familiar with the community, and as a team.

The Struggles We Shared

Janet

The bond between us was strengthened by some of the struggles we shared. Several issues became problems in our ongoing relationships with our informants and the fieldwork: differing conceptions of appropriate gender activity and behavior; overt sexism and racism expressed in our presence; our own muddled attempts to deal with subjectivity and objectivity in our field notes; and our continuing battle against weight gain.

I've already said how I worried about the women's feelings about me as a mother. We both realized that our status as professional women was not salient or prestigious in this community, but worse, any deviation from their view of appropriate female comportment made us ill at ease and made the fieldwork more difficult. As the study progressed, we focused on the ways in which we (as ethnographers, as middle-class "professional" women) differed from the women we were studying. We commented on the overt and covert sexism and racism in their talk. This brought us together.

Karen

We were engaged in an activity—research—that was very different from any of the jobs held or careers aspired to by any family member, male or female, in our study households. Our discomfort with the divergent views of race and of gender roles held by most members of the community increased. We were also increasingly pressured by our attempts to combine research and personal lives, particularly because of expectations by the first two study households that we would visit regularly. At this point, there were a number of occasions when after, or in the middle of, a day of fieldwork in the Felice household, we would spend time in one of the other study households assisting in planning, shopping, and preparing for a special event. We began to "talk" to each other more directly in the field notes by recording the multiple and competing responsibilities of our personal and professional lives. We became more intimate and had many discussions about the dilemmas we faced in our personal lives—especially those related to gender roles and expectations. I see our first few weeks in the Felice household as the point at or by which we viewed ourselves as connected both personally and professionally. Out of this connection we developed our shared interpretation of social life in the community.

In this community a woman is expected to marry and have children. Single adulthood is seen as a time of transition, preparatory to fulfilling this obligation. Professional aspirations, if any, are secondary to the central responsibilities of marriage and family life. Despite our contrasting marital and parental statuses, as graduate students pursuing professional status, we did not share this view of women's roles. Thus, our initial relationships were based in part on the contrast between their and our perceptions of appropriate gender roles, and this difference strengthened the bond between you and me. We were also different from the community in ethnicity, religion, class, and education. In combination, I believe that these distinctions between us as researchers and the community contributed to the creation of a joint fieldwork identity.

Janet

Acknowledging that there were aspects of our informants' values that we did not like raised issues of objectivity for us, as did the way we each used language in our field notes. In my notes, I refer to myself in the first person. This was actually consistent with my style as a fieldworker. I spoke more, expressed opinions, and later regretted that I had not listened more carefully. I wished sometimes that I were more like you. Silent.

In your notes, you and I are referred to in the third person. "Marcella went back to work at 1:05. Karen and Janet left." Later you wrote, "I (KC) watched Marcella fixing meatloaf." Perhaps you were not sure who would be reading the field notes and so you identified yourself for the potential audience—in this case, perhaps the principal investigator of the project. Even if this is something one would not want to trust to memory I don't think you wrote this for me; I would know that I had not written the notes by the handwriting, which was, obviously, not my own. Or were you objectifying yourself and me as was expected then of a social scientist? Were you positioning yourself and me to be a mirror or windowpane through which we could both view the culture clearly? How much did our different disciplinary training subtly influence and change the other's perceptions?

Karen

I was not sure who would read the field notes (aside from you and me). The principal investigator and the project funders had emphasized that a high level of specificity in recording eating and preparation activities was expected, and I think that I was more intimidated by their direction than you were; my early field notes reflect this. I was also influenced by graduate training, which called for a separation of self from experience in the name of objectivity. During fieldwork, however, while trying to understand "the community," I became more reflexive and less interested in objectivity or even the desirability of objectivity.

Janet

One of the most difficult aspects of fieldwork for me (and I thought much less for you) was the amount of food we were expected to eat in the course of our time with each family. You were petite and never seemed to worry about your weight. In fact, you gained very little during the fieldwork. For me, the upshot of all of this cooking and eating activity was a net weight gain of about ten pounds. I hated myself. Having spent more than half of my life battling my natural body shape (pear), I loathed gaining a few pounds. I resented the fact that this was not a problem for you This was more than I could tolerate. I became both angry and depressed.

Eventually, I found myself dreading meals that my friends would envy. I remember saying to one classmate that I was off to do fieldwork and was expecting a veal scaloppini meal. She cooed enviously. I grunted and told her that I felt like a stuffed pig; how I resented all of this focus on food and eating. She offered to go in my place. On January 15, I wrote a long set of field notes in which I muse about the growing feelings of resentment I felt. I could not understand the centrality of food in this culture. For me, health and image were more important. I had grown up with a mother who had dieted even during pregnancy to avoid getting fat. Growing up in a single-parent household, meals were expedient and solitary events rarely marked by the presence of guests or traditional dishes. Reared on a diet of yogurt and wheat germ, I worried about eating too much of the wrong foods and gaining weight.

Now I know that many of the women in the community fought this battle as well; they would eat large and delicious meals and then run "to spa" in an attempt to shed some pounds. Several of the women and a few of the men spoke and worried about their bodies and weight. In one or another way they attempted to keep themselves trim. It was a losing battle. I succumbed as they did. But I was desperately unhappy by the time we finished our work. And ten pounds heavier. You had better control and ate less. Or so I thought.

Our desire to keep in shape prompted a weekly visit to the gym where we met and talked about our work together. Here, too, we found a place of common interest and shared misery. It contributed to our growing solidarity.

Karen

After several months in the field, I also felt the burden of eating so many abundant, regular meals. Not only had both of us gained weight but we were also subject to uncomfortable physical reactions to the diet, which included more animal protein and fat than either of us normally ate. We were more frequently limiting portion size and refusing meals, or attempting to do so.

What Did We Leave Out?

Janet

Although we created a joint account of our experiences, it is also the case that there were some things we left out. For example, I never had the grasp of Marcella's family history that you had. Yet, I didn't want to ask what I thought was already known. You would list the members of each of Marcella's social groups and the large network of which she was a part, and although that helped me a lot, it also inhibited me. I felt foolish and thought to myself, "Karen knows these things"; I would simply ask you. This meant that there were also questions that I should have asked but did not. For my part I refrained from asking questions about who was what to whom. I saw that as your domain and steered clear of it. You focused on family history and networks—the very core of your dissertation though you may not have known it then. I chose to ask more about food events and their history. This was in line with my field's (folklore) emphasis at that time on performance and the similarity of this event to some such in the past. I was not aware of that either while we were in the field. So this is how we may have left things out. At the same time this was how our individual foci developed.

Our tenuous and fragile relationship with each other found us unwilling to question our own or our informants' motives. We could not discuss the differences between us and how they might affect our fieldwork; we were both too threatened and too vulnerable. It is with hindsight that I understand how the differences between us—your friendship with Marcella; my voluble and more gregarious personality; your listening skills and quiet demeanor; our life-style differences and familial responsibilities; my reluctance to eat too much and gain weight—helped and hindered our collaboration. We talked about a range of things, but we never discussed some of the more explosive issues such as fears of not being accepted or of being favored by one or another of the women. We also never argued; we were too insecure. Whatever tension and conflict we felt we kept to ourselves, except for some elaborate explanations for lateness or absenteeism that we provided for each other in our field notes. It was a safe way to communicate! The distance helped.

There were other questions neither of us asked at the time:

1. Why did they tell us the same stories? To ease the tension they may have felt between us? Were they creating a vision of themselves they wanted us to portray? What better way than to tell the stories twice. It reinforced the portrayal—their vision of themselves and their lives. We must have invested in that same story. I am reminded of Bruner's assertion that anthropologist and informant often seek each other out because they share the same story about the culture (1986: 150). Fieldwork is a collaborative effort. In this case the collaboration was between us and our informants. And it is this jointly constructed story that became the reality on which more fieldwork will be based. It is quite possible that you and I walked into the setting with a shared story—one shared first by the two of us. Then we collaborated with our informants to create the version we told in print, a story undisputed by any one of us.

2. Why were their stories not "modified" with each telling? We never even asked that question. Or if they were told differently, why did we not notice in the retelling and record or interpret the stories differently? I don't think we were critical enough of the fieldwork process to ask why we each were told the same story in the same way. Had we been more critical of our informants and more self aware we may have found this something to query.

3. Why did we not overtly comment on or question the bigotry we encountered? We let these comments slip away unmarked though we had felt uncomfortable and angry. How I hated the bigotry.

We never mentioned these experiences in any written or oral account of life in this community. These were moments deliberately left out and unanalyzed. I can write about it now, fourteen years later, though still with a sense of betrayal.

Karen

As a single woman, I felt a separation from the women in the community for whom such a status was undesirable. I believed that because you were a wife and a mother, you did not feel this kind of distance and lack of acceptance. I felt inadequate and unable to contribute to the many discussions about marriage and childrearing that were the anchor of conversation. You talked about your husband and child. Several of the women (Anne Cooper and others) asked me pointedly about my plans for marriage and made suggestions about the kind of man I should seek as a partner. The sooner the better, in their view. I rejected these suggestions and was frustrated by what I saw as their inability to adopt more extended views of women's roles.

I did not write or even talk about how I felt about being seen as a "deficient" single woman. I was hurt and angry. I felt submerged in a sea of marriage and maternity, from which I could not escape if I wanted to complete my graduate studies. Later, after we had completed fieldwork and I acquired nieces and nephews, I began to bring details of their lives to the many family-centered conversations.

What We Added:
Or How Our Presence Affected What We Saw

Janet

Our presence in the lives of the four families clearly affected what we saw. For example, our questions about celebratory meals were the impetus for recreated and reinvented traditions such as the St. Joseph's Day celebration I am about to describe; this occasion was only vaguely remembered by some of the adults, with the exception of Marcella. The children remembered nothing at all and asked what kind of special dinner this was.

It was St. Joseph's Day. A day that was no longer celebrated in Maryton, but a festival that once brought together the entire community. Since we had asked about how it was celebrated, Marcella promptly invited her family to a gathering to which each would bring a special dish associated with the holiday; Marcella would cook the especially esoteric dishes like macaroni and sawdust, rice pudding, and cavazumes, a special pastry. It was festive. At this event we were treated like siblings and Marcella's children. "I won't live forever," Marcella said unemotionally to all of us present but particularly to the two of us. "You have to learn how to make this." As she made the cavazumes she gave each of us a specific and childish task: You were permitted to break the eggs, and I was permitted to pour the water for the dough. Surely these trivial acts of sharing must have cemented our friendship. Once again we were treated as equal beings—young, untutored, and female.

At the beginning of each month the women wanted to show what they knew about food and how well they could cook. In addition, their friends and family were inviting us for meals and worrying about whether we were evaluating their competence in the kitchen. Introduced and becoming known as the girls who are studying the way people of different dialects cook and live produced a flurry of invitations to meals in competitive and frequent succession. Though we had attempted "to control" for this by offering payment at the end of our month's stay, nothing stemmed the tide of meal after succulent meal. Many of the women took great pride in their culinary skills and used this opportunity to show them off. Others paraded their best recipes and boasted of the ones at which they were most skillful.

It was also true that while we were learning about their food preferences they were checking on ours. During Roxanne and Robert's engagement period and the early days of Marcella's separation from her husband, the household was sparked with tension. There were frequent arguments—about Robert and Roxanne's wedding; about their father; about Marcella's clothes; about each other. Marcella was distraught. We sympathized.

One Friday evening shortly before the wedding, Marcella asked me to pick up some prepared fish and french fries for dinner on my way to their house. Friday was still "fish night" for this Catholic family. I arrived with their meal. Marcella had already set the table. She reimbursed me for my outlay. Roxanne, who was 23, and Jill, aged 19, sat down to dinner. Both of these young women were still living at home, though within a few months Roxanne would leave home for her new married life.

The food was passed from one of us to the other. The tension was palpable. Within minutes the two sisters were at each other about the manner in which they were eating. Roxanne looked with disgust at the amount of ketchup Jill had accidentally poured onto her plate. "That's ignorant," she said to her sister. "You don't know how to eat." Jill shouted back at her that she was annoying. Marcella looked dismayed. I tried to intervene as peacemaker. I said, "Oh, it's okay. Just pass the extra ketchup down to me and I'll use it." Both of the young women looked at me. Jill responded, "Janet, you don't even like ketchup." I had never told them this explicitly. There was silence. With that I had been put in my place as an outsider, a "stranger." (Earlier, Jill had explained to me, "In an Italian family you are either a stranger or family.")

This was a spat between siblings. I had been told to mind my own business. Further, I realized that they were monitoring my behavior as closely as I was observing theirs. This came as something of a surprise to me.

Karen

Because I was interested in the community's past and had already completed some historical research, I asked questions about migration patterns, family history, residential movement within the community, marriage, and other affiliations. In response, the women looked through closets, retrieved stored mementos, contacted older relatives, invoked their childhoods, and recalled earlier social life in the community. My queries prompted the women to reflect on social network relationships, current and past, that were usually taken for granted and not discussed. Their children did not understand my interest in the community's past, which they saw as foreign and bearing little relationship to their present lives. Marcella was particularly receptive to my inquiries and used her broad-based community knowledge to strengthen her position as a key informant in our study.

In the fourth household, we were relied upon as a source of information about other study households. Yvonne Weaver and her mother (one of Marcella's childhood friends) asked numerous questions about the timing, content, and execution of daily and weekend meals and celebratory food events in the other households. Our responses were part of our shared interpretation of community life. We reported our understandings—based on the reports made to each of us during the earlier phases of the fieldwork—to the Weavers, creating a "thrice-told tale."

A Common Voice and Still Separate but Equal

Janet

At the end of our fieldwork, each of us wrote a dissertation and received our doctorates. Each individual work shared our mutually developed interpretations and analyses although each concentrated on different aspects of community life and was framed by each discipline's peculiar stance. Interestingly, you were intrigued by the ways the women connected themselves in a social network. I was fascinated by the ways in which they nurtured their families and made meaning in their lives. Did this reflect our individual developmental histories and life-style choices?

Karen

As a consequence of our contrasting marital statuses and different personalities, we formed relationships with the women in the community differently and had different relationships with several of the women. You were friendly and talkative right away with all of these women, none whom you knew previously. With those I had not previously met, I was quiet at first and gradually became more comfortable, but never contributed as much to conversation as you did. My personality was (and is) different from most of the women in the community, for whom sharing food and nearly continuous conversation are the basis of social life.

In a recent volume on fieldwork, Caplan (1993:24) notes the tendency of ethnographers to "use the field to work through other parts of their lives." Although we did not discuss or acknowledge it at the time, I believe this is true of our experience. I focused on the complexity of social networks in part because such relationships were lacking in my own family, due to frequent job changes and residential relocations. You have commented on your mother's difficulties as a working single parent and neglect of more traditional family life.

Janet

It is still hard to separate which of us contributed what to our mutual understanding. Yet one thing is clear: Despite our common voice we did develop a unique position and perspective based on our personalities, our different statuses, and our disciplinary stances. We had a tacit agreement not to deal with our differences; we never discussed them. We did not probe or analyze our interpersonal relationship. Rather odd, don't you think, that two researchers trained to be reflexive did not reflect too much on their own relationship? Instead, we worked through our anxieties and vulnerabilities by doing our fieldwork. For better or for worse, we were silent about our disagreements. We gave priority to our collaboration and in so doing discovered that it is not possible to squelch entirely what is idiosyncratic and unique, and that it is possible to construct a common world view while maintaining individual perspectives.

Karen

Not only did we not analyze our own relationship, we ignored the ongoing conflict between Marcella and Anne, which continues to this day. Marcella and Anne vied for status as study participants and may have intentionally constructed and manipulated the competing alliance structure we described earlier. Over time, we became part of the "field," and the "field" became part of our lives. We are expected to visit regularly, exchange holiday gifts, celebrate birthdays and other life cycle events, and participate in community activities. As JanetKaren or KarenJanet, we maintain these relationships collectively; only rarely does one of us visit without the other. After nearly fifteen years, we have come to interact primarily with Marcella and her family, less frequently visiting members of the other households.

Janet

Learning is always facilitated by discussion and writing; it is what the academic enterprise is about. At least it should be. Though it is easier now to engage in collaborative work, academic writing is still often characterized as solitary activity, one in which an individual "genius" contributes to scholarship. A quick perusal of the prefaces and introductions of many scholarly writings indicates that the ideas written are not solely those of the author. Nor, indeed, is the text itself; thanks are frequently given to editorial and research assistants and typists for their contributions to the text's clear language and ideas.

Though we were not deliberately setting about the task of changing the nature of academic research and scholarship, we were among those who, by accident and of necessity, discovered that the ideals of solitary and competitive research proposed by the academy are not an honest description of the reality of the enterprise. After all, scholars contribute to an ongoing discussion aided and abetted by their students, spouses, and colleagues. Each single work reflects the ideas and musings, and the inventions and struggles of at least several people. In our own silent struggle to develop as fieldworkers and scholars we learned what feminist scholarship has now demonstrated; that the academic enterprise has favored a male orientation in its preference for recognizing a single individual as the scholar. Some women and men may, indeed, prefer another more communal stance, one that does not negate the individual but values and emphasizes the collaboration.

We did that and discovered that our ethnographies are enhanced by what we accomplished together and the experience we shared in its creation.

Karen

Despite the now-substantial literature on fieldwork, there is still relatively little to guide the prospective collaborative field team. We have found some similarities in the work of other women fieldworkers and those who work in their own countries.

This reflection on our field experiences and the way we constructed a joint interpretation of the community we worked in is the second time we have written about it. The initial paper, written only a few years after the fieldwork, was framed by the commonalities of fieldwork experiences among women anthropologists—protection, initial suspicion, conformity, reciprocity, and culture shock as described by Peggy Golde (1970: 5). Emphasizing our gender role and status differences, we described how these characteristics enabled us to learn more about gender roles and gender domains than either of us could have as a female researcher working alone. More recent considerations of the role of sex and gender in the field have emphasized the articulation of gender with age, sexuality, ethnicity, and class (Whitehead and Conaway 1986, Okely and Callaway 1992, Bell, Caplan, and Karim 1993).

In this chapter we have discussed some of the implications of doing fieldwork in our own culture, close to our homes, and the difficulties we had balancing competing personal and professional responsibilities. At the time, "the classic, exotic, other-cultural experience" was still the standard in the discipline (Messerschmidt 1981:3), and we were sensitive to the potential for devaluation of our work. In the end, having the field be "here" rather than "there" (cf. Geertz 1988) set the stage for the ongoing relationships with the women in the community that have enriched our lives.

5

Introduction to Chapter 5

Objectivity is often defined as a goal of social scientific research and writing. Researchers are expected to maintain a certain amount of distance or detachment from both the subject matter and the individuals they are studying. In effect, they are expected to remove personal issues and concerns from their work. As we noted earlier, Alma Gottlieb's early field notes (see Chapter 2) were devoid of personal content; she thought that was what her dissertation advisors expected. As a result, the notes were not a resource for writing the chapter in this volume; they lacked the emotional depth that the authors felt was necessary to recapture their first impressions of life in a Beng village.

Susan Krieger faced a similar dilemma as she sat down to write about the research she had done in a lesbian community in the midwestern United States during the late 1970s. Having been a participant in that community prior to being a researcher, she found it difficult to define the appropriate approach to take to her many pages of notes. As she describes, even having the notes laying on the kitchen table day after day (where she was more likely to see them) did not move her into action. Her initial attempts at sorting through and analyzing her data proved to be unproductive and frustrating.

In the chapter that follows, Krieger describes the process she went through. In the end, she found it necessary to reinject her self into the research and to understand her emotions and reactions as she was interviewing members of the community, some of whom she knew personally prior to knowing them as subjects in her study. Her book *The Mirror Dance: Identity in a Women's Community* ultimately offered a "birds-eye view" of a midwestern lesbian community that while known at one level is frequently "unobtainable" and "that in fiction and social science can be offered as a gift" (Krieger 1983: 192). She describes her study in the following way:

The study conveyed the central excitement of a community's gossip, of everybody talking about themselves and each other, who was going with whom, and why. It allowed a reader to follow "the hotline that went around all the time" in the community, to know the community from its center to its margins, to go to parties, visit bars, share in the breakups of couples and the raising of children, become immersed in the many internal dialogues and private social and sexual entanglements that knit the community together, and hear opinions about community leaders and norms that, because these opinions might be critical or sensitive, were not widely shared.

Krieger found that the sorting through of her own emotional reaction to interviewees was an essential element of her research process. In the end, however, the book offers an unusual approach to writing in that the authorial presence is not clearly visible in the book. Krieger reports (1983) that some readers saw her book as a "mere presentation" of the voices or experiences of members of the community. They longed for a more explicit analysis by the author.

This chapter, taken from her book *Social Science and the Self: Personal Essays on an Art Form* (1991), presents an honest, reflective, and insightful account of how she went about beginning to reflect on the data for her book. As she struggled to progress, she reflected on the role of the self in research. In what follows, she discusses why distance, objectivity, and convention were inappropriate to *her* unique analysis. These issues have taken on new urgency in the academy, particularly in the humanities and the social sciences. For some, the role of the self is simply part of the methodological steps in research; clarification of one's self can help the researcher to understand issues of bias, limitations on data collection, and the "vision" of the research as guided by the researcher. For others, however, the role of the self is part of a more formidable intellectual critique of the nature of knowledge or what Krieger terms the "fiction/social science ambivalence." As she states, "Social scientists often do what novelists do: they invent, they use illusion and inner vision, they focus on the unique and the particular. . . . Novelists, similarly, are often discoverers, testing ideas against evidence, developing generalizations, and seeking to be faithful to the details of external experience" (Krieger 1983: 176.) Here, some ethnographers argue (drawing from the philosophical roots of Derrida 1982 and other "deconstructionists") that the fundamental nature of the intellectual enterprise is not what those interested in social *science* believe.

In the discussion that follows, Krieger asserts the importance of ethnographers engaging in critical reflection of the role of the self in the research. Although some ethnographers are aware of the need for concern with the issue of "representation in ethnography" (Van Maanen 1995), others complain that the "over-abundance of concern with the reflexivity of their work and the task of writing ethnography . . . can lose the phenomenon of interest" (Mehan 1995, personal communication; see also Mehan 1992). Krieger, however, charges that efforts to avoid the role of the self are, essentially, a form of self-deception. She and others charge that ethnographers need to face up to the role of the researcher's self, as well as to the researcher's imagination (Atkinson 1990), in ethnography.

Beyond Subjectivity

SUSAN KRIEGER

In earlier chapters, I have referred to an article titled "Beyond 'Subjectivity': The Use of the Self in Social Science." I have mentioned that the article meant more to me than the book whose research and writing process it comments upon because the article speaks in a first-person voice and feels closer to me than the book. I have mentioned, too, that when I began writing *Social Science and the Self*, "Beyond 'Subjectivity'" was very much on my mind. It represented a kind of personal writing that I wanted my new work to live up to. I was afraid I would not be able to be as candid in my new work as I had been in that earlier article.

"Beyond 'Subjectivity,'" presented here, provides a specific discussion of research and writing in the case of *The Mirror Dance*. It also extends themes raised in previous chapters of this book. It is concerned with acknowledging one's involvement in one's work and with achieving some level of honesty in writing about that involvement. The article argues for use of insights about the self to help one understand others, and it advocates the development of a full enough sense of self, so that understandings of others will not be stilted, artificial, and unreal. Even more important in terms of the present work, "Beyond 'Subjectivity'" takes as central the problem of asserting oneself, and one's own vision, or voice, in the face of other voices that often seem to overwhelm and discourage the social scientific author. The most important feeling I arrived at after going through the exercise described in this article, which was aimed at helping me deal with my data, was that "I had a right to say something that was mine." I think that often we feel we do not have that right in social science, or we feel it is a right we have to earn. I think such attitudes toward the individual authorial perspective, while appealingly modest, are not very helpful. They encourage us to deny that we will speak of things in terms that reflect how we see them. The more important question, is How will we mold these terms? What resources will we use to make our language fit our experiences? Will we draw fully on our internal and individual sense of things? Will we learn how to make good use of ourselves, or will we primarily apply commonly held views because we know these are acceptable?

In part because it draws on notes about personal feelings that were not originally intended for publication, "Beyond 'Subjectivity'" gives a sense of an inner authorial voice. It is an inside story about a book and an author, however brief and well rationalized. (See chapter 5 on the "success" storyline.) The tradition for writing up personal accounts in social science says that our studies are about others, and that our methodological statements should describe how we came to know what we did about them. Dutifully, "Beyond 'Subjectivity'" does this, but the article interests me now less as an explanation of how I came to understand a lesbian community than as a statement in its own right that presents aspects of the private world of an author.

To take the internal life and make it external is important, in my view. The challenge of making a true portrait of one's experience remains, but at least the self is acknowledged. All of our statements about others are, very significantly, also about ourselves. We tend to provide little in terms of direct personal discussion when we write our studies, and I should like to see that little become a great deal more. Only with many stories will we get a good picture, since we each can speak only of our experience, and often we do this timidly, afraid of the outside world's tendency to deny us. This general tendency is well fueled by the many specific prohibitions against self-expression within social science. These prohibitions are particularly strong in their effects on the self-expression of women and of anyone not speaking a standard truth. The following article is not intended as a model of originality or correct personal expression, but it is a piece I found helpful, and I hope it suggests that there is more to do. Not only do we need to start talking about ourselves at greater length, but we need to experiment with different styles of self-understanding, for these can be keys to expanding our alternatives, both for being present in our works and for depicting experiences of others.

Beyond "Subjectivity":
The Use of the Self in Social Science

Recently, in both the social sciences and in related humanistic disciplines, there has been a restimulation of interest in the relationship between observer and observed.[1] Our attention is called to the many ways in which our analyses of others result from highly interactional processes in which we are personally involved.[2] We bring biases and more than biases. We bring idiosyncratic patterns of recognition. We are not, in fact, ever capable of achieving the analytic "distance" we have long been schooled to seek. While recognition of the interactional and contextual nature of social research is not new,[3] how we interpret ourselves during this new period of self-examination may, in fact, add something fresh and significant to the development of sophistication in social science.

I present the following account of my own work with the hope of contributing to a general sharing of personal stories about what we, as social scientists, now do. My account is one of backward beginnings, wrong ways of doing things, and problems I would rather not have had. Yet precisely because of these things, I think, the story is worth telling. In the following sections, I tell about some of what went into the writing of *The Mirror Dance: Identity in a Women's Community*,[4] a study of a midwestern lesbian social group I conducted during 1977–78. The book focused on problems of likeness and difference, merger and separation, loss and change, and the struggles of individuals for social belonging and personal growth.

I began my research unwittingly. I spent nearly a year participating in the community as a member without the slightest thought of studying it. The community was, for me, as for others, a home away from home, a private social world, a source of intense personal involvements and supportive social activity—a source of parties, dinners, self-help groups, athletic teams, outings, extended-family type ties, a place for finding not only lovers, but also friends. I had moved to a midwestern town to take a job as a visiting assistant professor and had found the community by accident and through need. My participation surprised me. "I did not become a lesbian," I wrote to myself in notes at the time, "to become one of a community." Yet the community won me over in the end, and three months before I was supposed to leave the job and town, I decided to study the community in which I was living, to ask questions of these bold midwestern women.

Data and the Problem of Interpretation

I had, for years, been interested in the subject of privacy, and I felt that this private, almost secret sphere of social activity would be a good place to talk to people about it. I wanted to learn about how individuals dealt with how they were known, or not known, to others. I then began two months of intensive interviewing with seventy-eight women who were either members of the community or associated with it. Someone joked that I had solved "the sampling problem" by interviewing the entire community "and then some," which was, by and large, what I did.

My interviews lasted an hour and a half each, were usually conducted in my own home, and focused on personal histories of self-other relationships in the community. I asked each interviewee four basic questions: (1) How would you define privacy (what images come to mind)? (2) How would you define the local lesbian community? (3) Within that community, how have you been concerned about boundaries between public and private, self and other (i.e., what has been your personal and social history)? (4) With respect to the outside world, how have you been concerned about protecting the fact of your lesbianism (who knows, who does not, and why)? Approximately 70 percent of the time in each interview session was spent on question 3, which concerned internal community relationships. Members of the community and others I approached showed me unusual cooperation. They typically came for interviews within a week of when I called. During the interviews, they spoke to me with great candor.

When I left the community, I took with me, along with my personal memories and accounts, four hundred pages of single-spaced typed interview notes, which were, I felt, "rich data" for a study I would soon write up. Then the unexpected happened. For a year I could do nothing with my notes. I picked them up; put them down; moved them around; took notes on the notes; copied them so that one set could sit in loose-leaf binders in my university office while the original set lay in binders on my kitchen table at home. (I had moved the notes to the kitchen table after realizing I kept avoiding them at my desk.) All the while, I kept trying to do simple things; to isolate themes; to find something to say that could be supported by my data. I thought of punching computer cards. I finally culled out the seven interviews with lesbian mothers and attempted to write about their experience, thinking that in some magical way the subject of motherhood would save me. It did not. Then I gave up. I closed the notebooks. I decided to write a novel. Occasionally, I thought about how despite the fact that I was now twelve hundred miles and many months away from the community, I still did not have a necessary analytic "distance" from the subjects of my study. However, that thought did not help.

Finally, a full year later, done with two drafts of my novel, and haunted still by those volumes of notes—the undefined "promise" of my data, the sense that I should not let the research go to waste—I decided, "I must write about what I can relate to. I must write a personal account." I began writing about what it had been like for me to live in that lesbian community. I wrote many pages, and then I shelved them. What I wrote was interesting, to me. Beyond recalling my experience, it enabled me to see that what I had thought of as a lack of analytic "distance" might more usefully be viewed as a lack of personal "separation" from my data, from all those "other women's voices" that rose up each time I took up my notes. But the account I had written was not social science in a conventional sense, and I wanted very much to be conventional.

However, writing the account did give me an insight. The most immediate problem, it seemed to me, was not that I did not have distance from my data, but that I did have, and probably always had, far too much distance. Before dealing with problems of "separation," I had to acknowledge that I was estranged.

I thought about estrangement.[5] I decided that to deal with my data in any "sociologically useful" fashion, I would have to get over my estrangement. I would have to feel that I could "touch" the experience of gathering my data, and in a way that I had not allowed myself before. I would have to begin by expanding my idea of my "data" to include not only my interview notes, but also my entire year of participation in the community. I would have to be willing not only to feel again what the experience of living in the community had been like for me, but also to feel it as fully and deeply as possible and to analyze my feelings. Why did certain things move me? What had unfolded over the year's time? Why had I felt estranged? What did I want? What did I receive? What was I afraid of? How could I bridge the gap between myself and my data?

Because I am not at ease simply "feeling" in an amorphous way, I went about "becoming in touch" with my data very methodically, in a highly disciplined and structured fashion. For the next four to five months, I devoted myself to an exercise which I called a "process of reengagement." The first stage of this exercise was a step-by-step analysis of my experience of involvement in the community, beginning with entry, progressing through entanglements in personal relationships, singling out key events and my emotional responses to them, reviewing the interview period, and ending with my feelings on leaving. The second stage was a step-by-step analysis of my experience in conducting the seventy-eight interviews which were the source of my notes. I later wrote a personal account of this process, called "'Separating Out': A Method for Dealing with Qualitative Data," from which the following is excerpted. This excerpt describes the second stage in my reengagement process and shows how an understanding of the self can help resolve the problem of interpreting one's data.

"Separating Out": A Method for Dealing with Qualitative Data

A Case-Analytic Technique

The strategy in the second part of my reengagement process required that I deal with each of my seventy-eight interview cases. First, I sought to identify and examine my responses to my interviewees as individuals. I reviewed feelings I had with respect to each interviewee, first, in anticipation of our interview session and, second, during the interview itself. Finally, I analyzed the data of my interview notes themselves. The analyses in each phase of this process were done by writing down my thoughts and feelings, taking up a separate sheet of paper for each interviewee at each step. When I was through, I had one set of notes reflecting my "preinterview self-assessment," another on my "interview self-assessment," and a third on responses to the interview notes.

Step 1: Preinterview Self-Assessment

During this preinterview self-assessment step, I recalled my acquaintance with each interviewee prior to our interview and reviewed how each interview appointment had been made. I remembered social occasions during which the interviewee and I had met and what the biases in introduction had been if the interviewee was known to me primarily through another person. Most important, I noted my personal expectations with respect to each interviewee immediately preceding the session: what I had anticipated with fear, and what with excitement, and what I felt I had wanted for myself in return. In doing this, I sought to identify those prejudices I brought to each interview. It seemed important to separate my personal disappointments and pleasures from my latter interpretations of my data. The following examples are indicative of the preinterview item self-assessment. They are excerpts from longer passages written about each preinterview experience.

> PREINTERVIEW 32: B. was one of my neighbors across the street who had been fairly open and friendly with me. I chose her to do one of the first interviews because she had been "public" as a lesbian and I felt she would be knowledgeable about the community and straightforward with me. Yet I was nonetheless concerned that she might not speak personally enough with me.

> PREINTERVIEW 44: I knew D. mainly through K. and was prejudiced against her, or, more accurately, I felt fear regarding her—that she was judgmental and did not like me because of my relationship with K. and its troubles—that she was primarily K.'s friend.

> PREINTERVIEW 67: I knew of V. that she was a straight woman in one of the core support groups in the community. Was afraid she would be distant and would withhold. Also, K. had told me V. played "poor me," so I worried I might get impatient with her.

Step 2: Interview Self-Assessment

A similar approach informed the next interview self-assessment step. Here, again, I wanted to identify my prejudices and any "hidden" personal agenda I might have had. Yet in this step, even more so than in the preinterview assessment, I was intent on recapturing the force of my emotions at the time, since they seemed to me to surround my waiting notes. For example:

INTERVIEW 32: This surprised my expectations, because B. was, it seemed, candid with me and more personal than I'd expected. I did not feel forced to adopt her views or anything of the sort. I really felt for her as a person at the end of the interview, as I had not before.

INTERVIEW 44: Interview was very tense for me. I felt D. being defensive. Felt pressure on her part that I join her—see it all her way. Felt she didn't want to be interviewed, felt I was pushing this upon her. I was angry with her because of all these things. When I really wanted to be friends, to win her, to have her like me. In the end, I felt she ran away, wishing she'd not said what she did, angry with me. I wished to run after her, to make it all right—to confront. This is the interview I felt worst about of all of them, it seemed so much a denial and rejection of me. Though I felt its content—what she said—was rich.

INTERVIEW 67: Was partly tense because I suspected my own motives about wanting to get to K. through V.—get inside information that would help me settle my troubled feelings. Felt partly pressed by V. to feel as she did. Also that V. was partly confused, yet that she felt she had a collar on rationality. The conversation was almost technical, in that she kept much emotion out. Did not like this (angry?—a little, but repressed it) in the end.

INTERVIEW 72: M. was the only one to really break down and cry at the time of the interview and want to be held. This scared me—because I did not want to get involved, and did not want her to become dependent on me. I tried to "handle" it by not making a big deal of it, by holding her and then letting her up when I felt she'd be okay. She had brought a tape recorder to record the interview for herself (only one who did this). When she started to cry and asked to be held, I pushed the recorder off. My leftover feelings were fear—that she'd call on me for more holding and that I'd say no. I might do it with someone but somehow I feared her, or she was not the one. I also had feelings that I invited this, with everyone. Then when I got it, drew back from it. This left me uneasy. Feeling angry (?), lonely. What if it were me who wanted to cry and be held?

It became increasingly obvious to me, as I recalled and noted my responses in each case, that I had felt much discomfort and that that had caused me trouble. Yet these were exactly the kinds of things I needed to articulate, since they had been crucial in frustrating my dealings with my data. For instance, the more I noted my responses, the more I became aware of how very often I had been afraid, both prior to the interview sessions and during them. What I had previously identified as anger was really fear. This, I think, was because each interview situation was an intimacy situation for me and an occasion which I felt required proof of myself. I wanted, during the interview sessions, not only to know each of my interviewees, but also for them to know and care about me. I reacted as if it were a denial of myself when an interviewee did not seem to care:

INTERVIEW 62: A disappointment. Because M. seemed to me a lot a front—how she wanted to appear, a line, not a real person. I didn't feel the intimacy, the honesty that I wanted. Felt she suspected that I found her false (unconvincing) in this way and that she was angry at this and defensive. When she left, I was let down and angry. Felt she had dealt with me formally, almost as a functionary for herself, rather than as a person. Which I wanted.

The interview self-assessment was difficult. I kept wanting to describe the interviewee and how she appeared to me when she arrived and as she was involved in the session. However, this seemed largely ungrounded, unless I also noted my own reasons for the response—the emotional issue, or issues, each session raised for me. I had to discipline myself to note a reaction of my own for every action of each interviewee that I noted. I had to take time to figure out the logic of my own reactions, for what they would tell me about barriers to dealing with my data. I had not expected the interview assessment to become highly self-analytic, since I felt I had already been extremely self-reflective during the earlier stage of reengaging with the entire research experience (step 1 of my exercise). Nonetheless, new things were brought to my attention in recalling my specific feelings in each of the interview situations.

My most important recognition occurred after going through approximately one-third of the cases. I began to notice that I could distinguish my responses in terms of whether I had felt pressure to become like a particular interviewee or whether I had felt I could "be myself" during the interview. I then began to look to characteristics of the different interviewees in relation to myself in order to understand why I would feel or not feel pressure. I realized that I would become angry and feel bad in those cases where I felt I had to be like the interviewee. My sense gained from these cases tended to overpower my sense of the actually larger number of cases in which I did not feel this threat. For example:

INTERVIEW 75: Went well. I was impressed with R. as a person—her independence, the carefulness of her thinking, her clarity. I got a good picture of her—because her words were honest?—and so did not feel threatened. Maybe this is mechanism: when the interviewees are confused (due to being defensive or otherwise inauthentic, or confused about themselves), I get threatened and confused about who I am, because the relationship is confused. I don't know what I am relating to; while if the interviewees are more clear about themselves, I can be more clear about myself.

I concluded that I had felt threatened where it seemed to me an interviewee was inauthentic in her presentation of self in ways that set off my own doubts as to who I was. I decided that my feelings concerning this were so strong because of the fact that I shared an intimate identity stake with all the women I interviewed. I looked to them, even in the ostensibly other-oriented interview situation, to help me solve the problem of who I was. Although the interviews were highly controlled and guided by me, my controls did not protect me from threats on a deeper level. The interviews were actually occasions of inner panic, occasions during which I feared that others would not allow me to be myself—to act as the person I truly felt I was. This feeling of threat to my sense of self had not been fully clear to me before I analyzed the individual accounts. But finally it was, and I could see in my responses how much I had wanted personal confirmation and acceptance:

> INTERVIEW 54: In her office. I was uncomfortable because of her power things—the phone, showing off stuff she'd written, her sensitivity. I felt she was trying to impress me with herself, that I was mostly a pawn to this, a person to be won over, not an independent person to be related to—one who had sensitivity, specialness, etc. And I wanted this other response from her. Perhaps because she was a peer at the university, and an unattached woman, recently out of a relationship. I think I had hopes we might be friends. With sexual possibilities maybe. But even if not, I wanted to be an equal, a real person to her. I left disappointed.

As I analyzed my responses in this way, I felt that my desires for confirmation, while perhaps extreme, might be more widespread in the community. The lesbian community might be functioning as an "identity community" for its members, one in which the most intimate sense of self was frequently on the line, a community in which the power to threaten by lack of confirmation was as strong as the power to confirm.

Reexamining my interview session responses made me aware of something else that was extremely important: the extent to which, even in those special-purpose sessions, I was engaged with the community and acting according to its rules, just as I had been outside the sessions. The interview situations were, in effect, small dramatic reenactments of the social dynamics of the larger community. They were microcosms providing specific examples of expected or acceptable community behaviors. In looking back on my responses, I was shocked, for example, to see how often my reactions to interviewees included an element of sexual expectation. In this way, I was clearly a member of the community:

> INTERVIEW 2: B. was younger than I had expected and very beautiful, with long straight dark hair. She reminded me of a woman I had been involved with back in California in the winter. I think I felt I would like her to fall in love with me.

> INTERVIEW 51: Knew E. casually, and occasionally, it seemed to me, she would be showing sexual interest in me. Some part of me, I think, wanted that more and also was repulsed and frightened by it.

The sexual expectation dilemma had been spoken of candidly by one of my interviewees:

It's like good old sex being such an important part of people's life. And coming to a place with that expectation. Like I am here because other people in this room are here because they have the same sexual orientation I do. It puts a great pressure on you as to what am I up to and what are these people in this room doing? A lot of heterosexual traps I tried to escape, I found here. Because of all those sexual tensions, nobody gets to really know each other or to feeling comfortable with each other.

In this same vein, this interviewee also articulated a predicament referred to in the accounts of others:

There isn't one woman in the community I haven't considered having a relationship with, just because you're in this community and because of all the pressure to need and want a relationship. Because you're in this community and because you have to relate some intimate details to get along, there is always the question of whether you want to be intimate. In a straight community, you have all these girlfriends who you tell things to. But in this community, you have to worry about whether it means you want to go to bed with them.

It was not easy for me or for my interviewees to acknowledge the pervasive and central sexual tensions of the community, since these were often subtle and personally sensitive. However, by examining my own responses, I was able to arrive at important insights. I concluded that my feelings of sexual expectation had less to do with actual possibilities for sexual relationship than with rules for defining the self in the community. For this was a community in which one's sense of personal identity was closely linked with one's feelings of sexual possibility and in which sexuality often appeared as a route to intimacy, as a means by which an individual might become truly known.

Step 3: Analyzing the Interview Notes

Once having completed both preinterview and interview self-assessments, and interpreting as many of my own responses as I could, I turned to the task of dealing with the content of my interview notes. Initially, I wanted to treat the accounts of my interviewees, as much as possible, as separate and different from my own. I wanted to see my interviewees as sharing my processes and reactions perhaps on occasion, but not as a rule. Yet as I began to review my notes, seeking concepts appropriate for categorizing and "making sense," I found that I was drawing on my understanding of myself with far greater facility than on anything else that came to hand. The task then reformulated itself as one in which I would seek to determine if and how my interviewees shared versions of the problems I had identified in myself.

I would look for words used by my interviewees that were reminiscent of my own, processes that were similar to mine, and assumptions about self in relation to others that were similar. Most centrally, as I read, I would imagine each individual as existing in a problem situation concerning differentiation of self in the community. I would view each individual as seeking, time and again, confirmation for who she was, all the while suspecting she might not belong.

Increasingly, as I examined the notes, I found what seemed to be parallels among the feelings expressed by the interviewees. For example, there was a frequent concern with possibilities for rejection by the community, whether rejection was or was not likely to occur:

> I have a yearning to be part of the community, but I feel, and I know by the grapevine, that I would be rejected.

There was a sense that the community had rules that excluded important aspects of the self, as these excerpts from different interviewees suggest:

> It's hard to capture because all that is implicit—a sense that the community does have these strong rules.

> There are some things you couldn't say.

A sense of the community as unreal or uncertain appeared often in the various accounts:

> The community, for me, became a monster.

> I see several different communities.

> Like the first two years I lived here, I was unaware there was one [a community].

> I think of them as a real tight closed group, that's closed until they know for sure that you're a lesbian, for one thing. And I don't think that you could just go meet them, go hang out with them. I think you have to join them.

In most of the accounts, there was a desire for the community to provide acceptance and self-confirmation:

> The community, to me, is a group of women who I could *know* that I could lean on for support.

> Here is a group of women who can understand me, touch me the way I want to be touched.

> When I had finally found these people, I felt I had finally found people who could accept my whole life.

Along with the need for confirmation were feelings of extreme disillu-
sionment and disappointment when the community seemed to have
failed a particular woman:

> You would think it would be easier to assert your differences in a commu-
> nity of women. But it's not. It's real disillusioning.

> I needed reassurance that I was doing all right. I needed some indication that
> I was appreciated. And they kept spewing forth this ideology of the commu-
> nity, the community, this axial of support when I felt totally abandoned.

During this data analysis step, I used my own insights and developed
them further with reference to analyses of the interview notes. This enabled me finally to write a paper about the collective reality of participation in the community.[6] The reality I described in that paper was, of
course, only part of the reality felt by community members, that portion I
could be in touch with as a result of my experience. But by now, as a result of clarifying my experience, I was no longer as frightened of my involvement as I had been initially. I could use my own recognitions as a
guide, a source not only of personal but of sociological insight.

This is not to suggest that my interpretations of the community were
merely interpretations of myself "writ large" and imposed on the testimony of others. I also had to follow additional rules that granted to other
members of the community feelings and responses that were different
from mine. Throughout the process of analyzing my notes, it was important for me to maintain a sense that there was much in each interview account that fell beyond my own limited experience. My task was to try to
uncover what I could with the tool of myself and my personal recognitions. I sought not simply to impose or to apply my newly developed
recognitions, but to expand those recognitions by constantly challenging
my existing understandings: challenging my perceptions of others with
what I now felt I knew about myself and, at the same time, confronting
my self-understanding with what my interviewees seemed to be telling
me that was different.

I think that often in social research, this is what we really do. We see
others as we know ourselves. If the understanding of self is limited and
unyielding to change, the understanding of the other is as well. If the understanding of the self is harsh, uncaring and not generous to all the possibilities for being a person, the understanding of the other will show this.
The great danger of doing injustice to the reality of the "other" does not
come about through use of the self, but through lack of use of a full
enough sense of self, which, concomitantly, produces a stifled, artificial,
limited, and unreal knowledge of others.

Conclusion

The preceding account describes an exercise that helped me to reengage with my data at the same time as I was "separating out" a sense of myself. The exercise proved immediately useful in generating insights. However, my problem of estrangement was not so easily solved. In 1980 when I returned to California, I again had trouble dealing with my data. I wanted to work with it and, simultaneously, to leave it—to begin new research. At that point, it helped for me to think back on the exercise I had engaged in during the previous year. That exercise had given me some confidence and an initial understanding of the nature of my problem. I knew I would have to "assert myself," even if my assertion felt uncomfortable, and even if I would continually feel I was illegitimately imposing myself on my data.

Two and a quarter years had passed since the original research for my study was completed. I finally began writing *The Mirror Dance*. I wrote it quickly, relying upon what now seemed deeply imbedded intuitions. The book was published in 1983. Responses from both reviewers and readers suggested that its portrayal was valid, to a surprising and somewhat uncomfortable degree. Yet I knew that what I said in *The Mirror Dance* was dependent on a very personal and idiosyncratic process of data gathering and analysis. Because that process was so personal and because it worked essentially "backwards"—to understand my community, first I had to understand myself—I have presented a partial description here of an analytic exercise that helped me greatly.

The exercise I engaged in was, for me, a way out of a problem. It was a source of insight both about others and about myself. It gave me some confidence when I needed it; it gave me a feeling that "I had a right" to say something that was mine. I had studied a community that I felt I was part of and, at the same time, that I felt estranged from. I was, at one point, overwhelmed by the voices of all the women in that community. They were all telling me what to do, and they were each telling me something different. It took a long time—longer than I had expected—to find, in myself, a voice by which I could speak back to them.

I found that voice and, as *The Mirror Dance* attests, I hid it. *The Mirror Dance* is written in an unusual ethnographic style, in which the voices of the women of a community interweave with and comment upon one another, analyzing their collective situation. The subjective "I" of the author is hidden in the book, never mentioned, merged finally back in with the community from which it emerged. It is precisely for that reason that the preceding account seems important to me, for it speaks to the origins of the book's inner voice. More crucially, it speaks of a personal process. In social science, I think, we must acknowledge the personal far more than we do. We need to find new ways to explore it. We need to link our statements about those we study with statements about ourselves, for in reality neither stands alone.

Notes

This article originally appeared in *Qualitative Sociology* 8:4 (1985): 309–324; it is used here by permission. For their help in preparing the original article, I thank Estelle Freedman, Marythelma Brainard, Nancy Chodorow, Meredith Gould, and Ann Swidler.

1. This restimulation of interest has been sparked most dramatically by the development of feminist scholarship across fields. This new scholarship has led to a reexamination not only of the difference that gender makes in determining what we see, and how we see it, but of other perceptual nets as well. In the recent literature, of great interest are Evelyn Fox Keller's writings on gender and science: "Feminism and Science," *Signs* 7:3 (1982): 589–602; "Feminism as an Analytic Tool for the Study of Science," *Academe* 69:5 (1983): 15–21; *A Feeling for the Organism: The Life and Work of Barbara McClintock* (San Francisco: W. H. Freeman, 1983); and *Reflections on Gender and Science* (New Haven: Yale University Press, 1985). Keller deals with notions of objectivity, subject-object splits, and gender in the work of scientists. See also Carol Gilligan, *In a Different Voice: Psychological Theory and Women's Development* (Cambridge: Harvard University Press, 1982), concerning women's distinctive developmental experiences and how these can lead to highly contextual ways of seeing; and Nancy Chodorow, *The Reproduction of Mothering: Psychoanalysis and the Sociology of Gender* (Berkeley: University of California Press, 1978), which provides a basic psychoanalytic statement concerning women's self-other relationships. Each of these works, to a significant degree, draws on theories of object relations, a field in which an important recent contribution is Margaret S. Mahler, Fred Pine, and Anni Bergman, *The Psychological Birth of the Human Infant: Symbiosis and Individuation* (New York: Basic Books, 1975).

For the past ten years, feminist anthropologists have been particularly articulate in encouraging the recognition of gender-related observer biases; a recent overview can be found in Jane Monnig Atkinson, "Review Essay: Anthropology," *Signs* 8:2 (1982): 232–258. Many of the earlier classic questions are framed in Michelle Zimbalist Rosaldo, "The Use and Abuse of Anthropology: Reflections on Feminism and Cross-Cultural Understanding," *Signs* 5:3 (1980): 389–417; Rayna R. Reiter, ed., *Toward an Anthropology of Women* (New York: Monthly Review Press, 1975); and Michelle Zimbalist Rosaldo and Louise Lamphere, eds., *Woman, Culture, and Society* (Stanford: Stanford University Press, 1974). Nonfeminist anthropologists interested in the "new ethnography" have also been concerned specifically with the observer-observed relationship, although in a different vein; see, for example, James Clifford, "Fieldwork, Reciprocity, and the Making of Ethnographic Texts: The Example of Maurice Leenhardt," *Man* 15 (1980): 518–532; Clifford, "On Ethnographic Authority," *Representations* 1:2 (1983): 118–146; Paul Rabinow, *Reflections on Fieldwork in Morocco* (Berkeley: University of California Press, 1977); Rabinow, "'Facts Are a Word of God': An Essay Review of James Clifford's *Person and Myth: Maurice Leenhardt in the Melanesian World*," in George W. Stocking, Jr., ed., *Observers Observed: Essays on Ethnographic Fieldwork* (Madison: University of Wisconsin Press, 1983), pp. 196–207; and the works of Renato Rosaldo and Clifford Geertz. An astute comparison of differences between the new feminist and nonfeminist anthropologists in their treatment of subject-object can be found in Marilyn Strathern, "Dislodging a World View: Challenge and Counter-Challenge in the Relationship between Feminism and Anthropology" (Draft of a lecture given in the series "Changing Paradigms: The Impact of Feminist Theory upon the World of Scholarship," at the Research Centre for Women's Studies, Adelaide, Australia, 1984). Finally, there is a category of other prominent recent works that either embody or call attention to subject-object and relational issues in a new way, for example, Barbara Myerhoff, *Number Our Days* (New York: Simon and Schuster, 1980); Arlie Russell Hochschild, *The Managed Heart: Commercialization of Human Feeling* (Berkeley: University of California Press, 1983); and Gloria Bowles and Renate Duelli Klein, eds., *Theories of Women's Studies* (London: Routledge and Kegan Paul, 1983).

2. Important discussions specific to sociology can be found in Dorothy E. Smith, "Women's Perspective as a Radical Critique of Sociology," *Sociological Inquiry* 44 (1974): 7–13; Smith, "A Sociology for Women," in Julia A. Sherman and Evelyn Torton Beck, eds., *The Prism of Sex: Essays in the Sociology of Knowledge* (Madison: University of Wisconsin Press, 1979), pp. 135–187; Marcia Millman and Rosabeth Moss Kanter, eds., *Another Voice: Feminist Perspectives on Social Life and Social Science* (New York: Anchor, 1975); Shulamit Reinharz, *On Becoming a Social Scientist: From Survey Research and Participant Observation to Experiential Analysis* (San Francisco: Jossey-Bass, 1979; reprint ed., New Brunswick, N.J.: Transaction Publications, 1988); Meredith Gould, "Review Essay: The New Sociology," *Signs* 5:3 (1980): 459–467; Helen Roberts, ed., *Doing Feminist Research* (London: Routledge and Kegan Paul, 1981); and Judith Stacey and Barrie Thorne, "The Missing Feminist Revolution in Sociology" (Paper presented at the Annual Meetings of the American Sociological Association, San Antonio, 1984; published in *Social Problems* 32:4 [1985]: 301–316).

3. Instructions to field researchers to acknowledge and deal with contextual effects and with personal roles and biases have long been common in sociological texts on qualitative method. Further, many of our classics in sociology have distinctly personal tones and styles. However, I believe there is something new being said today, and it is being said most prominently by feminist scholars. This new statement concerns both what a personal style can be and what we mean by the term "participant-observation." The feminists, in effect, are trying to point out that, traditionally, we have allowed the "personal" only if it was male; we do not even yet fully know what the female social scientist's voice might be. Further, it has never been at all clear exactly what we mean by participant-observation, but certainly the rational balancing of "distance" and "involvement" that is usually implied is something qualitatively different from what Keller, for instance, means when she speaks of "a feeling for the organism," and, indeed, of "love" (Keeler, *A Feeling* and "Feminism as Analytic Tool").

4. Susan Krieger, *The Mirror Dance: Identity in a Women's Community* (Philadelphia: Temple University Press, 1983).

5. I read Gearing on studying Fox Indians: "When one is estranged, he is unable to relate because he cannot see enough to relate to. . . . The opposite of being estranged is to find a people believable" (Fred Gearing, *The Face of the Fox* [Chicago: Aldine, 1970], p. 5).

6. Susan Krieger, "The Group as Significant Other: Strategies for Definition of the Self" (Paper presented at the Annual Meetings of the Pacific Sociological Association, San Francisco, April 1980).

Introduction to Chapter 6

Carrying out a research project is a journey, an intellectual journey. As with all journeys, it has unpredictable moments. Part of the way through the trip, participants often become discouraged. The moment of arrival—a finished paper, the end of the semester, graduation—seems far away. Some individuals may doubt the wisdom of having chosen the pathway at all. Although these "bumpy moments" are attached to almost all serious endeavors, research using ethnographic methods has more predictable moments of uncertainty, serendipity, and unavoidable error than do other research methods. These mistaken moments can be particularly painful to novice researchers. Newly minted researchers can ignore the special contributions they bring to a project as novices, including their enthusiasm, excitement, energy, and drive. They can, as Annette Lareau shows in her appendix, focus on the inevitable slips and problematic moments of the process.

Lareau, a sociologist, wrote the following piece as an appendix to her book *Home Advantage: Social Class and Parental Intervention in Elementary Education* (1989). Lareau's essay lays bare some of the common trials and tribulations faced by a graduate student engaging in his or her first field study. When she considered publishing the piece, she worried that her fieldwork mistakes were so serious that revealing them could have a negative impact on her scholarly reputation and, possibly, her future career. In the end, her frustration with the lack of frank appraisals in the field won out. She was also swayed by assurances from colleagues that all researchers face such dilemmas. In 1991, her book won the Willard Waller Award for Distinguished Scholarship by the Sociology of Education Section of the American Sociological Association.

Drawn from the research for her doctoral dissertation, Lareau's study examines social-class differences in parental involvement in schools. In the book she argues that educators and sociologists have failed to understand that social class provides parents with resources to comply with the request of teachers for assistance. Whereas teachers understand the tendency of working-class parents not to comply with their requests as a matter of parents' (lack of) concern for children's educational success, Lareau suggests that social class leads parents to mean different things when they assert they want to be helpful. For working-class parents there is a separation between home and school; these parents turn over responsibility for schooling to "educated people." They depend on the school to educate their children. They worry, at times correctly, that they are unable to help with school. Middle-class parents, by contrast, generally see an interconnectedness between home and school. Such parents view themselves as capable of helping with schoolwork as well as capable of critically assessing the professional competence of teachers.

Using case studies, Lareau shows positive consequences for some children from (middle-class parents) involvement as well as negative consequences when working-class parents adopt a separation between home and schooling. Using the work of Pierre Bourdieu and the concept of cultural capital, she argues that parents' strategies for family-school relationships draw on the resources of middle-class positions to boost their children's school experience.

Lareau's current project has involved a dramatic change in qualitative methods, with a heavy focus on participant-observation rather than interviewing and a much larger sample size diversified by class, race, and gender. She believes that there has been an ongoing "conversation" in herself, and her second project compensates, avoids, or overcompensates for weaknesses in the first project. Although new problems have developed, she still reports taking pleasure from removing or being able to avoid repeating some of the "thorns" that plagued her in her first major work.

Common Problems in Field Work: A Personal Essay

ANNETTE LAREAU

In his appendix to *Street Corner Society*, William Foote Whyte describes why twelve years after his book was originally published he decided to write a detailed portrait of how he did his famous study. He reports that he was teaching a methods course and had trouble finding 'realistic descriptions' of the field work process:

> It seemed as if the academic world had imposed a conspiracy of silence regarding the personal experiences of field workers. In most cases, the authors who had given any attention to their research methods had provided fragmentary information or had written what appeared to be a statement of the methods the field worker would have used if he had known what he was going to come out with when he entered the field. It was impossible to find realistic accounts that revealed the errors and confusions and the personal involvement that a field worker must experience (Whyte 1981, p. 359).

Three decades later the problem remains: realistic descriptions of how research data are collected are unusual. Most studies by sociologists who use qualitative methods devote a short section to the research methodology: they describe the number of respondents, the selection of the sample, and general procedures for data collection. But, as Whyte complained, these studies—some of which are exemplary works—rarely portray the process by which the research was actually done, nor do they give insight into the traps, delays, and frustrations which inevitably accompany field work (but see Walford 1987).

This lack of realistic portraits is a problem, for they are not simply to assuage readers' desires for more personal information about the author, or to get—for those of us with more malicious inclinations—'the dirt' on a project. Rather, they give qualitative researchers a formal avenue for reporting how they proceeded with data collection and analysis. Without these details, it is hard to tell when researchers did an exemplary job in the data collection and analysis and when they did a 'quick and dirty' job. It is agreed, of course, that one should establish a rapport with one's respondents, be sensitive to the field setting, take comprehensive field notes, analyze your data carefully, and write it up in a lively and accurate fashion. What that actually means, and what researchers actually do, is often anybody's guess. Most studies do not reveal their inner-workings, and good writing can cover up awkwardly collected and poorly documented field work.

In his appendix Whyte chose to do his 'bit to fill this gap' (1981, p. 359), and in this appendix I have decided to do my bit as well. One of the biggest problems is that this entails writing up my mistakes as well as my successes. In most lines of work, including teaching, almost everyone is forced to admit to having made mistakes from time to time. But admitting mistakes in field work seems more difficult. Partly, this is because we often have an overly romantic notion of field work, which emphasizes the glory of 'going native' and glosses over the difficulties and problems of the endeavor. The implicit message is that mistakes are rare. Partly, this reluctance is an artifact of a scholarly tradition in which a public discussion of 'inner-workings' is considered unseemly and unnecessary. Finally, admitting to mistakes in field work raises questions about the quality of the body of the research and the conclusions drawn from it. Given these considerations, it is hardly surprising that so little has been written about actual experiences in the field. Likewise, it is clear that all of us who are engaged in qualitative research could greatly benefit from a more frank sharing of our experiences.

My project has strengths as well as weaknesses. There are parts of the data set in which I am fully confident and parts which I think are considerably weaker. This assessment is implied in the way in which the work is written up, but in my view it is worth making this more explicit. So, in a fit of immodesty as well as honesty, I provide my own assessment of the strengths of the project, and I identify my successes as well as failings as a researcher.

This appendix consists of two parts. In Part I, I review the background for the study, access and entrance to Colton and Prescott, my role in the classroom, the selection of families, the interviews, and my assessment of the major mistakes I made in the research. I also briefly summarize the logistics of data analysis. In Part II, I turn to the development of the conceptual model and my struggle to formulate the research question.

It is my hope that readers will find this 'exposé' of a research project useful, not only for gaining insight into this particular study but for detailed examples of how to cope with common problems in field research. As I bumped about in the field not knowing what I was doing I often felt—incorrectly, as it turned out—that I was making a terrible mess of things, that my project was doomed, and that I should give up the entire enterprise immediately. This negativism came from my persistent feeling that, despite my having had a research question when I started, I didn't truly know what I was doing there. In part, my gloom signaled the continuing struggle to clarify the intellectual goals of the project.

As I have discovered, using qualitative methods means learning to live with uncertainty, ambiguity, and confusion, sometimes for weeks at a time. It also means carving a path by making many decisions, with only the vaguest guideposts and no one to give you gold stars and good grades along the way. It has its rewards. Yet, there were times in the field that I would have killed for an inviolable rule to follow—an SPSSX command to punch into the computer and let the results spill out. I found it exhausting, as well as exhilarating, to be constantly trying to figure out what to do next. It is unlikely that qualitative work will ever have specific research rules to punch into a computer, but it can—and in my opinion should—offer novice researchers more concrete guidance on matters of data collection, data analysis, and the writing up of qualitative work. This appendix is one, small contribution toward that process.

Part I: The Method of Home Advantage

Personal Background

I grew up in a white, upper-middle-class family; my father and mother worked as school teachers.[1] When I was in college, I spent three months in a small, predominantly black community in rural California, working in the schools as a teacher's aide and helping children with their homework in the evenings in their homes. After I graduated from college I thought about becoming a school teacher, and had there been jobs available I might have done so.

Instead, I got a job interviewing prisoners in City Prison for the San Francisco Pre-Trial Release Program. The program was commonly called the OR Project because it released defendants without bail on their own recognizance (OR).[2] Every day at 6.30 a.m. or at 5.00 p.m. I went inside City Prison. There, with one or two other co-workers, I made a record of who had been arrested, called them out to be interviewed, and spoke with them in the waiting room, through double-paned plastic windows and over telephones. Typically, I interviewed three to eight persons per day in the prison itself, then, in the office, I usually interviewed (by telephone) another ten or fifteen persons throughout the day. Each case needed three references—people who knew the defendant well and could verify the information collected, particularly the defendant's address, contact with relatives, and employment history. Over the course of two years, I did a lot of interviews.

The conditions for interviewing in this job were not exactly ideal. The telephones in City Prison did not work well; one or two were regularly out of order, and the ones that did work sometimes had static, so conversations were often conducted in a shout. Another OR worker was often sitting right next to me (about one foot away) also shouting interview questions. For each interview I would talk over the telephone (through the window) to a defendant, using my right hand to plug my ear so that I could hear her/his response. Once I heard the answer, I would balance the telephone on my left shoulder, use my left hand to secure the paper, and write down the answer. Throughout the interview other defendants stared down at the scene, and bailsmen, lawyers, families, and the guard with the door keys were all within ear shot. The defendants were often in crisis: many were dazed, angry, and adjusting to City Prison.

When I finished that job, I thought (modesty aside) that I had become an outstanding interviewer. I knew, particularly in telephone interviews with the families of respondents, that I often could get people to cooperate when other interviewers failed. I also knew that my interviews were very detailed, accurate, and, despite my truly terrible handwriting (a tremendous liability in field work), were considered to be among the best in the office. From that job I developed a love of interviewing as well as a firm desire to avoid ever being arrested and put in prison.

After I quit this job, I entered graduate school at the University of California, Berkeley, where I also worked intermittently as an interviewer. The twin experiences of working for two years as a full-time interviewer and working part-time on several research projects meant that I approached the field work for this study with uneven skills. In retrospect, I believe that this background had an important influence on the quality of the data I collected. I discovered I was more comfortable as an interviewer than as a participant-observer. While the months in the classrooms provided crucial information for this study, my field notes, for a complicated set of reasons which I explain below, were not as comprehensive, focused, or useful as they should have been. The interviews were much better. I felt I had a good rapport with the mothers and fathers I interviewed and I have confidence in the validity of the results.

The fact that the interviews were tape-recorded was also a major advantage. As my research lurched from studying everything in front of me in the field setting to a specific topic, my interests in a particular interview also shifted. Had I taken notes instead of tape-recording, I am certain that the comprehensiveness of my interview notes would have varied according to which question in the field setting seized my interest at that moment.[3] Although tape recorders do introduce an effect, particularly during the initial stages of an interview, I would not plan a new research project without them. In my opinion, they provide a form of insurance on the accuracy and comprehensiveness of data collected in the face of shifting intellectual concerns.

The Beginning of the Project

The research proposal, in its original formulation, was to study social class differences in family life and the influence of these family patterns on the process of schooling and on educational performance. I had grand plans. I was going to link class differences in family-school relationships to achievement patterns. I had hoped to study three rather than two schools; interview six families in each school; and I wanted to supplement the qualitative study with a quantitative analysis of a national data set of family-school relations. Almost immediately reality began to set in. Although I still think it would have been a good idea to have had a third school that was heterogeneous in students' social class, I also still think it would have been too much work. Without any real idea of where to begin, even comparing two schools seemed like two schools too many.

I did have a rough idea of what types of schools I wanted. I decided to study two specific social classes—white working-class and upper-middle-class parents. In this regard, as I note in the text, I followed in the footsteps of others in defining social class, notably Rubin (1976) and Kohn and Schooler (1983). I also wanted schools with a large number of white children to prevent the confounding influence of race. I ultimately sought two homogeneous schools with a concentration of children in each of the two social classes. Since most schools in the greater Bay Area are, in fact, segregated by social class, and to a lesser extent by race, this initial focus provided hundreds of schools as possible sites. I was timid about approaching schools. I worried about why a school would ever admit me. At times simply getting in seemed insurmountable, a problem discussed extensively in the literature.[4] In the end I used a different strategy for each school.

Access and Entrance at Colton

About two years before I began, I visited Colton school (and four other schools in the district) and interviewed the principal and vice-principal as a graduate research assistant on another project. The principal investigator of that project had asked for schools with a range of students by social class and Colton was the low socio-economic school. It was considered to be one of the best run schools in the district and I liked the principal and the vice-principal. In addition the school had a large number of white working-class students, a relatively unusual pattern. After a lot of stalling, I wrote the principal a letter (which unfortunately I have lost) asking for permission to visit one first grade classroom to learn about family-school relationships. I then called him and set up a time to talk about the project with him and the vice-principal.

To my astonishment, both of these administrators were very positive. We met for about fifteen minutes in the teachers' room (they had my letter in front of them) and most of the discussion centered on choosing a teacher. They had five teachers to choose from; I left the choice to them. They recommended one of their best first grade teachers, Mrs Thompson, and I accepted their choice. I knew it would be difficult to get one of their worst teachers and there were not, at least in my mind, any compelling analytic reasons for asking for one. (In fact, I preferred to have two good teachers in schools with good leadership. If I did, indeed, find class differences in family-school relationships, I didn't want those findings commingled with and confounded by questions about the quality of the teachers or administrators.) After our brief chat, the principal and the vice-principal said they would talk to the teacher for me and suggested that I return the following week. I left the school completely elated. I felt as if I might, after all, get this project off the ground.

The next week I returned, fifteen minutes late (I forgot my map and got lost), and the vice-principal took me to the classroom, where class was in progress. After the children went out to lunch, Mrs Thompson joined me at the table in the back of the classroom where I had been sitting. My notes from this encounter are sketchy at best:

> I summarize [the] project as an effort to learn about non-school factors [influence on achievement]. She says what do you want to do next; I say just observe, and then select five children and start to interview the parents. In the meantime, though, just observe and if I can help out in any way in the classroom then I am happy to do so. I also say that I realize that it is a busy time of year (tell her my mother was a teacher for 18 years) and that if I become a burden she should feel free to tell me. We then talk about when I will come next; she doesn't know exactly when class starts (she says, 'I just listen to the bells') and so checks chart on the wall. . . . We determine I will come Monday at 9.04.

From our first encounter on, Mrs Thompson was extremely nice, very friendly, and always tried to be helpful. Although I would like to think it is something I did to put her at ease, I think that basically she is a very nice person who goes through life being considerate and helpful.

In what became a play within a play, Mrs Thompson and other Colton staff were very helpful with the project and, without consulting parents, provided extraordinary materials. The teachers and staff simply gave me the test scores for all of the children in the class without any concern about consent forms or parents' permission. The principal, in considering the project, did not express any concern about the burden on parents and never suggested that I clear the project with the district office. And I never asked him if this was necessary. This was a mistake because for the rest of the project I was unnecessarily worried about what would happen if the district research officer found out about it. I also needed some district statistics and finally had to call the office and ask for them, without mentioning why I needed them. In addition, the principalship changed between the first and the second year of the study; both the principal and vice-principal left. I wrote a letter to the new principal and he agreed to cooperate and to be interviewed, but he might not have. This would have been extremely costly since I was almost one-half of the way through the study. As a result, I now believe in getting the highest official's formal approval for a project early on. I think it is very wise to contact respondents through informal channels but, once having secured access, it is important to gain official approval as well. This is usually not very hard to do (after you are already in the door).

Sometimes I puzzled about why Colton teachers and administrators cooperated so easily. The principal and vice-principal were interested in the research question; all of them thought family involvement in education was important but, although it was never articulated, they mainly seemed to think that being studied was part of their job. They had other researchers before me and expected others after me so they did not seem to treat it as a 'big deal' and were unruffled, helpful, and a bit *blasé* about the entire matter.

Access and Entrance at Prescott

At Prescott it was another story. There I was not given any real difficulty but the goals of the project were closely scrutinized. The district and school administrators expressed concern about the perspective of parents and the burden on parents, but the fact that both a district official and the principal were also graduate students appeared to be helpful in ultimately securing permission. Whereas I was never even asked about consent forms at Colton, the principal at Prescott asked that I get a separate slip from the six parents giving her their permission to release test scores to me. She felt that the human subjects permission form, although important, was not specific enough to cover the release of those materials. Knowing I had consent forms for only six families, the principal would never have released the test scores for the rest of the class to me.[5]

Part of this greater formality and rigidity at Prescott may have been related to my point of contact with the school. At Prescott I went through the district office which increased the emphasis on the procedures for approval of research projects (such as consent forms). I ended up at Prescott, rather than another school, through informal networks or the 'strength of weak ties' (Granovetter 1973). When I was looking for an upper-middle-class community Charles Benson, a very helpful member of my dissertation committee, suggested I think of Prescott. One of his graduate students (whom I knew slightly) worked as a district official, and at his suggestion I called her and then wrote her a letter.

That letter is reprinted in an end note.[6] It has many problems and it is much too long. Access letters should state the problem very briefly and then summarize accurately what the officials are being asked to do. In my letter the most important part (what I was asking them to do) is buried. The content of the letter I wrote to the district official was different than what I planned to tell the teacher and principal. Given that the district official was another graduate student I felt that I somehow owed her a longer, more academic explanation, but I had planned to adopt a much more vague approach with the teacher and parents. This strategy backfired because the district official forwarded the letter I wrote to her to the principal, who in turn gave it to the classroom teacher. I was quite upset at myself for this at the time as I should have known that might be a routine procedure. The lesson from this for me is that it is foolish to think, even if you are fellow graduate students, that one person should get one version of your project (when you are requesting access) and another person should get another. It is better to draft one version suitable for everyone.

Moreover in this age of bureaucracy, unless you are lucky, you will have to write a letter formally requesting access to a site. Another end note presents an introductory letter which, given what I know today, I wish I had written.[7] It is much shorter, more direct, and it focuses primarily on what I need from the site. Respondents do not need to be told, nor are they generally interested in, the details of the intellectual goals of the project (but see Walford 1987a). They seem mainly interested in knowing how much work you are asking them to do.

I now think that before I go into the field, I need a very short and very simple explanation for what I am doing there. When I began I had a one sentence description I was comfortable with: 'I want to learn more about how families help children in school'. If the listener wanted more information, however, I floundered. My answer, inevitably long and rambling, made both the person who asked the question and me squirm. Since that time I have been bored and perplexed when a simple question to a graduate student ('What are you studying?') produced a long, ambiguous, and defensive treatise.

As a matter of politeness, many people ask researchers what they are planning to do while in the field. It is essential to have a fleshed-out response prepared well in advance. In fact, in my bossy moments, I think that no researcher should begin a field study without memorizing a jargon-free summary of her/his intentions. This will save many awkward moments, increase rapport with people in the field, and help prevent the problem of respondents feeling particularly 'on stage' when they begin to engage in the activities in which they know that you are interested. A brief, accurate, and general statement will not of itself produce good rapport, but it is a better beginning point than a long and confused one.[8]

After receiving a copy of my letter (which was a mini-paper) the principal called me. She explained that the school was concerned about overburdening parents but that she was a graduate student as well and was sensitive to problems of research. Her biggest concern seemed to be the choice of the teacher. I wanted a self-contained first grade classroom; that year Prescott had only one first grade and one split classroom. There was only one choice and that was Mrs Walters.

I don't know what the principal, Mrs Harpst, told Mrs Walters. I do know that Mrs Walters was originally reluctant to have me in her classroom. As she told me later, she was afraid I would be a 'critical presence.' She agreed to participate, however, and the principal, in another telephone exchange, told me what day to begin the field work. Consequently I entered the school without ever meeting the principal face-to-face, and although I was at school regularly I did not meet her for several weeks.

The first day I appeared at school, Mrs Walters' welcome was cool. She showed me where to hang up my coat and put my purse but said very little in answer to my questions. Her aide, Mrs O'Donnell, was much warmer and bubbly. Mrs Walters told the children who I was while they were waiting in line outside the classroom. Her comments were:

> Today we have a visitor named Miss Lareau. She hasn't been in a classroom for a long time and so she wanted to visit our class and see how you work and talk and play.[9]

Mrs Walters' classroom was much smaller than Mrs Thompson's, and there was no free table at the back of the room. I felt painfully and obviously out of place that first day, as I listened to Mrs Walters talking to the children outside the classroom and watched Mrs O'Donnell work in the corner on some papers. They had not suggested where to sit or stand and I felt continually in the way. Finally, I found a chair in an empty space at the back of the classroom. When the children walked in they all stared at me intently and then walked to their seats, still staring. I was uncomfortable, Mrs Walters seemed uncomfortable, and the children seemed uncomfortable as well, although, as I explain below, they quickly adjusted to my presence.

My entrance to Prescott therefore was less smooth than at Colton for many reasons, including Mrs Walters' general discomfort at having me in the classroom, her lack of control over being selected as a research subject and, on top of that, her having been shown my overly complicated letter. I was worried that the focus on social class described in the letter might have had an important influence on Mrs Walters' behavior. She never seemed to remember what I was studying; she consistently treated me as if I were an educator studying the curriculum (which I was not) rather than someone interested in family involvement in schooling. As I noted in my field notes:

> Mrs Walters seems very interested in explaining the logic of learning activities to me. She carefully explains the bucket program and the 'hands on training' they are receiving. . . . This pattern, of Mrs Walters repeatedly telling me about the curriculum, makes me think that she sees me as an educator with the tools to evaluate a good or bad learning program. And/or, [it makes me think] she is worried about being evaluated.

Over time my relationship with Mrs Walters gradually warmed up. I considered the day she told me that she originally hadn't wanted me in the classroom to be a watershed. I felt that I had reached some level of acceptance but it took more time and more work than my relationship with Mrs Thompson. As I complained in my field notes, 'I often feel at a loss for words [with her].' Being somewhat shy myself, I felt ill at ease with her when we were alone together and I often seemed to fumble in my efforts to chat with her. But the aide was so friendly and got along so well with both Mrs Walters and me that, when she was there, the social interaction was quite comfortable and pleasant. During recess the three of us would go get a cup of coffee and visit together. When the aide was not there (in the afternoon or when she was sick) relations between Mrs Walters and me were much more formal. Like some older married couples, Mrs Walters and I both seemed to be more comfortable in the classroom with the children between us than trying to negotiate socializing together in a quiet classroom. At first I almost dreaded recess and lunch time with Mrs Walters, and I felt that I truly did not know what to do with myself. If Mrs Walters was doing an errand my choices were to sit in the classroom (which I felt self-conscious about since I never saw any aides or teachers do this), sit in the teachers' room (where I didn't know any of the teachers and conversation seemed to grind to a halt with my presence), or go to the bathroom and then return to the classroom looking busy (I did that a lot).

From this I learned that I had difficulty 'hanging out' and that I was happier in more structured situations, such as when class was in session or when I was interviewing someone. I also concluded that life would have been easier if, during the very first days in the field, I had come to school more frequently than twice a week for a few hours. If I had stayed all day and come three or four days in a row during the first week I would have been introduced to all of the staff and become more integrated. As it was I was introduced to a few staff members, but after that I saw a lot of familiar faces but was never introduced to them. Today I am much better at being able to say, 'I don't think we have met, although I have seen you around. My name is. . . '. But at that time I felt tongue-tied and often moved in and out of the teachers' lounges in both schools without talking or getting to know the other teachers.

Although I came to feel accepted in the classroom in both Prescott and Colton I never felt very comfortable outside of the classroom. This meant that my study was essentially restricted to single classrooms, and I lost the possibility of learning about the organizational dynamics at each school. Even today I feel that if I had been a more skilled field worker, had become more comfortable on the site, had been better at easing my way into informal settings and simply 'hanging out', that I would have learned more than I did. In particular I might have learned more about routine conflicts between parents and teachers in other classrooms, disagreements among teachers about how to manage parents, and principal-teacher relationships. I also might have gotten onto a more human footing with Mrs Walters and, for example, learned more about sensitive issues, including how she felt about parents breathing down her neck and who she really was. As it stands the manuscript treats these issues only superficially.

My Role in the Classroom

Someone told me once that in field work: *You need to know who you are and what you are doing there.* This is good advice, but such certainty is often hard to come by at the beginning since, even if you have one idea, the context may lead you to different ones. My role in the classroom differed between the two schools and this turned out to be another source of information about family-school relationships.

At Colton it was rare for adults to be in the classroom unless they were teachers or teachers' aides. In addition, children were almost always sitting at desks doing their work; they were not working on projects that needed individual supervision. As a result there was not much that Mrs Thompson needed me to do. Sometimes I would help out with art projects; for example, helping children open glue bottles and wiping up spilled glue. Mostly, however, I watched the lessons from the back of the classroom. This was facilitated by the fact that the classroom was quite large, there was a table in the back of the room at which I could comfortably sit, and the table was five or six feet from the nearest desk, giving me a little distance. I was not grossly disrupting the class by sitting there. I was not completely passive: I helped children line up, I went with them out to recess, I mediated disputes on the playground at children's requests, I went with them to the library, and frequently chatted with children in the class about things that were important to them (e.g., their toys, the pictures they drew). I knew the names of the children in the class and many of the children would wave and say hello to me when I walked across the playground as I came and went at school.

At Prescott, however, the classroom organization, spatial arrangements, and increased presence of parents on the school site led me to interact with children more and in different ways than at Colton. Mrs Walters wanted me to come to school to volunteer during 'independent time.' In these one hour periods three times per week, the class was divided into four 'stations' and different projects were available in each station. Mrs Walters scheduled a parent volunteer to be in the classroom during these times. This left four adults (including myself) to supervise the children as they worked independently. Children frequently had questions and particularly in the beginning of an hour in which the children were working on a new project all the adults were busy answering questions. Once the project got underway there was less to do as children went to work at their own pace.[10]

The problem was, as many parents so bitterly complained, that not all the children worked. Most did work consistently, but many would—for brief periods of time—break classroom rules by poking, hitting, or fussing at each other. Some children, including four or five boys, hardly did any work at all. The children seemed to operate under an implicit class-room rule that if an adult was watching you then you behaved and worked. I was ambivalent about what my role was to be; I didn't want to be a teacher or a disciplinarian. Like a favorite aunt or family friend, I was hoping to avoid discipline issues altogether. I wrote about this ambiva-lence in my notes:

> I am unsure as to what my role should be when children are not working productively or are 'acting out' with squabbles and minor fights. It is note-worthy that most of the children ignore me and continue their disputes in my presence (while with Mrs Walters and usually with Mrs O'Donnell the dispute is changed or is dropped).

The children quickly realized that I would not scold them and force them to work; as a result they would continue to misbehave in front of me. This made me uncomfortable. On the one hand I didn't want to be scolding children; on the other hand I didn't want Mrs Walters to feel that I was not helping out and doing what adults normally did in the classroom. Consequently I sometimes looked foolish and ineffective in the class-room, as this example makes clear:

> [Today] two boys were pushing each other in their chairs while they were supposed to be playing the numbers game. I came up behind them and said something weak/mild such as, 'Are you boys playing the numbers game?' They obviously were not as they continued to shove and push each other. Mrs Harris then saw them and came over and said harshly, 'Jonathan, Roger. Stop that this instant! Now sit up and sit in your chairs and behave!' (She physically pushed them apart and pushed their chairs closer to their desks).

Clearly, Mrs Harris was not ambivalent about controlling children. As my notes reflect, I began to think that I might have to get off the fence and take a more assertive role:

> When I started volunteering I wanted to disrupt the [classroom] activities as little as possible and so I made a concerted effort to stay away from the teacher/disciplinarian role. I am discovering, however, that in the world of children the adult/child split means I am often forced into the teacher/disci-plinarian role. Otherwise I am seen as powerless, not threatening, and the object of a great deal of acting out behavior when the children are not under the teacher's rule.

I didn't write down the actual date that I finally decided to abandon my passive role, but by about one third of the way through the field work I was controlling the children more and following the roles of the parents and teachers. This seemed to help; I felt more comfortable in the class-room and the children, Mrs Walters, and Mrs O'Donnell began to treat me like another parent or teacher's aide. I helped children with their stories, their art work, and various projects. I gave tests, I dictated problems which they wrote on the board, and supervised children, enforcing class-room rules when we went to the auditorium for a special event. When Mrs Walters left school to have an operation six weeks before the end of the semester, I continued to visit the classroom. By then I was integrated into the classroom, and Miss Chaplan, Mrs Walters' replacement, seemed to accept my presence. I helped organize the report cards and the games on the last day of school.

As I discuss in the text, my relationship to parents mirrored the pattern of family-school relationships in the two schools: I had much more con-tact with parents at Prescott than at Colton and the parents at Prescott scrutinized my activities much more closely than they did at Colton. There were advantages and disadvantages to this. The advantage of my more active role in the classroom at Prescott was that I worked with some of the parents and was, in many ways, a valuable assistant to Mrs Wal-ters, which she appreciated. The drawback was that I couldn't take notes in the classroom. I only tried that once in Mrs Walters' class. The room was too small to accommodate a desk for me so I had to write on my lap; and I was only two or three feet away from the children's desks so my note-taking distracted them. Also, I was often there for independent time and Mrs Walters needed adults to walk around and help children as they all worked independently. As a result I had to try to recreate notes after I left the site. This increased the amount of time that field work demanded and produced notes with fewer quotes than at Colton.[11]

Access and Entrance to the Families

When I entered the field I had planned to select the parents of children at the end of the school year, after I had observed in the classroom. Seeking a balance by gender and achievement levels, I decided to select a boy and a girl from the high, medium, and low reading groups for interviews. In each school, I wanted five children from intact families (although their parents could be remarried) and one child from a single-parent family. At Colton, since almost one half of the class was non-white, and around a quarter were from single-parent homes, only about one third of the chil-dren were potential candidates. One day after school, Mrs Thompson and I sat down with the reading groups. We chose a boy and a girl from each reading group. Whenever possible Mrs Thompson recommended chil-dren whose parents she knew from having interacted with them at the school. As a result, the Colton families I interviewed were somewhat more active in their children's schooling than the average parent. After we had made the choices, she gave me a booklet with the names, addresses, and telephone numbers of the families and I copied them out. She also gave me test scores for the entire class.

Mrs Walters was gone from Prescott by the end of the year. One afternoon after school, as we were cleaning up the classroom, the teacher's aide, the replacement teacher (Miss Chaplan), and I talked about whom to select for the study. The decisions were as follows, I selected Donald since he was clearly the highest achiever in the class and I had met his parents at Open House. Mrs O'Donnell also told me that Donald's parents were enthusiastic about the study and were hoping to be selected. Such flattery is hard to resist. I selected Carol and Emily because I had met their mothers and observed them in the classroom. I selected Jonathan, although I had not met his mother, because he was the lowest achieving boy. I added Allen in part because both Jonathan and Donald were well behaved and I wanted someone who was more of a troublemaker. Allen fitted that bill. The children represented almost one quarter of the class but, since five of the six mothers volunteered in the classroom, a slightly higher percentage of mothers active in school. After we selected the children I copied down the names and addresses of the families.

With these two sessions the sample was set. At Colton, however, two of the families moved during the summer after first grade before I had interviewed them. In the second year of the study I needed to add two more families, a boy and a girl, one of whom was from a single-parent family. Because I had not anticipated this, I did not have other names and addresses from which to choose. During the next year I visited Colton occasionally, and I discovered that Mrs Sampson's second grade class had a white girl, Suzy, who was a high achiever and whose parents visited the school frequently. Her father was a sheriff and her mother was a student. The teacher gave me their telephone number and I contacted them. Because of scheduling difficulties I had only one interview with them, but it was a long one and both the mother and father participated in it (with their eight-month-old girl sitting on my lap for much of the time).

The other child I added to the study, Ann-Marie, was in Mrs Sampson's class, and Mrs Sampson frequently mentioned her in informal conversations. I checked my field notes and I had a lot of notes about her from first grade. I decided to add her in the second year because I had been following her; she was from a single-parent family, and she seemed to exemplify important tensions that can occur between parents and schools. This choice was costly, however, as it upset the gender balance and left me with four girls and two boys in the Colton sample. Ann-Marie's mother did not have a telephone but Mrs Sampson told me when their parent-teacher conference would be held. So, with a show of confidence I didn't actually feel, I simply went to the conference and spoke to Ann-Marie's mother there. She agreed, with no resistance, to be in the study. This scrambling around to add respondents to the study could have been avoided if I had started the year by following a pool of ten or fifteen families, expecting that some would have moved (or dropped out for other reasons) by the second year.

In reflecting on the choice of families, I continue to feel that the children at both Colton and Prescott schools were a reasonably good sample of the classroom. There were no glaring omissions in terms of discipline problems, achievement levels, temperament, popularity, and parent involvement in schooling. At both schools I had a range of parents, from the most heavily involved to the least involved in school site activities and, according to teachers, in educational activities at home. Still, the sample was small and non-random so I cannot confirm this impression.

In addition to the twelve families in my sample I interviewed both principals, the first and second grade teachers at both schools, and the special education teacher at Colton. I interviewed the first grade teachers in the summer after first grade; the interviews with the second grade teachers and the principals were about a year later. The interviews ranged over a number of issues, including teachers' ideas of the proper role of parents in schooling, and their assessment of the level of educational support which the families were providing for their children. These discussions of the individual children were very helpful; they provided a useful contrast to parents' assessment of their behavior. At times teachers provided me with information which I would have liked to have asked parents about, as when Mrs Thompson told me she sent Jill to the nurse because of body odor. Unfortunately the demands of confidentiality precluded me from probing these issues as much as I would have liked. I did ask parents general questions; if they did not discuss the issue I was looking for, then I simply dropped it. To have done otherwise would have violated the teachers' confidentiality.

Requesting Interviews

In requesting interviews with parents I followed a different strategy for each school. In a qualitative methods class I took, Lillian Rubin cautioned against writing letters to working-class families asking them to participate in a study. She said that it was usually better to telephone, since working-class families did not read as much nor did they routinely receive letters on university stationery. This advice made sense to me and I followed it. I telephoned the Colton mothers, verbally explained the study and asked permission to visit them in their homes. At Prescott, I sent parents a letter describing the study and requesting their participation. I then telephoned a few days later and set up a time for the interview. These written requests for participation did not go out at the same time. They were sent out about a week before I was able to schedule the interview. At both schools the requests and the interviews were staggered over a period of several months.

All of the mothers at Colton and Prescott agreed to participate with little hesitation. The fact that I had been in Mrs Walters' and Mrs Thompson's classes seemed to help in gaining access to the children's homes. After I interviewed the mothers at the end of first grade, I told them I would like to return a year later. All of the mothers were agreeable to this. At the end of the second interview with each mother, I asked if I could interview the father as well. I interviewed all five Prescott fathers (Gail lived in a single-parent family). At Colton, I succeeded in interviewing only three of the five fathers. Mrs Morris and Mrs Brown were doubtful and reluctant to arrange for me to interview their husbands, and I did not press my request. I regret that now—I think with a bit of pressure I could have interviewed Mr Morris, since I met him at school once and at home once. I never even saw Mr Brown. He never went to school and his wife said that he was very shy. I doubt that, even if I had pursued it, I would have gained his cooperation. In addition, because of scheduling difficulties, I only interviewed Jonathan's mother (Prescott) once rather than twice.

In my telephone conversations and my letters to mothers asking for permission to interview them, I said the interviews would last about an hour and fifteen minutes ('depending on how much you have to tell me'). It turned out that the interviews took much longer; they always took at least ninety minutes and in most cases two hours. I discovered this very quickly and should have changed what I told parents but, again fearing rejection, I didn't. Now I would. It is a risk but, if it were happening to me, I would be irritated if I had set aside an hour and the interview took two. Furthermore, for reasons I don't completely understand, when I was in their offices or homes respondents rarely told me that it was time to go. Instead, adopting etiquette norms regarding guests, they seemed to wait me out. It was easy to delude myself and think that the respondents were enjoying the conversation so much that they didn't mind it going overtime, and in some cases that was true. But it was rude of me knowingly to conceal the true length of the interview (even by fifteen minutes to a half-hour) when I made my initial requests. It violated both the spirit and the letter of the notion that a researcher must respect her/his subjects.

My Perceived Role with Parents

The Prescott parents did not have any trouble figuring out who I was and what I was doing. They knew what graduate school was, they knew what a dissertation was, and they understood the concept of someone doing research on education without being an educator. Many had friends and relatives in doctoral programs. My general introduction was followed by questions from Prescott parents about my specific academic and career goals (e.g., 'Is this for your dissertation?').

The Colton parents did have difficulty figuring out who I was and what I was doing there. All of the mothers asked me if I was planning to become a teacher. When I said no, that I was working on a research project for the university, I generally drew nods accompanied by looks of confusion. In the beginning I often said I was a 'graduate student'. I dropped that description after a mother asked me if that meant I was going to graduate soon. From then on, I said that the university did a lot of studies and I was working on a research project to find out how families helped children in school. If mothers continued to ask questions about my plans I often took them through a brief explanation of the higher education system: 'After graduating from high school some people go to college. After four years of college people graduate and get a Bachelor's degree. After that, some people go on to more school, do research and get another degree. That is what I am trying to do now.' Overall, I would say that the Colton parents seemed to think that I was friendly, but that I was from a foreign land 'over there', a world they had little contact with and did not understand. Even without that understanding, however, they were willing to participate in the project.

One consequence of this confusion was that Colton mothers mistakenly thought I worked at the school. My efforts to establish myself as being independent of the school took on new vigor after my first visit to Jill's home, which was early in the interviews. I had finished the interview, had packed everything up, and was standing in the kitchen, chatting. Suddenly I saw that on the wall of the kitchen was a calendar, and on that day's date was written 'visit from school', with the time of our interview. I considered that to be very bad news; it could, and probably did, shape what the mother was willing to tell me. But the interview was over; it was too late to do anything more.

Thereafter, with parents, especially Colton parents, I stepped up my efforts to convince them that I was not from the school by stressing at the beginning of the interview, and repeating it in different ways at different times during the interview, that I did not work there ('Now, I am not from the school and there is something I don't understand very well. . . '). Although I can't be certain, I think these strategies worked; with some probing, all of the Colton parents did express criticisms of the school, although, as I show in the text, they were of a different character than at Prescott.

The Interviews

The interviews took place in the homes, in the living room or dining room. The interviews with mothers who worked in the home were often in the middle of the day, the ones with the fathers and the mothers who worked outside the home took place in the evening or at the weekend. In some cases the houses were quiet; in others children, dogs, house-cleaners, and the telephone frequently intervened. The interviews were open-ended and were set up to be more like a conversation than an interview. I had an interview guide but I sometimes varied the order of the questions, depending on how the interview was evolving. I had a tape recorder and I did not take notes during the interview. Instead, I tried to maintain eye contact, nod frequently, and make people feel comfortable. In the course of these and other interviews, I have discovered that each interview guide has its own rhythm. I have found that there is a particular time (often one eighth of the way through the interview) when the respondent should be 'with you.' If the respondent is not 'with you', it usually means that the interview is in trouble.[12]

In my interviews in people's homes, I found that within fifteen minutes of my arrival we should be set up and ready to begin the interview. Fifteen minutes into the interview things should be more relaxed; the respondent should look less tense and be sitting more comfortably in the chair; the original tension in the room and interpersonal awkwardness should be easing up; and there should be a sense of movement and revelation. Usually that happened, occasionally it did not. Some respondents (like some students in an examination) never seemed to settle into the rhythm. The situation remained awkward all the way through. In those instances I often discontinued the interview and started chatting. I asked the respondents questions about their house, their dog, their clothes, their pictures, their car. (Or I talked about myself, my clothes, local shopping malls I have been in, my family, my childhood fights with my brothers and sisters.) My goal was to try to put these people at ease, make myself seem less intimidating, find something that we had in common, and—I suppose—to portray myself as a 'regular person', one that they could talk to easily. In addition, I was interested in hearing them talk about something they cared about and could discuss with ease. That was helpful, for it gave me a sense of the tone and demeanor which I was striving for when I went back to the interview questions.[13]

Sometimes these conversational diversions, while hardly subtle, did seem to help. Respondents seemed to relax and began to forget the tape recorder. (Noticing that I didn't turn off the tape recorder or apparently mind wasting tape on a discussion of the family dog seemed to help some respondents to relax.) A few interviews—my first interview with Laura's mother at Colton and my interviews with Gail's mother at Prescott—never seemed to 'click' fully. There were good moments followed by awkward ones. For example, when I arrived at Laura's house the television was on and the mother didn't turn it off; in fact, she continued to stare at it from time to time, and comment about it during the interview. It was one of my first interviews in a home and I didn't have the nerve to ask her to turn it off. Now I always make sure that the television is off or, if others are watching it, I move the interview to another room. One of the first things I say after I get set up with the tape recorder is, 'Do you mind if we turn off the television for a while? I'm afraid this tape recorder is quirky and the television really causes problems. It shouldn't be too long'. I also thank them when they do turn off the television and again, when I am leaving, apologize if they missed any of their favorite programs because of the interview.

Considering the number of interviews, having two or three awkward ones was not very many, but I found such occasions to be extremely depressing. I tried to take comfort in Lillian Rubin's comment that it 'happens to everyone'. She confided that, after trying everything she could think of to enliven a failing interview with no success, she would simply finish the interview as quickly as possible and 'get out of there'. I still consider that to be good advice.

Data Analysis

I did two data analyses on this project. The first was half-hearted; the second time I was more systematic as I followed many of the ideas in Matthew Miles and A. Michael Huberman's (1984) very good book on data analysis, *Qualitative Data Analysis: A Sourcebook of New Methods*. Fortunately, the results did not change when I analyzed the data more carefully, although the second attempt did highlight themes I had not seen before. Readers interested in data analysis generally are referred to Miles and Huberman. In this section, I simply summarize the steps I took in the two analyses.

In my first effort, I finished collecting the data and then, based on what I had learned, I wrote it up. I felt that I had to portray the data accurately and I carefully reviewed my interviews and field notes. I also drew heavily on the notes I wrote after each interview: a short statement (usually three pages, single-spaced) which summarized the key issues in the interview.[14] During this period I transcribed sections of tapes where I felt there were important quotes, making carbon copies of these transcriptions. One copy of these quotes was put into a file, with the folders organized by child; the carbon copy was cut up and glued onto index cards. I also made numerous charts, sketching out the responses of parents to different issues, a precursor to 'data displays'. But the entire process was informal.

The second time I analyzed the data, the analysis was much more comprehensive and systematic. First, I spent hours listening to tapes: I purchased a portable tape recorder (a 'Walkman') and listened to tapes in the house, as I rode my bike, made dinner, and went about my life. In addition, all of the interviews were transcribed verbatim. It took an average of ten to fifteen hours for me or the secretaries in my department to transcribe a two hour interview, depending on sound quality. The shortest interview was ten pages, single-spaced: the longest was twenty-five pages, single-spaced. For a few interviews, only critical sections (anywhere from seven to fifteen pages of single-spaced quotes per interview) were transcribed. In all, I had thirty-seven interviews with typed quotes, each interview quite lengthy.

I cut these single-spaced transcriptions up into individual quotes (with a code name on each quote) and glued them on five by eight inch index cards. Colton was yellow, Prescott was white, and the teachers in both schools were blue. I ended up with over one thousand index cards. At first the cards were simply in groups by school and by child. Then they were sorted by basic categories: parents' view of their proper role, their educational activities in the home, and their complaints about Mrs Walters. I also had categories for family life, including children's lessons outside of school and the social networks among parents in the community. Teachers' cards were grouped according to what educational activities they sought from parents.[15]

As the analysis continued, I tried to clarify my research question in the light of the literature. In particular I tried to see how my data could modify, challenge, or elaborate known findings. The cards continued to be in piles by major analytic categories (all over the living room floor), but the composition of these groups shifted as I reviewed the quotes, thought about the research question, looked for negative examples, and tried to clarify the differences within the schools as well as between them. For example, during the first analysis I focused on parents' educational activities at home and their attendance at school events. Gradually I realized that Colton and Prescott parents' actions went beyond helping at home. Parents in the two schools differed in how much they criticized the school and supplemented the school program. I also found omissions in the literature on this issue. This shifted the focus from looking at social class differences in parents' support (i.e., how much parents complied with teachers' requests) to the more inclusive notion of linkages.

As I pursued this idea the analytic categories became more numerous: teachers' wishes for parent involvement; parents' beliefs regarding their proper role, information about schooling, scrutiny of teachers, interventions in school site events, criticisms of teachers, educational aspirations for their children; and possible explanations of why parents were—or were not—involved in schooling. Differences between mothers and fathers and the disadvantages of parents' involvement were two other categories.

During this time I maintained index cards about each child in the study. These quickly became inefficient and cumbersome because the case studies of children were incomplete and I was 'borrowing' cards from the analytic piles to supplement information on each child. Finally I developed a dual system. For each child I had a collection of transcribed interviews on paper for the mother (both interviews) and the father. I also had the comments that the teacher had made about the child. These typed interviews were all paper-clipped together and put in three piles (Colton, Prescott, and educators). In addition, copies of all of the interviews were cut and pasted onto hundreds of index cards which were kept in analytic categories within open cardboard boxes (with rubber bands grouping cards in subcategories), and rearranged slightly as the analysis developed. Ultimately the chapters of this book mirrored the boxes of cards.

Following Miles and Huberman, I also made numerous 'data displays'. For example, I created matrices with the children listed in rows and various types of parent involvement in columns (i.e., reviewing papers after school, reading, attending Open House, attending conferences). I also produced matrices on select issues: in one chart I compared the criticisms Colton and Prescott parents had of school, in another I displayed what parents said was their proper role in schooling. The information on the cards duplicated the data displays (on large pieces of poster board) which provided a quick, visual overview of the evidence. Put differently, the cards showed me what I had, as the groups of cards provided stacks of evidence in support of ideas; the data displays showed me what I didn't have—as the cells revealed missing cases or showed exceptions to the pattern. Producing these matrices was time-consuming, but they were very helpful in displaying the strengths and weaknesses of the argument. Together the coding categories, sorting system, and dual system of case studies and analytic categories gave me a chance to look for other patterns, and increased my confidence in the accuracy of my interpretation of the data.

Mistakes: Lessons from the Field

I made one very serious mistake in the field; I fell behind in writing up my field notes. Writing up field notes immediately is one of the sacred obligations of field work. Yet workers I have known well all confessed that they fell behind in their field notes at one time or another. Researchers are human:—we get sick; we have an extra glass of wine; we get into fights with our spouses; we have papers to grade, due the next day; or we simply don't feel like writing up field notes immediately after an interview or a participant-observation session. On top of that, at least for me, writing field notes is both boring and painful: boring, because it repeats a lot of what you just did and it takes a long time to write a detailed description of a fifteen-minute encounter/observation; painful, because it forces you to confront unpleasant things, including lack of acceptance, foolish mistakes in the field, ambiguity about the intellectual question, missed opportunities in the field, and gaping holes in the data. To be sure, there is a tremendous sense of satisfaction in having placed on paper the experiences of the day and then adding these to the top of a neat and growing pile. But the time! Initially, one hour in the field would take me three hours to write up. Missing sessions of writing field notes can, like skipping piano practice, get quickly out of hand . . . exponentially, in fact.

If I wrote up my interviews two or three days later, I put 'retrospective notes' (or retro for short) at the top of the first page. In many cases I believe that I could have recreated, even several weeks later, a good account of what happened in the classroom, but I imposed on myself a certain 'code of honor'. If I missed my deadline and didn't write the event up within a few days of its occurrence, I wouldn't allow myself to write it up a week or two later and use my recollections as field notes. I was sure that the information would be distorted. So there were notes that I never wrote up despite my best intentions. My delinquencies multiplied because I didn't stop going into the field; gaining acceptance in the field is dependant on being there and being part of things. The more I went the more interesting things I saw, and the more people told me about upcoming events that they encouraged me to attend (i.e., the Easter Hat parade, a play coming to school). Like a greedy child on Christmas Day who keeps opening package after package without stopping to play with them and then asks for more, I kept going to the field, didn't write it up, but went back to the field anyway for fear of missing something really important. I usually went to the field three times per week (alternating schools), or about a dozen times per month. I don't know exactly how many transgressions I committed. My best estimate is that I completed about 100 hours of observation, with more hours at Prescott than at Colton, and I failed to write notes on about one eighth of my field work. Today I faithfully record in my calendar when I go into the field, where I go, and how long I stay. In my current and future work I want to be able to state, as Lubeck (1984; 1985) did, how many hours of field work the study is based on. This record of visits to the field also helps me keep track of sets of field notes and interviews.

In spite of these omissions I had, of course, quite a large amount of data. I was in the classrooms for several months and had stacks of carefully written notes of routine activities. Many studies (Lightfoot 1983) have been based on far less, but it was a serious breach of field methods and, although I cannot prove it, one that I am convinced is more common than is noted in the literature. In hindsight, the writing up of field notes was linked to the renowned problem of 'going native'. I liked being in the classrooms; I liked the teachers, the children, and the activities—making pictures of clovers for St Patrick's Day, eggs for Easter, and flower baskets for May. I liked being there the most when I felt accepted by the teachers and children. Thinking about taking notes reminded *me* that I was a stranger, forced me to observe the situation as an outsider, and prevented me from feeling accepted and integrated into the classroom. Writing up my field notes was a constant reminder of my outsider status. It was also a reminder of the ambiguous status of my intellectual goals; I knew only vaguely where I was going with the project. I also worried I might be making the wrong decisions, such as when I began to take a more active role in the class at Prescott or spent most of the time at Prescott during independent time (when Mrs Walters needed help) rather than visiting the classroom regularly at other points in the day. There was a lurking anxiety about the field work: Was it going right? What was I doing? How did people feel about me? Was I stepping on people's toes? What should I do next?—and this anxiety was tiring.

The few times when I forgot about note-taking and observing and just enjoyed being there, I felt a tremendous sense of relief. I liked the feeling of giving up being a researcher and simply being a teacher's aide. The seduction of participation sometimes overshadowed the goal of participation; and the cost was a lack of carefully collected information. If I could do it over, I would arrange things so that I had a different set of choices. I would change my schedule and slow down the project. Although it was advantageous to be in both schools at once, in the interest of completeness I would now probably do one school at a time. I was also in a hurry to get through graduate school, a goal that now seems short-sighted. As a result I have developed what I call the Lareau Iron Law of Scheduling:

> Never (and I mean never) go into the field unless you have time that night, or in the next twenty-four hours, to write up the notes.

Such rigidity may seem hard to enforce because presence in the field is critical to sustaining access and rapport. There is also the 'somewhere else' problem (Walford 1987) that something critically important will take place and you will miss it. But whatever happens will often happen again, particularly if it is part of the routine social interaction that qualitative workers are usually trying to study.

This iron law of scheduling can be carried out, it just takes self-restraint. And it is crucial: field work without notes is useless and destructive. It is useless because without documentation the observations cannot and should not be incorporated into the study; it is destructive because worrying about missing notes takes away valuable time and energy from the project, creates new problems, undermines competence, and turns a potentially rewarding process into a burdensome one. In my experience at least, it is not worth it.

A Hybrid Pattern

In most of the classic studies, the researchers were sustained by grants and field work was all that they did. Today such full-time devotion to field work is uncommon because difficulty securing full-time funding means that researchers are balancing other economic commitments while in the field. For graduate students, making ends meet often means working as a research assistant on someone else's project. For faculty, it means continuing to meet teaching obligations while doing field work. Although researchers would love to face only a computer when they leave the field, many in fact must go to committee meetings, write lectures, go to work, pick up children, fix dinner, etc. For many researchers, a hybrid pattern of commitments has replaced the single commitment model of field work that characterized the community studies of the past.

This new hybrid pattern affects the character of field work in many ways. In my case other obligations severely curtailed the amount of time I could spend in the field. I was working twenty hours per week, I had many school obligations, I had to run my own household, and I was living in an area with family and friends in the immediate vicinity. It was often hard to find six to ten hours a week to go to the schools. In addition I felt the strain of straddling two different worlds. I would leave Prescott school and, with my head swimming with thoughts about how I should have handled Allen poking Jonathan, drive to the university, try to find a parking place in the middle of the day, and go to work as a sociology teaching assistant. It was disorienting. Because being in the field required more formal attire than was the norm among students at the university, I found myself constantly explaining to people I met in the hallway why I was so dressed up. I felt on stage and out of place when I was visiting the classroom, but I also felt myself a misfit at the university. I had trouble getting used to this; it seemed as if I could never establish a routine.

I think that researchers need to take seriously this hybrid pattern of research and analyze the differences it makes in access, entrance, rapport, data collection, and data analysis. It seems to me, for example, that access must be negotiated over longer periods of time, and more often, when the worker is moving in and out of the field than when she/he is living there (see Bosk 1979). Data collection is slower when the researcher is in the field less often, and moving in and out of the field is a strain, though possibly less of a strain than living in an unfamiliar environment for months at a time (Powdermaker 1966). Although data collection takes longer, data analysis and the clarification of the research question may move along more quickly under this hybrid pattern. Being in a university environment as well as in a field setting provides more people with whom to discuss the research question. This ready availability of sounding boards may help the researcher move ahead more rapidly with the data analysis.

Whether a commitment pattern is hybrid or single, all qualitative researchers inevitably experience errors and confusion in their research. In the course of defining the problem, negotiating access, beginning observations, and conducting interviews, many decisions must be made, some of which—in retrospect—are regrettable. This is true in all research, but in qualitative methods the mistakes are usually carried out and observed by the researcher first hand (rather than being committed by others and reported—or not reported—to the principal investigator by subordinates). Qualitative researchers also work in naturalistic settings and they lack opportunities to 'rerun' the data. Moreover, overwhelmed by the immediacy of the field setting, the sheer amount of data collected, and the many possibilities which the project offers, some researchers—temporarily or permanently—lose sight of their intellectual question(s). I turn now to a discussion of this problem.

Part II: Problems with the Research Question

Blinded by Data

Two months into my field work, a graduate seminar on participant-observation was offered by Michael Burawoy. Thinking that it might be useful to have others to talk to about the project I enrolled in the course.[16] As I soon discovered, Burawoy (1979) viewed qualitative data as data that tried to help answer a question. He allowed that the mode of inquiry might be very different than the mode of presentation in the final report, but he was interested in having us—all of us—answer sociological questions. 'So what?' was the question of the quarter.

As Burawoy soon discovered, I resisted this approach. More precisely, I was ambivalent and confused about how to write up the data I was collecting, which grew, literally, by the hour. Data collection is an absorbing process and it pleased me to add more and more field notes to the pile and make arrangements to complete interviews. Still, the sheer amount of data sometimes seemed overwhelming and I did not feel prepared to analyze it. I had unconsciously accepted the methodology of survey research which consists of four steps: a) formulate a problem; b) collect data; c) analyze it; and d) write it up. I was overextended simply trying to get to both schools, take notes, write up the notes, work as a teaching assistant, and keep up with Burawoy's class. As far as I was concerned, the analysis could wait.

My ambivalence, however, centered less on the problem of not having time to do it and more on the proper strategy for analyzing and writing up qualitative research—a problem which ultimately haunts almost all qualitative researchers. I wanted to describe social reality, to supply the details and the vivid descriptions that would draw my readers in and carry them along; I hoped to produce the holistic and seamless feeling of many of the ethnographies that I had read. Some of the many works in this genre are analytical. *Tally's Corner* (Liebow 1968), *Worlds of Pain* (Rubin 1976), and *Everything in Its Path* (Erikson 1976) all have arguments—but the analysis seems subordinate to the data. They certainly aren't written in the 'now-I-am-going-to-discuss-three-ideas' style which characterized everything I had written during graduate school. Captivated by some of the ethnomethodology and anthropology I had read, I was eager to abandon explicit intellectual questions and 'simply' describe social reality. More to the point, I believed that was what good ethnographers did. Describing reality provided intrinsically interesting information. The intellectual ideas, tucked away in a concluding chapter or footnotes, did not spoil or constrain the novelistic portrayal of reality. I had hoped to use my own data to draw compelling pictures which would not—to use a favorite expression of mine at the time—violate the complexity of social reality. But I was also interested in ideas. I had waded through Bourdieu and found his approach useful. I was genuinely interested in the way in which social stratification was reproduced, and in the contribution made to children's life chances, by the interactions between parents and teachers.

As my field work progressed I struggled to determine the 'proper' relationship between theory and qualitative data. I had framed a question before I began my field work, but once I got caught up in the drama of actually being in the field my original question became hazy. I had trouble linking the data back to the original question or modifying the original question. Instead, I was preoccupied by the characters—Mrs Walters, Mrs Thompson, the children, and even my own role in the research process.

This intellectual confusion is reflected clearly in my field notes. My notes—and I know that I am not alone in this—had some sensitive concepts (Glaser and Strauss 1967) but then were all over the map. They were a hodgepodge of observations made on the basis of shifting priorities. One day I recorded the curriculum and how children interacted with the materials, their skills and how they displayed them. Another day I looked at how the teacher controlled the classroom and her methods of authority. Another day I looked at my role in interacting with the children, how I responded when children started breaking classroom rules in front of me, and my relationships to the teacher and the aide. Observations on the relationships between the aide and the children, the aide and the teacher, the parents and the children, all flow indiscriminately through my field notes. I wrote detailed descriptions of special events (e.g., a school play, a description of an easter egg dyeing project). I also watched for and noted hallmarks of social class: labels on clothing, vacation plans, parents' appearances in the classroom, and different relationships between parents and teachers. Anything and everything that went on in the classroom I tried to record. In my efforts to capture social reality as comprehensively as possible, I forgot about the need for a focus.

Burawoy had no such memory lapse. He read a sample of my field notes and promptly advised me to narrow my interests. He also asked me (as well as the other members of the class) to spend a paragraph or two at the end of each set of field notes analyzing what was going on in the notes. After each session of observation, we were to write out our notes and then evaluate them in light of our question. We were expected to assess what we had learned, what new questions had been raised by our observations, and how we planned to proceed. Burawoy's advice was excellent. Today I make my graduate students do the same thing, but, as with much, if not most, good advice (i.e., to lose weight or stop smoking) it was easier to give than to follow. I found the required analyses extremely difficult to do. I hated them. Worse yet, I did them only when I had to—the ten times I was required to give them to Burawoy.

Part of the reason that I avoided these analyses was that they highlighted the murkiness of my intellectual purpose. Methodologically I was clearer; I wanted to provide a rich description of social reality. The problem was that my romance with ethnomethodology didn't help me frame my research question in a way that would allow an answer that made a theoretical contribution. I was asking, '*How* does social class influence children's schooling?' The answer was supposed to be a description of social reality. What I lacked was another, more conceptual, question: 'Do these data support one interpretation and suggest that another interpretation is not as useful?' or to be more specific, 'Can we understand parents' involvement in schooling as being linked to their values? Does cultural capital provide a better explanation for why parents are involved in school?' These questions have 'yes' or 'no' answers which can be defended using data from the study. By framing a 'how' question I could not provide a similarly defensible answer. I could not show that one explanation was superior; I could not demonstrate that these data helped to address an important issue. In short, I could not answer the 'So what?' question.

At the time I did not really understand the implications of posing the 'wrong' question. I analyzed my notes as rarely as possible and I didn't really notice that my goals changed hourly. I was more focused on building rapport with the teachers, taking comprehensive notes, trying to get the notes typed up, and getting permission to interview parents and teachers so I could complete the next stage of the project.

Burawoy, however, *was* concerned about the way I framed my study. He expressed this in all of our meetings. From our first discussion (following his review of my field notes), he repeatedly cautioned me to think the study through 'in greater analytical detail'. This advice sailed right by me or more accurately I ignored it. In the sixth week of the quarter I wrote a paper on what I had learned from my observations. It was long and my first effort to assess what I had learned from almost five months of research. It was all description: how teachers at Prescott and Colton looked, how they interacted with the children, how much math the children knew, where the children took their vacations, and a little about children's feelings about their academic ranking in the class. I discussed parents, noting that Colton parents were rarely there, seemed more deferential, and didn't seem to know as much as Prescott parents. The paper was vivid in parts and dull in others but it didn't define a question. It was an unfocused description of classroom life in two schools.

Burawoy's reaction to the paper, strongly worded and highly critical, proved to be the turning point in the conceptual development of the project. His comments made it clear that I could not continue to conduct a study that posed no problem and articulated no argument. He noted:

> One's reaction to what you have written has to be, so what? What is so surprising? At no point do you attempt to present plausible alternatives to your findings. . . . I would like to see you produce a theoretical beginning to this paper. I want you to use the literature to highlight the significance of the data you have collected. . . . I really think you have to develop an argument, particularly as I presume this will be part of your thesis.

The chair of my dissertation, Troy Duster, gave me the same feedback although in a different way. Slowly I began to realize that quotes and field notes (which I found fascinating of course) would have to be applied to an intellectual problem. An unfocused 'thick description' would not do.

Using my original formulation of the problem and my conversations with others in my department, I began to try to link up the data with the intellectual problem. I wrote another, much shorter, paper noting the significant correlation between social class and educational achievement and arguing that this correlation was linked to parent involvement in schooling. This attempt was, as Burawoy commented, 'a major advance' over my earlier paper, but I still had a long way to go.

In retrospect, part of my problem was that the question I was framing was too heavily embedded in quantitative models. I was trying to unravel the way in which class difference in family life influenced schooling *and shaped achievement*. I seriously thought I could provide some kind of causal model using qualitative data. Today, that goal strikes me as outlandish. The strength of qualitative data is that it can illuminate the *meaning* of events. It cannot demonstrate that parent behavior 'a' has a stronger effect on achievement than parent behavior 'b' in a sample of two classrooms.

This preoccupation with achievement as a dependent variable and steady immersion in the quantitative literature made me overlook qualitative sociological studies that could provide a suitable framework for my project. I had not read many of the socio-linguistic studies that had been done in the United States, nor was I familiar with the work of cultural anthropologists. I unwittingly ignored the work of potential role models—people who had used similar methods successfully and whose studies could provide valuable examples.

I also failed to realize that just as an individual develops a personal identity most researchers develop an intellectual identity, one that often includes a theoretical as well as a methodological orientation. This identity does not usually change significantly over a single research project, although it might be modified in some ways. I began my project admiring radically different types of qualitative research; my own intellectual identity was in flux. I failed to realize that my multiple admirations were prompting me to strive for mutually incompatible goals. This was not, I have come to realize, an idiosyncratic pattern for I have observed many novice researchers do the same.

For example I admired many ethnomethodological and phenomenological studies in which the flesh and blood of real life is portrayed in vivid detail. Yet most of these studies emphasize that it is critical that the researcher's description remains true to the actor's subjective experience. I do not embrace this view. I believe my respondents should be able to agree that I have portrayed their lives accurately, but I do not want to restrict myself to 'folk explanations'. It does not trouble me if my interpretation of the factors influencing their behavior is different from their interpretation of their lives. Parents at Prescott and Colton schools cannot be expected to be aware of the class structure of which they are a part, nor of the influence of class on behavior. I want to be able to make my own assessment, based on the evidence I have gathered and my understanding of social structural factors. It is difficult, if not impossible, to provide a detailed, comprehensive portrayal of social reality (particularly using the actor's subjective experience) which also selects out elements of that experience to build a focused, coherent argument. A comprehensive portrait and a focused argument are different goals. As with many things in life, you cannot do everything. You have to choose.

This is why it is very helpful for a researcher to know her/his intellectual identity at the beginning of a research project. If you know what you believe in, what type of work you are trying to do, what you would consider acceptable and what you would consider unacceptable, you have a framework and general parameters for your research. You are also better prepared to make compromises: what kinds of weaknesses in your research are you willing to live with and what are completely unacceptable? Being clear about matters such as these can improve both the quality and the quantity of data collection. Well-defined, mutually compatible goals make it easier to focus in the field and also contribute to better organized data.

The Lone Ranger Problem

Even with a clear intellectual identity and a general theoretical question, almost all research questions undergo modification in the light of the data. A favorite description for this in qualitative methods courses is that the research 'evolves'. Many researchers adopt the myth of individualism here. The lone researcher collects the data and, aided by her/his powers of sensitive observation and skill in writing up field notes, the researcher's initial question 'evolves' and becomes more focused. After having collected the data, the researcher retreats into her/his study to write it up and then emerges with a coherent work.

This is a mistaken view of the research process. Research, like everything else, is social. Ironically, this is more obvious in the physical sciences, where researchers must share expensive laboratory equipment, than it is in the social sciences. In the physical sciences, faculty, post-doctoral fellows, graduate students, technicians, and (occasionally) undergraduate assistants all share the same work space—and equipment. Lab interactions and lab politics are a routine part of the work process. Social scientists, even those collaborating on large research projects, rarely work together in such a way. Usually the research team meets periodically for a couple of hours and co-workers may share a computer or an office, but they spend much more of their work time alone than do their colleagues in the physical sciences. Still, the research process in sociology is social. Researchers do not get ideas from vacuums; they arise from a social context. The impact of historical factors on academic agendas is testimony to that fact (Karabel and Halsey 1977). And the ideology of individualism notwithstanding, advances in conceptual models also depend crucially upon an exchange of ideas.

In my own case, my argument (and the relationship between the conceptual model and the data) went through four or five stages, becoming narrower and less sweeping at each point. As the question became clearer my data collection became more focused as well. I began to collect information about parents and I looked closely at the differences between the two schools. I ultimately dropped my effort to explain achievement, and developed an interest in the debates on cultural capital and, to a lesser extent, parent involvement in schooling. To say that my research question 'evolved' is true, but this is far too passive a description. Just as reproduction of the social structure does not happen automatically, so the narrowing and refining of a research project is not an automatic process. Qualitative researchers take steps to *produce* a more focused research question. Participant-observation, writing up field notes, and reflecting on field notes are the steps which are normally emphasized in the literature but there are others. Talking to colleagues is critical to the development of a question. Writing up the results and having the work critically reviewed is another important step. Comparing your findings to the literature and seeing how your conclusions modify the literature is also useful.

Today my rule of thumb is that every third visit to the field should be followed by some kind of effort to push the question forward. This can be a one hour conversation with a colleague (by telephone if necessary), a comparison with other studies, or a long memo which is then reviewed and criticized by others. Such efforts must include reflections on the overall goals of the project, the theoretical question, the data, and the remaining gaps. The analysis at the end of field notes and this 'state of the question push' are similar but not identical. The former is focused around a particular event or dynamic in the field setting; the latter is broader, more reflective, and—most importantly—more social. It is an effort to reach out and place the study in a social context, to get others' feedback, to evaluate the study in terms of its contribution to the field. It is not usually very difficult to arrange this social interaction, but it must be solicited by the researcher; it will not happen automatically.

Thus, all of the conceptual advances in this project were linked to the production and criticism of written work. Writing was helpful because it required that I organize, systematize, and condense volumes of information. It helped me struggle to build the argument and it allowed me to assess the evidence in a new way. The criticism of others, particularly the comments of colleagues around the country, challenged me to rethink some of my ideas. Although I had many enjoyable sessions talking about the project and bouncing ideas around, I learned less from talking and listening than I did from writing. One consequence of this is that every few months or so (depending on the pace of data collection) I write a paper about my current project. (A deadline, such as giving a talk about the research, is helpful here.) These working papers are not polished and in most cases are not publishable.

Overall it was the social interaction (especially the criticism from others) that helped advance my work. While the lone scholar image has its appeal, it does not accurately portray the actual process in qualitative—or quantitative—research.

Writing It Up

After I signed a book contract and was committed to finishing this project, I began to ask colleagues who did qualitative research what books they considered exemplary models of writing up a qualitative project. I was shocked at how much trouble people had thinking of exemplary books. Moreover, when they did recommend books they were not usually within the field of the sociology of education. Several people recommended *Tally's Corner* (Liebow 1967). One colleague recommended Charles Bosk's book *Forgive and Remember* (Bosk 1979), a study of the socialization of medical residents into surgery. It is a compelling book and, I believe, a useful model. Another suggested *Everything in Its Path* (Erikson 1976), an award winning book which portrays the destruction of a community by the failure of traditional support systems following a dam burst.

When I began to reflect on the books that didn't make the list (only 99 per cent of the available literature), it became clear that there were many ways that qualitative researchers could end up producing mediocre books—even those beginning with interesting ideas and good evidence. Many studies represent good solid work but they have a plodding tone and analysis; they lack lively writing. Others seem as though the author(s) had not accurately represented the community under investigation and/or had missed important things in field research. Some books had good ideas and an interesting argument but seemed to be unsystematic in the analysis and portrayal of evidence. Others were long on ideas and short on data, while some lacked an argument all together.

The downfall of many of these books lies in their failure to integrate theory and data. In my own case, as I began to try to write up the results of this study, I would career rather abruptly from discussions of theory and the research problem to presentation of the data. I also presented very few quotes. Detailed—and negative—comments from reviewers helped me see the error of my ways. Mary Metz, a guest editor for *Sociology of Education*, summarized the complaints of reviewers, complaints that I have echoed in my own reviews of other manuscripts using qualitative methods:

> You need to work with your data and decide what can be learned from it and then present your theory tersely as it will help us understand those findings and put them in context.

The reviewers also complained that I made sweeping generalizations without enough evidence to back them up, another common problem in manuscripts based on qualitative research.

I used the reviewers' and the guest editor's criticisms to improve my dissertation. I cited and used more qualitative research and I worked to change the focus from a heavily theoretical piece to a more empirically grounded one, but problems remained. I over-shortened the literature review and the quoted material was not integrated with the text. Following Aaron Cicourel's advice, I labored to integrate the data with the analysis, supply more data and be more 'aggressive' in showing 'what is missing empirically and conceptually' from other studies.

Cicourel's advice was useful again as I prepared to write this book; it reminded me to use the data to build an argument. Nevertheless, while I knew that adding more data would strengthen my argument, I wasn't clear how much additional data to include. I had an urge to add almost everything. Finally, in a move of some desperation, I turned to books and articles that I admired and counted the number of quotes per chapter or page; most averaged one quote per printed page. The quotes were not evenly spread throughout the chapters; there would be pages without any quotes and then three or four quotes per page. Most of these studies also provided examples in the text. Of course the right number of quotes depends on many factors, but the count gave me a ball park figure for my own writing which I have found useful. The problem of linking theory and data is an ongoing struggle. I made a rule that every chapter had to have an argument. I also remembered, although I did not always follow, the advice that someone passed on to me that every paragraph should be linked to the argument. I tried to show that my interpretation was a more compelling way of looking at the data than other interpretations. In other words I tried to answer the question, 'So what?'

It will be for others to judge how well I have done in connecting the theoretical argument and the research data. I know that I have done a better job of integration with this book than I did with the written work that preceded it, notably drafts of papers and the dissertation. I used almost none of my dissertation in preparing this book. Instead I began again, adding probably three to four times as many quotes and streamlining and increasing the aggressiveness of the thesis. This pattern of modest improvement in linking theory and data gives me hope: maybe experience will help. In fact a comparison of first and second books does suggest that some people get much better at this as they go along; others however do not, and a few seem to get worse.

Reflections on the Making of Home Advantage

This project had its share of mistakes but it also had its successes. The design, which included interviews with both parents and teachers, is unusual as most studies do one or the other. This yielded insights that would not have been possible if I had studied families or schools. It was also helpful to follow children over time and clarify that parents adopted similar modes of interaction regardless of the teacher. It was very important to supplement the interviews with classroom observation which improved the interviews and enabled me to 'triangulate' in a way that would have been impossible with interviews alone.

In the end I did have a good rapport with the staff, particularly the classroom teachers I worked with most closely. On her last day of school Mrs Walters gave me a hug goodbye; Mrs Thompson thanked me warmly for being in her classroom. In both schools children ran up and gave me a goodbye hug on the last day of school. By the end of the interviews I felt I had genuinely come to know and enjoy many of the mothers and fathers, and I was also certain that in several cases the feelings were mutual. This was a reward. There are plenty of awkward moments in field work, even among the best researchers, but there are also rewards and signs, little and big, of acceptance. These are important to notice and remember. This is harder to do than one would think. Moments of foolishness and the damage they have wrought are easy to worry about. I spent a lot of time fretting about the mistakes I made in this study. They scared me so I wanted to try to hide them; I worried about each and every one of them, and they overshadowed my assessment of the project. This kind of self-criticism, in which the impact of each criticism is five times that of each compliment, is not productive.

It was productive, however, to spend time thinking about the strengths and weaknesses of the study and the confidence which I have in the results. As this appendix and the format of the book make clear, I have confidence in the validity of the interviews. I feel that I was helped by my previous experience as an interviewer. Although it is difficult to prove, I am confident in the quality of the data—that I did not lead, badger, or trap respondents in interviews, that I listened to them carefully and was able to get them to talk in an honest and revealing way. The field notes were also carefully recorded. When I went into the field I thought I would find evidence of institutional discrimination. I thought, as Bowles and Gintis, Cicourel and Kitsuse, and others had suggested, that the teachers were going to differ significantly in their interactions with parents of different social class. I did not find evidence to support this position. When I did not find it I looked for other explanations rather than trying to force the evidence into that intellectual frame. The project did not have as many field notes focused directly on the intellectual problem as I would have liked, but the ones that were there were carefully done.

Can we learn anything from a study of two first grade classes, twelve families, four teachers, and two principals? Yes, I think we can use a small, non-random sample to improve conceptual models. This study shows that a very high proportion of parents would agree that they want to be 'supportive' of their children's schooling but that they would mean very different things by this. It suggests that family-school models are inadequate. Researchers do not spend enough time addressing the differences in objective skills which social class gives to parents. Independent of parents' desires for their children, class gives parents an edge in helping their children in schooling. My confidence in the validity of the findings is bolstered by the fact that they elaborate a pattern that has been noted by many researchers, although often only in passing. They also mesh with the conclusions of other recent works (Baker and Stevenson 1986; Stevenson and Baker 1987; Epstein 1987).

Although not a form of systematic evidence, I must add, that just as after you learn a new word you see it everywhere, after I finished this study I began to notice that social class differences in family-school relationships are as evident in the Midwestern city where I now live and work as it was in the West Coast communities I studied. I see working-class neighbors and friends take a 'hands-off' attitude toward their children's schooling, emphasizing their own inadequacies and turning over responsibility to the school. I see upper-middle class families, particularly academic couples, trying to monitor and control their children's schooling. I think that while there may be aspects of the argument that need modification, the overall pattern, that class gives people resources which help them comply with the demands of institutions, is really there. Other research, using multiple methodologies, is necessary to establish that and to illuminate the interactive effects of class and parent involvement; for example, working-class parents are much less likely to make requests of the school staff, and when they do make such requests are more likely to have them honored than upper-middle-class parents.

What this study cannot do is provide an assessment of how important individuals' competencies are relative to other factors influencing parent involvement (i.e., values, teachers' roles), nor can it evaluate how common parents' actions are, including parents' supervising teachers and compensating for weaknesses in the classroom. A small sample imposes restrictions that cannot be surmounted with felicitous phrases such as 'one half of the sample believed . . .' Large-scale, representative studies are much better for describing the proportion of people who share certain beliefs, and internal variations, while addressed here, can be better elaborated with a larger group. What qualitative methods can do is illuminate the meanings people attach to their words and actions in a way not possible with other methodologies. Although I admire many quantitative studies, they are in some ways 'unnaturally' straightforward. Data analysis and computer analysis have a much smaller range of options and there is less of a domino effect than occurs in qualitative work. Quantitative research does not have the ambiguity and uncertainty of field work.

In my view qualitative work is more cumbersome and more difficult than survey research at almost every stage: formulation of the problem, access, data collection, data analysis, and writing up the results. It is more time consuming; it is harder to spin off several publications; and, to add insult to injury, it is considered lower status by many members of the profession. But it adds to our knowledge in a critical and important way. It is that pay-off that draws me back, despite all I have learned about the enormous commitment of time and energy that qualitative research demands. If it were not one of the only ways of gaining insights into the routine events of daily life and the meaning that makes social reality, qualitative methods would not have a lot going for it. It is too much work. But it is one of the only ways, and possibly the only way, to achieve such insights. The usefulness of these insights rests, however, on the character of our research. Exchanging notes on our disappointments and successes in field research is an important step in increasing the quality of our work.

Notes

1. I am indebted to William F. Whyte's work not only for the idea of writing an appendix but also for providing a model of how to write one. I have shamelessly adopted elements of his organizational structure, including this one, in my appendix. Readers will note, however, a difference in the content and goals of the two appendices. Whyte's appendix elaborates issues of access, entry, and the formulation of the intellectual problem. He also provides a very good discussion of ethics and holding the line between researcher and native. My goals are somewhat different. Although I briefly review the issues of access and entry, my focus is on the practical considerations of data collection, data analysis, and the writing up of the results. I do, however, also discuss the task of formulating an intellectual problem in qualitative research.

2. My job was to help determine if recently arrested defendants were qualified to be released on their own recognizance. To help indigent defendants save bail money, the Own Recognizance Project (OR Project) would prepare cases by providing a summary of the social ties a defendant had to the area, including her/his correct address, contact with relatives, and employment history. Unlike bail, which was simply a matter of producing the money and the collateral, OR cases required judges' signatures. Primarily because of negative publicity, many judges were very reluctant to exercise the OR option. Although the San Francisco City Prison was not as bad as some prisons, most people found prison so uncomfortable that they wanted to get out as soon as possible. For them OR was too slow and too chancy so they bailed out instead.

3. Unfortunately for those of us not trained in shorthand, it is not possible to write down every single word and idea in an interview, particularly if you are trying to maintain eye contact and build a rapport with the subject. Without a tape recorder researchers must do some editing while taking notes. For most of us this means that some particularly interesting passages are written in more detail than others. Yet what is considered interesting changes as the project and the research question develop, thus note-taking is inevitably altered by these intellectual questions.

4. Whyte (1981) has a good discussion of the problems of access, but almost all books on qualitative research methods discuss the problems. The writing on qualitative methods has increased radically in recent years and there are many good

pieces around. Bogdan and Biklen (1982), while directed at research in education, is a useful overview. Other works include Silverman (1985), Agar (1986), and from a somewhat different perspective Glaser and Strauss (1967). Although older, Schatzman and Strauss (1973) provide a succinct discussion of key issues. In more specialized discussions, Gorden (1987) focuses on interviewing, Kirk and Miller (1986) the problems of reliability and validity in qualitative work, Macrorie (1985) the task of writing up one's results, and Punch (1986) on the politics of field work. Erickson (1986) also has a useful overview of the steps in a qualitative research project using studies of teaching as an example. Finally, for reflections on the research process, see Rabinow (1977), Georges and Jones (1980), Van Mannen (1988), Simon and Dippo (1986), and Schon (1987).

5. As part of the human subjects approval process at the university, I wrote consent forms for all of the parents, children, teachers, and others I interviewed. [Since I was not disrupting the classroom activities, I was not required to gain consent forms from all of the children in the classes.] These forms briefly described the goals of the project and the methodology, including that parents and teachers would be interviewed. Before I gave parents and teachers the forms I stressed that these forms were routine and added that they were developed after serious abuses by researchers, such as prisoners being given drugs without being told. Although I agonized over the content of the form almost no one read it. Only two parents—a lawyer and his wife—read the form carefully before signing; the remaining parents and educators signed it with only a glance.

6. My letter to Prescott was as follows:

Dear Mrs Finnegan:

This letter is in regard to our recent telephone conversation regarding my request to conduct a small research project in your district. As I mentioned, I am a graduate student in a doctoral program at University of California, Berkeley, in the sociology department. As part of my dissertation research, I am conducting a study on social class variations in the family-school relationship for young children. As you probably know, the social standing of a child's family is a key predictor of educational outcome. The purpose of the research is to examine the process through which social position affects the educational process. In particular, the research will focus on the impact which the social position of professional-middle-class and working-class families has on day to day experience of school life.

I would like to conduct a very small pilot study on these issues in Prescott School District. The research would involve one first grade classroom in your district. The study would include interviews with the teacher, principal, school secretary, and five families of the children in the classroom. In addition, I would like to observe the children in the classroom for a short time, perhaps amounting to six or eight visits. All of the interviews would be 'semi-structured' interviews with open-ended questions. The interviews would last a little more than one hour and would be tape recorded. All of the persons in the study would be assured of confidentiality.

The interviews will cover a number of issues in family life and school life. The study will ask both parents and the child questions about the family's approach towards schooling. The parents' view of schooling, the way in which the parents convey this view to the child and the behavior of the parents will be explored. In addition, the conflicts between parents regarding education and the proper type of educational experience will be studied. The purpose of this study is to *compare* differences between working-class and professional-middle-class families in their view of the ideal family-school relationship. The interviews in your district will provide a basic description of the family-school relationship for a small number of families of relatively high socio-economic status.

A slightly different set of issues will be taken up with the teacher, principal, and school secretary (the secretary is included as the front office often is the first point of contact between families and schools). First, it is important to note that I would like to request that the school send a letter to the families indicating that the researcher has the permission of the district to conduct the interviews. I would be happy to contribute in any way possible to the writing and mailing of such a letter.

Secondly, the interviews with the teacher, principal, and school secretary will focus on the amount of information which school personnel have about family life. Questions will focus on the types of information which school staff learn about families, and the informal ways in which this information is gathered. In addition, the research will solicit the perceptions of school staff regarding the way in which family life shapes the day to day educational experience for young children. It is important to emphasize that the purpose of the study is *not* to evaluate teachers, schools, or parents. Indeed, the specific teaching style of a teacher is really of very limited interest as the study seeks to understand social class patterns of family-school interaction.

These brief comments are intended to provide you and your colleagues with better insight into the concerns of the research project. If you or anyone else in the district has further questions, I would be happy to provide additional information. I appreciate your consideration of this request and look forward to hearing from you in the future.

Sincerely,
Annette Lareau

7. With hindsight, this is the letter I would write today:

Dear Mrs Finnegan:

Thank you for taking the time to speak with me the other day. As we agreed, I am writing to request permission to conduct a study in your school district.

In this project, I am interested in learning more about how families help children in school. I would like to visit one first grade classroom in the district on a regular basis this school year (e.g., two times a week). My visits would be scheduled to be at a convenient time. Having worked in classrooms, I know how important it is to take an unobtrusive role in the classroom. I would be happy to work as a classroom volunteer if the teacher would like.

In addition, at a convenient time, I hope to interview the parents of five children in this classroom, as well as the teacher, principal, and school secretary. The interviews will last an hour or so. All information collected would be kept confidential; neither the identity of Prescott school district, nor that of any parents or teachers, would ever be revealed.

I am requesting permission to observe in the classroom and for you, or the school staff, to supply names and addresses of parents, with the understanding that parents may refuse to cooperate in the study. For your information, I have attached a sample copy of the letter which I would mail to parents.

I know that you, and the teachers, lead busy lives. Teachers have reported that the experience of working on this research project was interesting and pleasant. If it would be helpful, I would be happy to make a brief presentation about the project to school staff. If you would like any other information, please feel free to contact me at (618) 453–2494.

Again, I appreciate your consideration of my request. I look forward to hearing from you in the future.

Sincerely,
Annette Lareau

8. I always told people that there was another school involved and that the school was of a different level of affluence. In the beginning I used the term 'socioeconomic status'; that really raised eyebrows. I now realize that it is much too long a term and much too academic to be useful.

9. Having come from Berkeley I found this 'Miss Lareau' title to be astounding in the 1980s, but it happened in all of my interactions in the school. No one called me Ms Lareau, and many people asked me: 'Is it Miss or Mrs?' Unmarried teachers, including Miss Chaplan, used the term Miss in all of their interactions. It didn't really bother me, however, and I never asked to be called Ms. I didn't really care what they called me. I was just glad to be in a school doing field work.

10. I met several mothers, including Allen's and Emily's, during these periods. As children's work got underway the mothers would often chat with me and ask me questions about my study. They also observed me in the classroom and my interactions with the children. Mrs Walters often complained about mothers visiting during volunteering saying, 'You get more work out of one parent than two.' In my own case it meant that mothers were watching me just as they watched Mrs Walters. There were also indications that mothers discussed me and my study in their conversations with one another. Thus my role with parents paralleled that of the teachers; Prescott mothers knew more about me, scrutinized, and questioned me much more closely than Colton parents.

11. If there was a statement which I thought was important I would repeat it to myself over and over again while in the classroom and write it down immediately after I left—usually in my car before I drove away. Most of the field notes from Prescott do not have direct quotes; if there are quotes, however, I am quite confident of their accuracy.

12. While interviewing defendants in City Prison for the OR Project I found that by two or three minutes into the interview I needed to have the defendant calmed down, no longer trying to tell me the story of his or her arrest, and concentrating on the names of three persons (with telephone numbers) who could act as references, otherwise I felt the interview was in trouble. This 'transition point', therefore, varies from study to study, depending on both the length and the substance of the interviews.

13. Although I believe I was almost always genuine in my admiration for aspects of the respondents' lives, the content of my compliments and 'fishing expeditions' varied according to social class. In Colton I found myself discussing television programs, admiring respondents' house plants and, to a lesser extent, their clothes. In Prescott I talked about classical music preferences, houses, and house decorations.

14. In these summaries I wrote a description of the respondents, the house, and key parts of the interview. I also listed critical quotes and their location on the tape (i.e., 'good quote about criticisms of school, end of side one').

15. These categories had been the analytic structure of my dissertation which had seven chapters: 1) a literature review and statement of the problem, 2) a description of the research methods, 3) a description of the two schools and the amount of parent involvement in each school, 4) parents' attitudes towards their role in schooling and the degree to which they complied with teachers' requests, 5) family life (i.e., lessons, gender roles, kinship ties) and the influence on family-school relationships, 6) teachers' wishes for parent involvement, and 7) the importance of cultural capital in shaping family-school relationships.

16. The class had a distinct (and very effective) structure. We were divided into groups of four, in roughly similar intellectual areas. We were to meet twice a week outside class to compare and discuss each other's field notes and problems in the field. Twice during the quarter we made presentations in class and shared our field notes with the entire class. Burawoy also read our field notes and commented on them. Course requirements included a critical literature review to help formulate a problem, a paper based on the field work, and ten sets of field notes.

Epilogue: A Selective Guide to the Literature

Research using ethnographic techniques has become fashionable. In the past twenty years there has been a dramatic increase in the number of published works in the field. For persons who want to get familiar with major issues in the field but have limited amounts of time for training, the literature can be overwhelming and frustrating. In this short, closing piece, we offer a friendly guide to this literature where we briefly discuss works we have found helpful or have known to be helpful to others. We stress the selectivity and, in some respects, arbitrary nature of the guide. We are certain that there are excellent works omitted; pieces we have found helpful may lack usefulness for others.

Textbooks

For novices, there are a number of excellent textbooks that provide an overview of the field. Martyn Hammersley and Paul Atkinson provide a solid overview in *Ethnography: Principles in Practice* (1983). Another useful guide is *Ethnography and Qualitative Design in Educational Research* (1993) by Margaret LeCompte, Judith Preissle, and Renata Tesch. Anselm Strauss's comprehensive book *Qualitative Analysis for Social Scientists* (1987) provides the definitive methodological overview of the inductive "from the ground up" approach he made famous with Barney Glaser in the work *The Discovery of Grounded Theory* (1967). Some people are fond of the older but still useful book by Steven Taylor and Robert Bogdan, *Introduction to Qualitative Research Methods* (1984).

In this thin textbook department, there is the widely used (and recently revised) piece by John Lofland and Lyn Lofland, *Analyzing Social Settings* (1984), which provides a nice summary of the key issues in the field. An older but still handy small book is *Field Research* (1973) by Leonard

Schatzman and Anselm Strauss. See also David Fetterman, *Ethnography: Step by Step* (1989). All of these books are technical ("how to") as well as reflective.

A popular approach has been the development of a reader with selections from multiple authors. The collection by Robert Emerson, *Contemporary Field Research* (1983), is particularly good but there are many others, including George Spindler, *Doing the Ethnography of Schooling* (1982) and Paul Rabinow and William Sullivan, *Interpretive Social Science* (1987). Written in 1966, the book *Stranger and Friend: The Way of an Anthropologist* by Hortense Powdermaker is widely seen as a classic work. Quite dated but still quite good is the book by Rosalie Wax, *Doing Fieldwork: Warnings and Advice* (1971). A long essay by Frederick Erickson (in Linn and Erickson 1990), although focused on the study of teaching, provides an excellent beginning-to-end discussion of ethnographic methods. Two large handbooks, *Handbook of Qualitative Research* (1994) edited by Norman Denzin and Yvonna Lincoln and *The Handbook of Qualitative Research in Education* (1992) edited by Margaret LeCompte, Wendy Millroy, and Judith Preissle offer a comprehensive overview of the field.

Also useful are books about doing fieldwork, especially Michael Agar's *The Professional Stranger* (1980). A group of graduate students at the University of California, Berkeley, wrote up their experience of doing fieldwork in a semester with their professor. The product, *Ethnography Unbound* (Burawoy, 1991), provides a realistic portrait of student ethnography, including the hurdles of entry, access, ethics, and exit all within the course of one semester.

Reflections

Ethnographic methods involve reflections and interpretation; reflections on the fieldwork experience remains a popular genre. Paul Rabinow's short book *Reflections on Fieldwork in Morocco* (1977) remains a compelling treatise. In a different vein, James Clifford (1988) has a series of essays reflecting on *The Predicament of Culture: Twentieth-Century Ethnography, Literature, and Art* (1988). See also the writing of Clifford Geertz (1973, 1983). For a particularly thoughtful reflection on ethical issues, see Charles Bosk's (1992) appendix to *All God's Mistakes*. The diaries of Bronislaw Malinowski (1967), not originally written for public consumption, also offer insights into the frustrations of the process.

One-Topic Pieces

In addition to the overviews there are a number of books on selective topics. Raymond Gorden (1969) has written a very good (fat) book titled *In-*

terviewing. Although written for survey research, *The Art of Asking Questions* by Stanley Payne (1980) is a thoughtful and careful book that is helpful in constructing an interview guide for open-ended interviews. There is a recent book on *Writing Ethnographic Field Notes* (Emerson et al. 1995); Blanche Greer's essay "First Days in the Field" (1964) remains a thoughtful reflection on the first hours of a project. The discussion of "thick description" by Clifford Geertz that was originally written in his book *Interpretation of Cultures* (1973) is a short, classic, and compelling treatment of an essential piece of this methodology; it has been widely reprinted (e.g., Emerson 1983). The issue of feminist methodology generally has been taken up in a collection by Sandra Harding (1987); Dorothy Smith's book *The Everyday World as Problematic: A Feminist Sociology* (1987) provides a reflection on ways to integrate a feminist analysis of institutional relations with an ethnography of daily life. *Women in the Field* provides insights into the experience of female anthropologists (Golde, 1986). Innovative techniques including the use of photographs and video in ethnography have gained attention; for discussions and examples see Howard Becker (1982, 1986) and Robert Bogdan and Sara Biklen (1982). In a different vein, sociolinguistic approaches or "microethnography" are discussed by Gee (1992) and Erickson (1992). Exemplars of sociolinguistic analysis can be found in Frederick Erickson and Jeffrey Shultz, *The Counselor as Gatekeeper* (1982), Hugh Mehan, *Learning Lessons* (1979), and Shirley Heath, *Ways with Words* (1983).

Data Analysis

One of the first and still best detailed "cookbook" discussions of the topic is the book *Qualitative Data Analysis* by Matthew Miles and A. Michael Huberman (1984). A more reflective "immerse yourself" in the process can be found in Frederick Erickson's long essay in *Handbook of Research on Teaching* (Wittrock 1986). The edited collection by Charles Ragin and Howard Becker (1992), *What Is a Case?* provides a careful analysis of some of the theoretical issues in data analysis. On the practical level, *Qualitative Research: Analysis Types and Software Tools* by Renata Tesch (1990) reviews common software programs for ethnographic research. The "NUDIST" package (not reviewed by Tesch) as well as other computer issues are taken up in the expanded edition of *Qualitative Data Analysis* by Miles and Huberman.

Writing

John Van Maanen's short book *Tales of the Field* (1988) lays out three common genres for writing up the results of fieldwork. The book provides an unusual integration of the literature in sociology and anthropology. *A Thrice Told Tale* (Wolf, 1992) also makes the point of subjectivity in writing through the compelling story of an event in a Chinese village. Clifford Geertz writes of the importance of "being there" in the text in his short book *Works and Lives* (1988). Having a presence in the book (as one had in the field) without lapsing into narcissism or boredom is a challenge; *Never in Anger* (1970) is a beautifully written book where Jean Briggs, as ethnographer, is highly visible in the text in a very effective fashion. *Translated Woman* (Behar 1993) addresses this problem in a different way but provides an honest wrestling with the issue of subjectivity. Regarding the juxtaposition of the author in the text see also Paul Atkinson, *The Ethnographic Imagination: Textual Constructions of Reality* (1990).

Writing is difficult. In his book *Writing for Social Scientists*, Howard Becker (1986) provides a fine overview of the writing process. For undergraduates, there is the excellent *A Guide to Writing Sociology Papers* (Sociology Writing Group, 1994), which has a section on writing an ethnographic paper. The issue of turning papers into published articles is taken up by Robert Bogdan and Sari Biklen (1982) in *Qualitative Research for Education;* the book also presents a concrete discussion of journal expectations. Many people have difficultly writing. *Writing Without Teachers* (Elbow, 1973) proposes the importance of "free writing" to help students reclaim writing. Technical sources, including the *Chicago Manual of Style* (1993) and *Publication Manual* of the American Psychological Association (1994), reveal standards for decisions in writing, helping students who copy each citation down in a different fashion introduce order into the text by smoothing out the style of the text and references. For students who feel inadequate about their spelling or grammar, *The Random House Handbook* (Crews 1992) is a useful resource. Finally, the ever-classic *The Elements of Style* (Strunk and White, 1979) provides a succinct guide to better writing.[1]

Notes

1. A number of journals specialize in ethnographic methods, including *Journal of Contemporary Ethnography* (formerly *Urban Life*). The official journal of the Council on Anthropology and Education (a division of the American Anthropological Association), *Anthropology and Education Quarterly,* often has high-quality articles using ethnographic techniques. The American Sociological Association also has a growing number of panels at annual meetings with a methodological focus; the American Educational Research Association has a division (Social Context of Education) that often features work in this approach.

Bibliography

Achebe, Chinua. *No Longer at Ease*. London: Heinemann Educational Books, 1960.

Adler, Patricia A. *Wheeling and Dealing: An Ethnography of an Upper-Level Drug Dealing and Smuggling Community, 2nd Edition*. New York: Columbia University Press, 1993.

Adler, Patricia A., Peter Adler, and John M. Johnson. "Street Corner Society Revisited: New Questions About Old Issues." *Journal of Contemporary Ethnography* 21, no. 1 (April 1992).

Agar, Michael. *The Professional Stranger: An Informal Introduction to Ethnography*. New York: Academic Press, 1980.

Agar, Michael H. *Speaking of Ethnography*. Beverly Hills, CA: Sage, 1986.

Amadi, Elechi. *The Great Ponds*. London: Heinemann Educational Books, 1969.

American Psychological Association. *Publication Manual, 4th Edition*. Washington, DC: American Psychological Association, 1994.

Anderson, Elijah. *A Place on the Corner*. Chicago: University of Chicago Press, 1978.

Arensberg, Conrad M., and Solon T. Kimball. *Culture and Community*. Gloucester, MA: P. Smith, 1972.

Atkinson, Jane Monnig. "Review Essay: Anthropology." *Signs* 8, no. 2 (1982): 232–258.

Atkinson, Paul. *The Ethnographic Imagination: Textual Constructs of Reality*. London and New York: Routledge, 1990.

Baker, David, and David Stevenson. "Mothers' Strategies for School Achievement: Managing the Transition to High School." *Sociology of Education* 59 (1986): 156–167.

Becker, Howard Saul. *Art Worlds*. Berkeley: University of California Press, 1982.

Becker, Howard Saul, with a chapter by Pamela Richards. *Writing for Social Scientists: How to Start and Finish Your Thesis, Book, or Article*. Chicago: University of Chicago Press, 1986.

Behar, Ruth. *Translated Woman: Crossing the Border with Esperanza's Story*. Boston: Beacon Press, 1993.

Bell, Diane, Patricia Caplan, and Wazir Jahan Karim, Eds. *Gendered Fields: Women, Men and Ethnography*. London and New York: Routledge, 1993.

Bernstein, Basil. *Class, Codes and Control*. London: Routledge and Kegan Paul, 1975.

_____. "Social Class, Language, and Socialization." In *Power and Ideology in Education*, edited by J. Karabel and A. H. Halsey. New York: Oxford University Press, 1977, 473–486.

Bogdan, Robert C., and Sari K. Biklen. *Qualitative Research for Education: An Introduction to Theory and Methods*. Boston: Allyn and Bacon, 1982.

Bosk, Charles L. *Forgive and Remember*. Chicago: University of Chicago Press, 1979.

_____. *All God's Mistakes: Genetic Counseling in a Pediatric Hospital*. Chicago: University of Chicago Press, 1992.

Bourdieu, Pierre. "Marriage Strategies as Strategies of Social Reproduction." In *Family and Society*, edited by R. Forster and O. Ranum, 117–144. Baltimore, MD: Johns Hopkins University Press, 1976.

_____. "Cultural Reproduction and Social Reproduction." In *Power and Ideology in Education*, edited by Jerome Karabel and A. H. Halsey, 487–511. New York: Oxford University Press, 1977a.

_____. *Outline of a Theory of Practice*. Translated by R. Nice. London: Cambridge University Press, 1977b.

_____. "The Specificity of the Scientific Field." In *French Sociology: Rupture and Renewal Since 1968*, edited by C. C. Lemert, 257–292. New York: Columbia University Press, 1981a.

_____. "Men and Machines." In *Advances in Social Theory: Toward an Integration of Micro- and Macro-Sociologies*, edited by K. Knorr-Cetina and A. V. Cicourel, 304–317. Boston: Routledge and Kegan Paul, 1981b.

_____. *Distinction: A Social Critique of the Judgment of Taste*. Edited and translated by R. Nice. Cambridge: Harvard University Press, 1984.

_____. "The Social Space and the Genesis of Groups." *Theory and Society* 14, no. 6 (1985): 241–260.

_____. "Forms of Capital." In *Handbook of Theory and Research for Sociology of Education*, edited by J. G. Richardson. New York: Greenwood Press, 1987a.

_____. "What Makes a Social Class? On the Theoretical and Practical Existence of Groups." *Berkeley Journal of Sociology* 32 (1987b): 1–17.

_____. *Homo Academicus*. Stanford: Stanford University Press.

_____. *The Logic of Practice*. Cambridge: Polity Press, 1990.

Bourdieu, Pierre, and Jean-Claude Passeron. *Reproduction in Education, Society, and Culture*. London: Sage, 1977.

Bourgois, Philippe. "Crack in Spanish Harlem." *Anthropology Today* 5, no. 4 (August 1989): 6–11.

_____. "Just Another Night on Crack Street." *New York Times Magazine*, November 1989, 52–94.

_____. "In Search of Horatio Alger: Culture and Ideology in the Crack Economy." *Contemporary Drug Problems*, Winter 1989, 619–649.

_____. "Growing Up." *The American Enterprise* 2, no. 3 (May/June 1991): 28–33.

_____. "In Search of Respect: The New Service Economy and the Crack Alternative in Spanish Harlem." Russell Sage Foundation Working Paper #21, 1991.

_____. "Shooting Gallery Notes." Russell Sage Foundation Working Paper #22, 1991.

_____. "From Jibaro to Crack Dealer: Confronting the Restructuring of Capitalism in Spanish Harlem." In *Articulating Hidden Histories: Festschrift for Eric Wolf*, edited by Jane Schneider and Rayna Rapp. Berkeley: University of California Press, 1995.

_____. *In Search of Respect: Selling Crack in El Barrio*. Cambridge: Cambridge University Press, 1995.

Bowles, Gloria, and Renate Duelli Klein, Eds. *Theories of Women's Studies*. London: Routledge and Kegan Paul, 1983.

Bowles, Samuel, and Herbert Gintis. *Schooling in Capitalist America*. New York: Basic Books, 1976.

Briggs, Jean L. *Never in Anger: Portrait of an Eskimo Family*. Cambridge: Harvard University Press, 1970.

Bruner, Edward. "Ethnography as Narrative." In *The Anthropology of Experience*, edited by Victor Turner and Edward Bruner, 139–155. Urbana: University of Illinois Press, 1986.

Burawoy, Michael. *Manufacturing Consent*. Chicago: University of Chicago Press, 1979.

_____. *Ethnography Unbound: Power and Resistance in the Modern Metropolis*. Berkeley: University of California Press, 1991.

Caplan, Pat. "Introduction 2: The Volume." In *Gendered Fields: Women, Men and Ethnography*, edited by Diane Bell, Patricia Caplan, and Wazir Jahan Karim, 19–27. London and New York: Routledge, 1993.

Chapple, Eliot Dismore, and Carleton S. Coon. *Principles of Anthropology*. New York: H. Holt & Company, 1942.

Chodorow, Nancy. *The Reproduction of Mothering: Psychoanalysis and the Sociology of Gender*. Berkeley: University of California Press, 1978.

Cicourel, Aaron Victor, and John T. Kitsuse. *The Educational Decision-Makers*. Indianapolis: Bobbs-Merrill, 1963.

Chicago Manual of Style, 14th Edition. Chicago: University of Chicago Press, 1993.

Clifford, James. "Fieldwork, Reciprocity, and the Making of Ethnographic Texts: The Example of Maurice Leenhardt." *Man* 15 (1980): 518–532.

_____. "On Ethnographic Authority." *Representations* 1, no. 2 (1983): 118–146.

_____. *The Predicament of Culture: Twentieth-Century Ethnography, Literature, and Art*. Cambridge: Harvard University Press, 1988.

Crews, Frederick C. *The Random House Handbook, 6th Edition*. New York: McGraw-Hill, 1992.

Dadie, Bernard Binlin. *The Black Cloth: A Collection of African Folktales*. Translated by K. C. Hatch. Amherst: University of Massachusetts Press, 1987.

Denzin, Norman K., and Yvonna S. Lincoln, Eds. *Handbook of Qualitative Research*. Thousand Oaks, CA: Sage, 1994.

Derrida, Jacques. *Margins of Philosophy*. Translated by Alan Bass. Chicago: University of Chicago Press, 1982.

Durkheim, Emile. *The Division of Labor in Society*. Glencoe, IL: Free Press, 1961.

Elbow, Peter. *Writing Without Teachers*. New York: Oxford University Press, 1973.

Emerson, Robert M. *Contemporary Field Research: A Collection of Readings*. Prospect Heights, IL: Waveland Press, 1983.

Emerson, Robert M., Rachel I. Fretz, and Linda L. Shaw. *Writing Ethnographic Field Notes*. Chicago: University of Chicago Press, 1995.

Epstein, Joyce L. "Parent Involvement: What Research Says to Administrators." *Education and Urban Society* 19, no. 2 (1987): 119–136.

Erikson, Frederick. "Qualitative Methods in Research on Teaching." In *Handbook of Research on Teaching,* edited by Merlin C. Wittrock, 119–162. New York: Macmillan, 1986.

_____. "Ethnographic Microanalysis of Education." In *The Handbook of Qualitative Research in Education,* edited by Margaret D. LeCompte, Wendy L. Millroy, and Judith Preissle, 201–225. San Diego: Academic Press, 1992.

Erickson, Frederick, and Jeffrey Shultz. *The Counselor as Gatekeeper: Social Interaction in Interviews.* New York: Academic Press, 1982.

Erikson, Kai T. *Everything in Its Path.* New York: Simon and Schuster, 1976.

Fetterman, David M. *Ethnography: Step by Step.* Newbury Park, CA: Sage Publications, 1989.

Gearing, Fred. *The Face of the Fox.* Chicago: Aldine, 1970.

Gee, James Paul, Sarah Michaels, and Mary Catherine O'Connor. "Discourse Analysis." In *The Handbook of Qualitative Research in Education,* edited by Margaret D. LeCompte, Wendy L. Millroy, and Judith Preissle, 227–291. San Diego: Academic Press, 1992.

Geertz, Clifford. *The Interpretation of Cultures: Selected Essays.* New York: Basic Books, 1973.

_____. *Local Knowledge: Further Essays in Interpretive Anthropology.* New York: Basic Books, 1983.

_____. *Works and Lives: The Anthropologist as Author.* Stanford: Stanford University Press, 1988.

Georges, Robert A., and Michael O. Jones. *People Studying People.* Berkeley: University of California Press, 1980.

Gilligan, Carol. *In a Different Voice: Psychological Theory and Women's Development.* Cambridge: Harvard University Press, 1982.

Giroux, Henry A. "Theories of Reproduction and Resistance in the New Sociology of Education." *Harvard Educational Review* 53 (August 1983): 257–293.

Giroux, Henry A. *Theory & Resistance in Education.* London: Heinemann Educational Books, 1983.

Glaser, Barney G., and Anselm L. Strauss. *The Discovery of Grounded Theory: Strategies for Qualitative Research.* New York: Aldine, 1967.

Golde, Peggy, Ed. "Introduction." In *Women in the Field: Anthropological Experiences,* 1–15. Chicago: Aldine, 1970.

_____, Ed. *Women in the Field: Anthropological Experiences, 2nd Edition.* Berkeley: University of California Press, 1986.

Gorden, Raymond L. *Interviewing: Strategy, Techniques, and Tactics.* Homewood, IL: Dorsey Press, 1969.

Gottlieb, Alma, and Philip Graham. *Parallel Worlds: An Anthropologist and a Writer Encounter Africa.* New York: Crown Publishers, 1993.

Gould, Meredith. "Review Essay: The New Sociology." *Signs* 5, no. 3 (1980): 459–467.

Granovetter, Mark. "The Strength of Weak Ties." *American Journal of Sociology* 78 (1973): 1360–1380.

Greer, Blanche. "First Days in the Field." In *Sociologists at Work: Essays on the Craft of Social Research,* edited by Phillip E. Hammond, 322–344. New York: Basic Books, 1964.

Hammersley, Martyn, and Paul Atkinson. *Ethnography: Principles in Practice.* London and New York: Tavistock, 1983.

Hammond, Phillip, and Robert N. Bellah. *Sociologists at Work: Essays on the Craft of Social Research.* Edited by Phillip E. Hammond. New York: Basic Books, 1964.

Harding, Sandra, Ed. *Feminism and Methodology: Social Science Issues.* Bloomington: Indiana University Press, 1987.

Heath, Shirley Brice. *Ways with Words: Language, Life, and Work in Communities and Classrooms.* Cambridge: Cambridge University Press, 1983.

Hochschild, Arlie Russell. *The Managed Heart: Commercialization of Human Feeling.* Berkeley: University of California Press, 1983.

Jones, James Howard. *Bad Blood: The Tuskegee Syphilis Experiment.* New York: Free Press, 1981.

Karabel, Jerome, and A. H. Halsey. "Educational Research: A Review and Interpretation." In *Power and Ideology in Education,* edited by Jerome Karabel and A. H. Halsey, 1–86. New York: Oxford University Press, 1977.

Keller, Evelyn Fox. "Feminism and Science." *Signs* 7, no. 3 (1982): 589–602.

_____. *A Feeling for the Organism: The Life and Work of Barbara McClintock.* San Francisco: W. H. Freeman, 1983.

_____. "Feminism as an Analytic Tool for the Study of Science." *Academe* 69, no. 5 (1983): 15–21.

_____. *Reflections on Gender and Science.* New Haven: Yale University Press, 1985.

Kirk, Jerome, and Marc L. Miller. *Reliability and Validity in Qualitative Research.* Beverly Hills, CA: Sage, 1986.

Kohn, Melvin L., and Carmi Schooler, Eds. *Work and Personality.* Norwood, NJ: Ablex, 1983a.

_____, Eds. "Stratification, Occupation, and Orientation." In *Work and Personality,* 5–33. Norwood, NJ: Ablex, 1983b.

_____, Eds. "The Reciprocal Effects of the Substantive Complexity of Work and Intellectual Flexibility: A Longitudinal Assessment." In *Work and Personality,* 103–124. Norwood, NJ: Ablex, 1983d.

_____, Eds. "Occupational Experience and Psychological Functioning: An Assessment of Reciprocal Effects." In *Work and Personality,* 55–81. Norwood, NJ: Ablex, 1983c.

_____, Eds. "Job Conditions and Personality: A Longitudinal Assessment of Their Reciprocal Effects." In *Work and Personality,* 125–153. Norwood, NJ: Ablex, 1983e.

_____, Eds. "Class, Stratification, and Psychological Functioning." In *Work and Personality,* 154–190. Norwood, NJ: Ablex, 1983f.

_____, Eds. "The Cross-National Universality of the Interpretive Model." In *Work and Personality,* 281–295. Norwood, NJ: Ablex, 1983g.

Komarovsky, Mirra. *Women in College: Shaping New Feminine Identities.* New York: Basic Books, 1985.

Krieger, Susan. "The Group as Significant Other: Strategies for Definition of the Self." Paper presented at the Annual Meetings of the Pacific Sociological Association, San Francisco, CA, April 1980.

_____. *The Mirror Dance: Identity in a Women's Community.* Philadelphia: Temple University Press, 1983.

_____. "Beyond 'Subjectivity': The Use of the Self in Social Science." *Qualitative Sociology* 8, no. 4 (1985): 309–324.

_____. *Social Science & the Self: Personal Essays on an Art Form.* New Brunswick, NJ: Rutgers University Press, 1991.

Lareau, Annette. *Home Advantage: Social Class and Parental Intervention in Elementary Education.* London and Philadelphia: Falmer Press, 1989.

LeCompte, Margaret D., Wendy L. Millroy, and Judith Preissle, Eds. *The Handbook of Qualitative Research in Education.* San Diego: Academic Press, 1992.

LeCompte, Margaret D., Judith Preissle, and Renata Tesch. *Ethnography and Qualitative Design in Educational Research, 2nd Edition.* San Diego: Academic Press, 1993.

Liebow, Elliot. *Tally's Corner.* Boston: Little, Brown and Co., 1967.

Lightfoot, Sara Lawrence. *The Good High School.* New York: Basic Books, 1983.

Linn, Robert L., and Frederick Erickson. *Quantitative Methods/Qualitative Methods.* New York: Macmillan, 1990.

Lofland, John, and Lyn H. Lofland. *Analyzing Social Settings: A Guide to Qualitative Observation and Analysis, 3rd Edition.* Belmont, CA: Wadsworth, 1995.

Lubeck, Sally. "Kinship and Classrooms: An Ethnographic Perspective on Education as Cultural Transmission." *Sociology of Education* 57 (1984): 219–232.

_____. *Sandbox Society.* London and Philadelphia: Falmer Press, 1985.

Lynd, Robert Staughton. *Middletown: A Study in Contemporary American Culture.* New York: Harcourt, Brace and Company, 1929.

Lynd, Robert S., and Helen M. Lynd. *Middletown in Transition: A Study in Cultural Conflicts.* New York: Harcourt, Brace and Company, 1937.

MacLeod, Jay. *Ain't No Makin' It: Aspirations and Attainment in a Low-Income Neighborhood,* Revised Edition. Boulder, CO: Westview Press, 1995.

Macrorie, Ken. *Telling Writing.* Upper Montclair, NJ: Boynton/Cook, 1985.

Mahler, Margaret S., Fred Pine, and Anni Bergman. *The Psychological Birth of the Human Infant: Symbiosis and Individuation.* New York: Basic Books, 1975.

Malinowski, Bronislaw. *Argonauts of the Western Pacific.* New York: Dutton, 1961.

_____. *A Diary in the Strict Sense of the Term.* Translated by Norbert Guterman. New York: Harcourt, Brace and World, 1967.

Mayo, Elton. *Some Notes on the Psychology of Pierre Janet.* Cambridge: Harvard University Press, 1948.

Mehan, Hugh. *Learning Lessons: Social Organization in the Classroom.* Cambridge: Harvard University Press, 1979.

_____. "Understanding Inequality in Schools: The Contribution of Interpretive Studies." *Sociology of Education* 65 (1992): 1–20.

Messerschmidt, Donald, Ed. "On Anthropology 'at Home.'" In *Anthropologists at Home in North America: Methods and Issues in the Study of One's Own Society,* 3–14. Cambridge: Cambridge University Press, 1981.

Miles, Matthew B., and A. Michael Huberman. *Qualitative Data Analysis: A Source Book of New Methods.* Beverly Hills, CA: Sage, 1984.

Miles, Matthew B., and A. Michael Huberman. *Qualitative Data Analysis: An Expanded Sourcebook.* Thousand Oaks, CA: Sage, 1994.

Millman, Marcia, and Rosabeth Moss Kanter, Eds. *Another Voice: Feminist Perspectives on Social Life and Social Science.* New York: Anchor, 1975.

Moffatt, Michael. *Coming of Age in New Jersey: College and American Culture.* New Brunswick, NJ: Rutgers University Press, 1989.

Myerhoff, Barbara. *Number Our Days.* New York: Simon and Schuster, 1980.

Okely, Judith, and Helen Callaway, Eds. *Anthropology and Autobiography.* London and New York: Routledge, 1992.

Pareto, Vilfredo. *The Mind and Society: A Treatise on General Sociology.* Edited by Arthur Livingston. Translated by Arthur Livingston and Andrew Bongiorno. New York: AMS Press, 1983.

Payne, Stanley Le Baron. *The Art of Asking Questions.* Princeton: Princeton University Press, 1980.

Powdermaker, Hortense. *Stranger and Friend: The Way of an Anthropologist.* New York: W. W. Norton, 1966.

Punch, Maurice. *The Politics and Ethics of Field Work.* Beverly Hills, CA: Sage, 1986.

Rabinow, Paul. *Reflections on Fieldwork in Morocco.* Berkeley: University of California Press, 1977.

_____. "Facts Are a Word of God: An Essay Review of James Clifford's 'Person and Myth: Maurice Leenhardt in the Melanesian World.'" In *Observers Observed: Essays on Ethnographic Fieldwork,* edited by G. W. Stocking Jr., 196–207. Madison: University of Wisconsin Press, 1983.

Rabinow, Paul, and William M. Sullivan, Eds. *Interpretive Social Science: A Second Look.* Berkeley: University of California Press, 1987.

Ragin, Charles C., and Howard S. Becker, Eds. *What Is a Case? Exploring the Foundations of Social Inquiry.* Cambridge and New York: Cambridge University Press, 1992.

Reinharz, Shulamit. *On Becoming a Social Scientist: From Survey Research and Participant Observation to Experiential Analysis.* New Brunswick, NJ: Transaction Publications, 1988.

Reiter, Rayna R., Ed. *Toward an Anthropology of Women.* New York: Monthly Review Press, 1975.

Roberts, Helen, Ed. *Doing Feminist Research.* London: Routledge and Kegan Paul, 1981.

Rosaldo, Michelle Zimbalist. "The Use and Abuse of Anthropology: Reflections on Feminism and Cross-Cultural Understanding." *Signs* 5, no. 3 (1980): 389–417.

Rosaldo, Michelle Zimbalist, and Louise Lamphere, Eds. *Woman, Culture, and Society.* Stanford: Stanford University Press, 1974.

Rosaldo, Renato. *Culture and Truth: The Remaking of Social Analysis.* Boston: Beacon, 1989.

Rubin, Lillian B. *Worlds of Pain.* New York: Basic Books, 1976.

Rynkiewich, Michael A., and James P. Spradley. *Ethics and Anthropology: Dilemmas in Fieldwork.* New York: John Wiley and Sons, 1976.

Schatzman, Leonard, and Anselm L. Strauss. *Field Research.* Englewood Cliffs, NJ: Prentice Hall, 1973.

Schon, D. A. "The Art of Managing: Reflection-In-Action Within an Organizational Learning System." In *The Interpretive Turn: A Second Look,* edited by P. Rabinow and W. M. Sullivan, 302–326. Berkeley: University of California Press, 1987.

Silverman, David. *Qualitative Methodology and Sociology.* Brookfield, VT: Gower Publishing, 1985.

Simon, Roger I., and Don Dippo. "On Critical Ethnographic Work." *Anthropology and Education Quarterly* 17, no. 4 (1986): 195–202.

Smith, Dorothy E. "Women's Perspective as a Radical Critique of Sociology." *Sociological Inquiry* 44 (1974): 7–13.

_____. "A Sociology for Women." In *The Prism of Sex: Essays in the Sociology of Knowledge,* edited by Julia A. Sherman and Evelyn Torton Beck, 135–187. Madison: University of Wisconsin Press, 1979.

_____. *The Everyday World as Problematic: A Feminist Sociology.* Boston: Northeastern University Press, 1987.

Sociology Writing Group. *A Guide to Writing Sociology Papers.* New York: St. Martin's Press, 1994.

Soyinka, Wole. *Myth, Literature, and the African World.* Cambridge and New York: Cambridge University Press, 1976.

Spindler, George, Ed. *Doing the Ethnography of Schooling: Educational Anthropology in Action.* New York: Holt, Rinehart, and Winston, 1982.

Stacey, Judith, and Barrie Thorne. "The Missing Feminist Revolution in Sociology." *Social Problems* 32, no. 4 (1985): 301–316.

Steffens, Lincoln. *The Autobiography of Lincoln Steffens.* New York: Harcourt, Brace, World, 1958.

Sterne, Laurence. *The Life and Opinions of Tristram Shandy, Gentleman.* San Francisco: Arion Press, 1988.

Stevenson, David L., and David P. Baker. "The Family-School Relation and the Child's School Performance." *Child Development* 58 (1987): 1348–1357.

Strauss, Anselm L. *Qualitative Analysis for Social Scientists.* Cambridge: Cambridge University Press, 1987.

Strunk, William Jr., and E. B. White. *The Elements of Style, 3rd Edition.* New York: Macmillan, 1979.

Taylor, Steven J., and Robert Bogdan. *Introduction to Qualitative Research Methods: The Search for Meanings.* New York: Wiley, 1984.

Tesch, Renata. *Qualitative Research: Analysis Types and Software Tools.* Bristol, PA: Falmer Press, 1990.

Tutuola, Amos. *The Palm-Wine Drinkard and His Dead Palm-Wine Tapster in the Dead's Town.* London: Faber and Faber, 1952.

Van Mannen, John. *Tales of the Field: On Writing Ethnography.* Chicago: University of Chicago Press, 1988.

_____, Ed. *Representation in Ethnography.* Thousand Oaks, CA: Sage Publications, 1995.

Venolia, Jan. *Rewrite Right! How to Revise Your Way to Better Writing.* Berkeley: Ten Speed Press, 1987.

Wacquant, Loïc J. D. "The Puzzle of Race and Class in American Society and Social Sciences." *Benjamin E. Mays Monograph Series,* vol. 2, 1989.

Wacquant, Loïc. "The Ghetto, the State, and the New Capitalist Economy." *Dissent,* Fall 1989, 508–520.

_____. "Sociology as Socioanalysis: Tales of Homo Academicus." *Sociological Forum* 5 (1990): 677–689.

_____. "Making Class: the Middle Class(es) in Social Theory and Social Structure." In *Bringing Class Back In,* edited by Scott G. McNall, Rhonda F. Levine, and Rick Fantasia. Boulder, CO: Westview Press, 1991.

Wacquant, Loïc J. D. "'The Zone': Le Métier De "hustler" Dans Le Ghetto Noir Américan." *Actes de la recherche en science sociales* 93 (June 1992): 39–58.

Wacquant, Loïc. "On the Tracks of Symbolic Power: Prefatory Notes to Bourdieu's 'State Nobility.'" *Theory, Culture, and Society* 10 (August 1993): 1–17.

_____. "Bourdieu in America: Notes on the Transatlantic Importation of Social Theory." In *Bourdieu: Critical Perspectives*, edited by Craig Calhoun, Edward LiPuma, and Moishe Postone. Cambridge: Polity Press, 1993.

_____. "Urban Outcasts: Stigma and Division in the Black American Ghetto and the French Periphery." *International Journal of Urban and Regional Research* 17, no. 3 (1993): 366–383.

_____. "The State and Fate of the Ghetto: Redrawing the Urban Color Line in Post-Fordist America." In *Social Theory and the Politics of Identity*, edited by Craig Calhoun. New York: Basil Blackwell, 1994.

Wacquant, Loïc J. D. "Morning in America, Dusk in the Dark Ghetto: the New 'Civil War' in the American City." *Revue française d'études américaines* 60 (May 1994): 97–102.

Walford, Geoffrey, Ed. *Doing Sociology of Education.* Philadelphia, Lewes: Falmer Press, 1987.

Ware, Caroline Farrar. *Greenwich Village, 1920–1930: A Comment on American Civilization in the Post-War Years.* Boston: Houghton Mifflin Company, 1935.

Warner, W. Lloyd. *The Social Systems of American Ethnic Groups.* New Haven: Yale University Press, 1945.

Wax, Rosalie H. *Doing Fieldwork; Warnings and Advice.* Chicago: University of Chicago Press, 1971.

Whitehead, Tony Larry, and Mary Ellen Conaway, Eds. *Self, Sex, and Gender in Cross-Cultural Fieldwork.* Urbana and Chicago: University of Illinois Press, 1986.

Whyte, William Foote. *Street Corner Society, 3rd Edition.* Chicago: University of Chicago Press, 1981.

Willis, Paul E. "Youth Unemployment: Thinking the Unthinkable." mimeo.

_____. *Learning to Labor.* New York: Columbia University Press, 1977.

_____. "Cultural Production Is Different from Cultural Reproduction Is Different from Social Reproduction Is Different from Reproduction." *Interchange* 12 (1981): 48–67.

_____. "Cultural Production and Theories of Reproduction." In *Race, Class, and Education*, edited by Len Barton and Stephen Walker. London: Croom Helm, 1983.

_____. "Youth Unemployment and the New Poverty: A Summary of a Local Authority Review and Framework for Policy Development on Youth and Youth Unemployment." Wolverhampton Information Center, June 1985.

Wolf, Margery. *A Thrice-Told Tale: Feminism, Postmodernism, and Ethnographic Responsibility.* Stanford: Stanford University Press, 1992.

Notes on the Book

Learning how to carry out research projects using participant observation and in-depth interviews has become a priority for scholars in a wide range of fields, including anthropology, sociology, education, social work, nursing, and psychology. This book, a collection of well-known fieldwork accounts covering the qualitative research process, aims to help undergraduate students, graduate students, and scholars in the social sciences understand common problems in the research process and learn strategies for resolving them.

Unlike methods books that treat research issues in a superficial or prescriptive fashion, this book realistically portrays, through researchers' own accounts, the process of discovery and resolution of conflicts involved in fieldwork. It also shows the costs involved in the choice of solutions. Students and seasoned scholars alike will find the collection a source of knowledge, inspiration, and comfort concerning the complexity of conducting fieldwork.

Notes on the Editors and Contributors

Karen Curtis is policy scientist and assistant professor in the College of Urban Affairs and Public Policy of the University of Delaware. She completed her dissertation, "I Never Go Anywhere Empty-Handed: A Study of Women's Social Networks," in 1983. She is editor, along with Anne Sharman, Janet Theophano, and Ellen Messer, of *Diet and Domestic Life in Society* (1991).

Alma Gottlieb is associate professor of anthropology at the University of Illinois at Urbana–Champaign. In addition to *Parallel Worlds,* she has written a full-length ethnography of the Beng entitled *Under the Kapok Tree: Identity and Difference in Beng Thought* (1992). She is currently working on a study of Beng infants.

Philip Graham is associate professor of English at the University of Illinois at Urbana–Champaign. He has published several works of fiction, including a novel, *How to Read an Unwritten Language: A Novel* (1995), poetry, and a collection of short stories. Most recently, he has been working on a novel inspired by Beng conceptions of spirits and the afterlife that takes place in the city of ghosts that surround every city.

Susan Krieger teaches in the Feminist Studies Program at Stanford University. She is the author of *The Mirror Dance: Identity in a Women's Community* (1983) and *Social Science and the Self: Personal Essays on an Art Form* (1991). She recently completed a book manuscript entitled "The Family Silver: Essays on Relationship Among Women."

Annette Lareau is associate professor of sociology at Temple University in Philadelphia. She is the author of *Home Advantage: Social Class and Parental Intervention in Elementary School* (1989). Currently, she is engaged in a study entitled "Managing Childhood: Social Class and Race Differences in Parents' Management of Children's Organizational Lives" in which she compares parental involvement in school with their involvement in other aspects of their children's lives, including church, sports, music, and other after-school activities.

Jay MacLeod is an Anglican priest living in Chesterfield, England. The second edition of *Ain't No Makin' It* was published in 1995 by Westview Press.

Jeffrey Shultz is professor and Chair of Education at Beaver College. He is coauthor of *The Counselor as Gatekeeper: Social Interaction in Interviews* (1982) with Frederick Erickson. Currently, he is exploring middle school students' perceptions of schooling.

Janet Theophano is associate director of the College of General Studies and adjunct assistant professor of folklore at the University of Pennsylvania. The study discussed in her chapter, in which she collaborated with Karen Curtis, led to her dissertation, "It's Really Tomato Sauce but We Call It Gravy: A Study of Food and Women's Work in an Italian-American Community" (1982). She is editor, along with Anne Sharman, Karen Curtis, and Ellen Messer, of *Diet and Domestic Life in Society* (1991).

William F. Whyte is Professor Emeritus in the School of Industrial and Labor Relations at Cornell University. A former president of the American Sociological Association, he is the author of more than a dozen books including his autobiography, *Participant Observer* (1994).

Index